WILSON LINE
DELAWARE-NEW JERSEY FERRY CO.
WASHINGTON
POCAHONTAS
WILDWOOD
NORTHAMPTON
ACCOMAC
CHICAGO
R.V. Elliott 6/20/70

# Last of the Steamboats

*The Saga of the Wilson Line*

# *THE SAGA OF THE WILSON LINE*

# Last of the Steamboats

RICHARD V. ELLIOTT

TIDEWATER PUBLISHERS
Cambridge, Maryland 21613

ISBN 0-87033-149-3

Library of Congress Catalog Card Number: 70-124312

Printed in the United States of America

To my late grandmother

IDA HEDDEN ELLIOTT

# Contents

# Acknowledgments

PREPARATION of any history requires extensive information retrieval. This can only be done by locating and delving into a vast variety of books, magazines, newspapers, records and files of all sorts. To do so one invariably depends on the cooperation of many people, people who have access to relevant information that is not readily available to the researcher, or people who can provide leads, suggestions or information to assist in evaluating and piecing together a meaningful and complete history.

Fortunately a great deal of information and many rare photographs have been carefully maintained by the various Wilson Lines during the past 88 years. Most of this material is now maintained by Wilson Shipyard, Inc., at Wilmington, Delaware's historic Fourth Street Wharf. John W. Gravdahl, president of the shipyard, extended every hospitality and made company records and photographs available to the author.

When it was possible to locate people who were once intimately associated with one of the Wilson organizations, I endeavored to contact them for insights or information which would not have been available through other sources. In this regard I found a consistent, enthusiastic welcome and was given considerable help by a number of Delaware Valley people. Among them were Mrs. R. Frances Wilson Richardson, daughter of the late Captain Horace Wilson and granddaughter of J. Shields Wilson, founder of the Wilmington Steamboat Company of 1882; George B. Junkin, former president of Wilson Line, Inc.; the late Frederick K. Reybold, former public relations director of Wilson Line, Inc.; Frank Weber, former general manager of the line; Captain Arthur M. Knight, former marine superintendent of Wilson Line, Inc., and now vice-president of the Mystic Steamship Corporation; Frank Santosuosso, former chief purser on *Boston Belle;* Mrs. H. F. Walsh, former Wilson agent at Yonkers, N.Y.; Joseph I. Goldstein, current president of Wilson Line of Washington, now Wilson Boat Line, and many other people who had been associated with one of the Wilson Lines. It would be difficult to find more helpful or friendlier people than the men and women of Wilson Line.

I appreciate too the kind assistance provided by many other busy people who serve in various capacities with a number of other business organizations, federal, state and local agencies, as well as libraries and historical societies, in the United States and abroad. Among them are the late Edward K. Laux, retired executive of The Port of New York Authority, who had served with the U.S. Rubber Development Corporation in Brazil during World War II; B. B. Wills, president of Wills Excursion Lines; Mr. and Mrs. James T. Wilson, who maintain the library of The Steamship Historical Society of America in Staten Island, N.Y.; A. Spencer Marsellis, president of the society; John D. Kilbourne, curator of The Historical Society of Pennsylvania; Mrs. Gladys M. Goghlan, manuscript librarian of The Historical Society of Delaware; Mrs. Marie E. Windell, librarian of Eleutherian Mills Historical Library; Anthony Higgins, associate editor of the Wilmington *Evening Journal;* Mrs. Helen Delich Bentley, marine editor of the Baltimore *Sun* and current chairman of the Federal Maritime Commission; Leon de Valinger, Jr., state archivist of the State of Delaware; Donald P. Will, comptroller of the Chesapeake Bay Bridge and Tunnel Commission; Nolan C. Chandler, general manager of the Cape May-Lewes Ferry of the Delaware River and Bay Authority; John Blackeby, vice-president of the American Bureau of Shipping; John L. Lochhead, librarian of The Mariners Museum; Robert Ware, managing editor of *Marine Engineering/Log;* P. C. Mello, president of Titanium Industries of Rio de Janeiro, Brazil; and Paul F. Van Wicklen, supervising editor of *Via Port of New York,* The Port of New York Authority.

Appreciation must also be expressed to numerous staff members of other organizations, including the Yonkers Public Library, the Philadelphia Free Public Library, the Enoch Pratt Free Library of Baltimore, the Trenton Free Library, the New York, Wilmington, Delaware, and Wilmington, North Carolina public libraries, Bethlehem Steel Corporation, the National Archives, Maryland Shipbuilding and Drydock Co., Sun Shipbuilding & Dry Dock Co., the New York Historical Society, the World Ship Society, the Railroadians of America, the Penn-Central Company, the Ocean Hiway Association, the Cunard Steam-Ship Co., Ltd., the U.S. Merchant Marine Academy, the U.S. Naval Academy, Servicios de Navegacao da Amazonia e de Administracao do Porto do Para, Brazil; Moore-McCormack Lines, United States Lines, Lloyd Brazileiro, Actor's Equity Association, the American Swedish Historical Foundation, the E. I. du Pont de Nemours Company, the Peabody Museum of Salem, Massachusetts, Seafarers International Union, Long Island Historical Society, The Mariners Museum, of Newport News, Virginia, the British War Veterans of America, the U.S. Maritime Administration, the Library of Congress, Home Insurance Company, the U.S. Department of State and the staffs of many eastern newspapers.

Among steamship fans, fellow members of the Steamship Historical Society of America and others who have given help in various ways I must also thank photographers Edward O. Clark, R. Loren Graham, Harry Cotterell, Jr. and Edward Gibbs; Herman Langer, Francis Palmer, John Blake, Mary I. Doran, Jack C. Mills, Eugene McDonald, John H. Shaum, Jr., Professor Frederick C. Shipley, Paul Abels, Ronald R. Klages, Peter T. Eisele, C. Spanton Ashdown, Charles Greenberg, Mrs. C. Bradford Mitchell, Mrs. Margaret Layton O'Neill, Mrs. Gayle Motes Baron, Misses Patricia Ryan, Carole Ann Flanagan, Linda Trees, Leslie Sloane and Kathleen Wise; Philip Craig, Louis L. Calta, Mathew Bruccoli, Ronald Girimonti, Mario Trombetta, Salvatore Bottone, J. Joseph Fitzgerald, Elmont Nelson, John D. Rainer, M.D., Professor Bernard Rosenberg, E. Boyd Schroeder, Thomas D. Carver, Charles Gablehouse, Daniel E. Keough, Jerome Press, Robert Leydenfrost, Jack Marshall, Myron L. Hurwitz, Harry Jones, Terry Graham, Howard Kennedy, Lloyd D. Schwalb, Donald B. Roberts, Harrison Bullock, Donald C. Ringwald and George Foster.

I also especially appreciate the time given to me by members of my family who have always encouraged my interests and who had accompanied me on trips during that period of youth when such was necessary for a day out on one of the steamboats. Deepest thanks go to my late grandmother, Ida Hedden Elliott, my father, George F. Elliott, my mother, Eileen Higgins Elliott, my brother, George F. Elliott, who is now preparing his first book, my sister, Mrs. Maureen Elliott Russo, my brother-in-law, Perry V. Russo, my nephew, Gregory Elliott Russo, my aunt, Mrs. Marie Higgins Haring, and uncles Joseph, John, Francis and the Rev. Edward Higgins.

Finally, I would like to thank William G. Muller, who painted the handsome view of *State of Pennsylvania* appearing on the jacket; Franklin B. Roberts, Jr., Frank O. Braynard and Professor C. Bradford Mitchell, whose steadfast help and encouragement reinforced my determination to complete this volume. A last word of appreciation goes to the Wilson Liners themselves. They gave me an interest in the maritime world and the field of transportation in general.

Richard V. Elliott

# Foreword

MANY KNOW the lower Hudson River by its ancient name of North River, but not many know the Delaware by its equally old name, South River.

By the same token many know of the Wilson Line but perhaps few know enough about this great steamboat institution to recognize it as "in many ways the greatest of all American steamboat lines." This is author Richard Elliott's contention, and his fascinating, humorous and thoroughly delightful book is convincing.

From tugboat to hydrofoil, the Wilson company through its various corporate management groups, pioneered and survived, rose and fell. For nearly 100 years it had operated more than 100 steamboats and other vessels and had carried over 250,000,000 people.

As Dick sums it up: "Wilson Line may not have looked or acted quite like other steamboat lines, nor did it fit the popular notion of what a steamboat line should be. It was itself . . . it was steamboating determined to survive, and it lived to operate the last of the steamboats."

This is a grand book as well as a revealing one. Its more than 225 illustrations alone make it a collector's item for every ship lover, historian or student of Americana. Dick's own excellent line drawings used as endpapers are crackerjack; you'll find yourself turning to them constantly. Bill Muller's beautiful cover painting is a fitting introduction to a colorful and dramatic story.

Imagine a company that was loath to run "moonlight" cruises and only did so because the competition introduced them so successfully, but, even then, allowed no drinking or dancing. This is the early Wilson Line that from 1882 to 1918 carried 50,000,000 passengers.

Dick's liberal use of interesting quotations takes you back to the handbills of the day, to the glowing tributes when new boats came out, to the launching parties and rescues and to the occasional explosions and fires. His style of writing is clear and you won't want to put the book down. It reads like a novel, and, since the best novels are autobiographical, this is in a way the autobiography of a steamboat line, the "nation's greatest excursion line."

Would you believe that in 1926 the company had 200 sailings a day!

The steamboats are the people of this autobiography, and you, dear reader, will feel like crying with the famous old captain when you see his *City of Washington* a burned-out wreck. But don't worry, a major characteristic of this company, which itself survived so many competitive and business disasters, was its ability to rebuild its veteran steamboats. Once the decision was made, it took only $150,000 and sixty days to return the *City of Washington* as good as new.

"Amazingly she had 'replaced herself,'" Dick writes.

The influence of famed naval architect George Sharp on the Wilson Line's story may be new to some readers. The length of his remarkable career was surprising to me. His functional design and streamlining were far ahead of his time.

Good chapter titles give this book a fine quick-glance appeal. Splendid chapter summaries tie up the story just told and hint at what's to come. Grand capsule sentences pack a wallop, such as: "Since Wilson usually introduced new developments in steamboating, it enjoyed a perennially modern image."

There are many opportunities for bits of humor to peak through the story, such as when in the late 1930s the steamers were painted bright colors and had floor shows and showgirls to lure passengers. The boat's captain was the "only sour face" aboard, and he was heard to bemoan the fact that after being a riverman for 30 years he'd be "skipper of a boat painted aquamarine and carrying a bunch of dancing cuties!"

To provincially-minded me, the Swedish background of the Wilmington, Delaware, area was something completely new. How the Swedish American Line, Swedish royalty and even President Roosevelt all joined in anniversary ceremonies before the war makes an interesting section. The Wilson Line, of course, was a major contributor to the festive occasion.

The exciting stories of how the Wilson boats got to the Amazon and elsewhere and what they did there during World War II make good reading. A full-length book could be devoted to this one episode, not to mention a movie or two.

In addition to George Sharp's pioneering work with the Wilson Line, the company made many other contributions to modern ship design and operation. When the *State of Pennsylvania* was rebuilt in 1944 she was given a synchronized whistle-light system, a safety innovation hailed as new 20 years later and still not as widely adopted as it should be, many say. Radar was also used on Wilson steamers before most others dreamed of investing in it.

Yesterday, when aboard the tug *Kerry Moran*, we tied up below the Colgate clock at Jersey City. As we entered the slip, we passed the decrepit remains of the Wilson Line pier. The name is still clearly evident on the outer pier end. Alongside lay the former Wilson steamer *Bay Belle*, and she looked pretty good . . . still very much alive and steaming, although over 60 years old.

This book is an important book because it tells an important story that is already becoming ancient history. Let's hope that Dick Elliott and others will do similar social histories of such famous companies as the Ward Line, the Merchants & Miners Line, the Morgan Line, the Clyde Line, and the Savannah Line, to list a few of the other major Atlantic Coast Lines.

FRANK O. BRAYNARD

# Last of the Steamboats

*The Saga of the Wilson Line*

## Chapter I

# The Pioneers and "Wilson's Line"

DEVELOPMENT of the steamboat in eighteenth-century America centered on the Delaware and Hudson Rivers. When the region between them was first settled, the Dutch named them the South and North Rivers. In fact, Henry Hudson, an English navigator employed by the Dutch, first called the Delaware the "South" River when he found it by chance while in search of the "North" River that later bore his name.

Quite naturally, rivers were principal arteries of transportation in early America and it was along the banks of the two rivers that centers of rudimentary culture and commerce developed. In the 1700s sailing vessels carried much of the commerce between cities and towns on and between the North and South Rivers. From the earliest times a close relationship existed between New York on the Hudson and Philadelphia on the Delaware, the first capitals of independent America.

Men of ideals as well as those of trade frequently traveled between the two key centers of early American civilization. They traveled to promote their ideas, inventions and hopes in this vibrant period. In an interesting irony of history, John Fitch, a young Yankee, came to be regarded as the father of Delaware River steamboating, while another young man, from the vicinity of the South River, has been hailed as founder of Hudson River steamboating. The latter, Robert Fulton, born in 1765 in Lancaster County, Pennsylvania, has been credited as the inventor of the first successful steamboat. However, the steamboat evolved through the efforts of many men. One of them has all but been completely forgotten. That man was William Henry, who, like Fulton, was born in Pennsylvania of Irish background. Fitch and Fulton owed a great debt to this enthusiastic pioneer who had built a steamboat of sorts as early as 1763. The transportation revolution brought by the steamboat in the 19th century was developed largely from the ideas of William Henry.

John Fitch, born in 1743 at East Windsor, Connecticut, was the first man to demonstrate effectively the steamboat in America. Fulton's predecessor had operated a steamboat on the Delaware in 1785. Fitch earnestly sought support for his concept and generally was either ignored or regarded as insane. He was too far ahead of his contemporaries and too little understood. According to marine historian John H. Morrison, Fitch continued his experiments and his 45-foot steamboat, built by Brooks and Wilson of Philadelphia, made her trial trip on the Delaware on August 22, 1787 at the grand speed of 3 miles per hour. She was powered by two sets of oars or paddles on either side, and, crude though her canoe-style propulsion was, she *was* a steamboat. That same year, Fitch won recognition for his labors and received a patent to operate steamboats in New York, New Jersey, Pennsylvania, Virginia and Delaware.

Another steamboat, the 60-foot *Perseverance,* was built in 1787 and the following year ran a trip from Philadelphia to Burlington in three hours and twenty minutes. Still another steamer,

*Thornton,* was built in 1789. In 1790 she made 8 miles per hour on her trials; this was far better than Fulton's first steamboat. Fitch's boat was placed in regular day service from Arch Street, Philadelphia, to Bordentown, New Jersey, returning every other day. She also made occasional trips to Chester and Wilmington, astonishing the Delaware Valley.

John Fitch, born in 1743, was the first man to demonstrate the steamboat effectively. One of his vessels regularly steamed the Delaware in 1787. The Steamship Historical Society of America, Inc.

In the *Life of John Fitch* by Thompson Westcott, Fitch's steamboat, driven by stern paddles, is said to have traveled up to 3,000 miles without a serious mishap in her first season. Exultantly, Fitch proclaimed: "We reigned Lords High Admirals of the Delaware." His vessel, the first placed in regular commercial service, was an operational success. However, the boat failed financially and Fitch's remaining supporters mistakenly abandoned him. That the venture died through loss of monetary backing in no way detracted from Fitch's technological accomplishment. His patrons and society had failed. As early as 1778 Thomas Paine had called for a national subsidy to develop the steamboat. However, the steamboat concept was not well understood and the nation at that time was engaged in the American Revolution, a vastly more pressing matter.

Fitch then turned to New York and, in 1796, operated a propeller-driven steamboat, New York's first, on Collect Pond in Manhattan. This was seven years before John Ericsson, the Swedish inventor of the screw propeller, was born. Unfortunately Fitch met with continued disappointment, but so convinced was he of the future of the steamboat that he predicted that vessels powered by steam would cross the Atlantic "whether I shall bring it to perfection or not." Despite unshakable faith in the concept, Fitch became ill and despondent. In 1798 he committed suicide, tragically unaware that future generations would believe in his ideal.

Although Fitch had passed from the scene, others in the United States and abroad forged ahead with experimental steamboats. Besides Fitch, America's pioneers included James Rumsey of Maryland, Oliver Evans of Delaware, New York-born Colonel John Stevens and Nicholas Roosevelt of New Jersey, Robert Livingston of New York and Robert Fulton of Pennsylvania. Rivalry and disputes were the order of the day as competition both spurred and blocked their efforts.

After Fulton allied himself with the brilliant and wealthy Livingston in France, the future of the steamboat became more certain. In contrast to Fitch, who had not profited from previous studies, Fulton, while an art student in Paris, had reviewed Fitch's papers and patents which had been left in the hands of the American consul. Joint Fulton-Livingston experiments followed in France, and these led to utilization of the paddle wheel, the best means yet employed to propel a steamboat up until that time.

In selecting the paddle wheel drive Fulton finally achieved success when his *North River Steam Boat* of Clermont, N.Y. made her historic trip up the Hudson on August 7, 1807. The engine of this vessel was built by James Watt in England. Yet even the water or paddle wheel, which was the key to Fulton's success, was not a new development, experiments having been made in America as early as 1789. While no part of the *North River Steam Boat,* later dubbed *Clermont,* was an original invention, Fulton's indisputable genius was his ability to creatively synthesize results from his predecessors' experiences. His vessel became the world's first commercially successful steamboat. Fulton was the man who proved beyond any doubt that the steamboat could be a practical means of transportation. However, even this was not immediately acknowledged by the public. Fulton and "Fulton's Folly," as his boat came to be called, were also ahead of the times. True recognition did not come until years later.

Fulton and Livingston, however, had won the first steamboat "race" against Colonel John Stevens whose own steamboat was completed about two weeks later than *North River Steam Boat.* Stevens first became interested in the steamboat concept when he accidentally discovered Fitch's steamer in 1785. His boat, *Phoenix,* might have been better named "South River Steamboat," for Fulton had secured an exclusive monopoly to operate in New York. (Seventeen years later Fulton's monopoly was to be overturned by the noted *Gibbon vs. Ogden* case in the Supreme Court, but New York Harbor was Fulton's in 1807.)

Under Captain Moses Rogers, John Stevens' *Phoenix* pioneered deep-sea transportation by steamboat and launched steamboat service between Wilmington and Philadelphia. Courtesy: The Mariners Museum, Newport News, Va.

After operating *Phoenix* briefly between New York and New Brunswick, New Jersey, Stevens quit the region ordering his steamboat to the Delaware, and Delaware River steamboating was reborn—due to Fulton's monopoly at New York. Under Captain Moses Rogers, *Phoenix* made the first ocean trip by a steamboat to Philadelphia in 1809, a forerunner of his memorable voyage on *Savannah* which made the first transatlantic crossing of a steamship in 1819.

Arriving on the Delaware, *Phoenix* was placed in regular service between Philadelphia and Trenton, beginning July 5, 1809. In 1813, the new steamboat *Eagle,* in which Captain Rogers had an interest, entered competition against *Phoenix* on the Upper Delaware, but not doing well, was returned to the Wilmington-Philadelphia trade for which she was intended. For this work the forerunner of the Wilmington Steamboat Company was formed by Captain Rogers and the Bristol and Partridge Company, a Philadelphia-Baltimore sailing packet line. At that time the fleet included *Eagle, New Jersey, Superior* and *Vesta.*

In this era, the main line of trade from Pennsylvania to New York was across New Jersey from Bordentown and Trenton to New Brunswick. This was the route of the stagecoach and later of early steam railroads. The Stevens-controlled Union Line, running from Philadelphia to Trenton, was the first major steamboat line on the Delaware. From the earliest days, the Upper Delaware was the river's busiest area. *Philadelphia,* built in 1813, replaced *Phoenix* on the Trenton line in 1815. She proved popular and became affectionately known as "Old Sal." In days before steamboats carried whistles, she sounded a small cannon to announce her landings. (The practice was abandoned after one of her crewmen was accidentally killed by a cannon blast.) "Old Sal" was followed by a number of fine early steamers, most of which were built at New York or New Jersey shipyards.

From 1831, Robert L. Stevens controlled the Delaware and Raritan Canal and the United New Jersey Railroad, which carried the cargo and passenger trade from New York to the Delaware and thence to Philadelphia. The railroad met his Union Line steamers at Bordentown. In fact much of the history of Upper Delaware steamboating for the first half of the 19th century is that of Stevens' Union Line which was to be related to the Camden & Amboy Railroad. The latter evolved into the Central Railroad of New Jersey. Steamboating on the Lower Delaware grew more slowly.

The earliest recorded steamboat service from Philadelphia to Wilmington was provided by Captain Moses Rogers' *Eagle* in 1814 and by the converted sailing ship *Vesta* in 1815, the year Fulton died. The same year the company transferred *Eagle* to Baltimore and ran her between Baltimore and Elkton, *Eagle* becoming the pioneer of both the Wilmington Steamboat Company and the Old Bay Line.

Five years earlier, Major Philip Reybold of the U.S. Army, a Philadelphian of Dutch background, had purchased a large tract of land at Delaware City, Delaware. There he began farming and raising thoroughbred livestock. By 1829, he and his son-in-law, John C. Clark, oversaw the completion of the Chesapeake and Delaware Canal, the eastern terminus of which was at Delaware City. The canal opened an all-water route from Baltimore to Philadelphia and spurred steamboat operations on the Lower Delaware. Wilmington and New Castle become important rival ports.

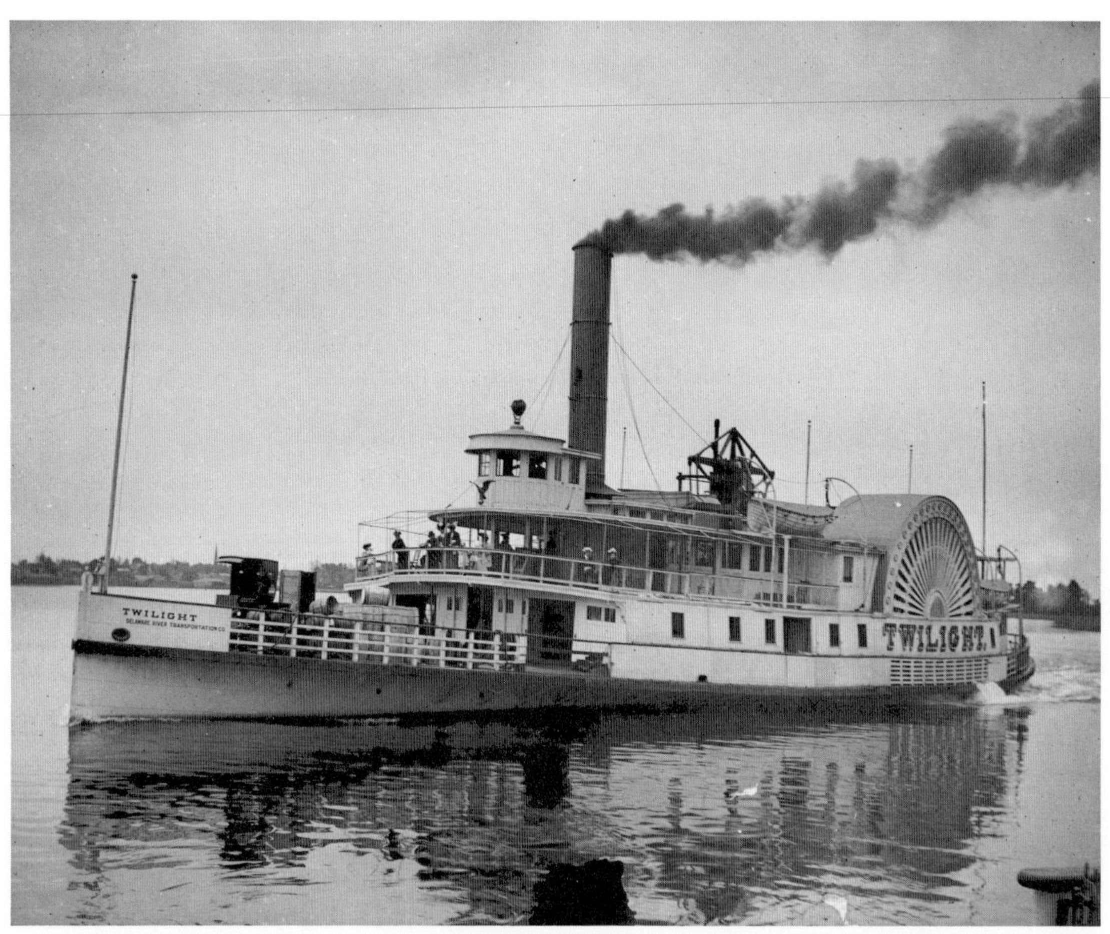


Beam-engined *Twilight* of 1868 was built for Captain Henry Crawford. She usually ran on the Philadelphia-Trenton route during her 55-year career. Courtesy: The Mariners Museum, Newport News, Va.

In 1820 the steamer *Superior,* formerly operated by Captain Rogers' group, began regular sailings from Philadelphia to Wilmington. She was operated by the Wilmington Steamboat Company of which William Young was president. For a dollar, *Superior* offered an eight-hour trip between Wilmington and Philadelphia. In 1828, the 156-foot beam-engined *Wilmington,* built at Philadelphia, also entered the trade. She was variously recorded as owned by Wilmington and Philadelphia Steamboat Company or Wilmington Steamboat Company. She was sold to southerners about 1840 but was lost en route to her new owners.

Meanwhile, sail packet service between Wilmington and Philadelphia continued as it had since colonial times. The two best known Wilmington lines were the Warner Line and the Bush Line. Warner was the pioneer, established in 1773, while Bush Line began in 1776. Both lines were maintained for over a century and during that time Warner Line continuously operated a sloop named *Fame.* Wilmington Steamboat Company also faced competition from horse-drawn wagons on shore and from steamboats controlled by the railroads.

By 1838, the new Philadelphia, Wilmington and Baltimore Railroad had completed the construction of tracks from Baltimore to Philadelphia and eventually became an important carrier. Captain Wilmon Whillden was one of the important Lower Delaware steamboatmen. He built *Delaware* in 1816, coordinating his steamboat services with those of the railroads. At one point he was a partner of Commodore Vanderbilt and operated steamboats on both the Delaware River and Chesapeake Bay. He introduced the 169-foot *Telegraph* in 1836 and ran her for the railroad in competition with Wilmington Steamboat Company. The 192-foot *W. Whillden* entered the trade in 1845 under an arrangement with the Philadelphia, Wilmington and Baltimore, which later became the powerful Pennsylvania Railroad.

Shipbuilding was just becoming a major industry on the Delaware. One of Wilmington's earliest yards was operated by Enoch Moore at the foot of East Fourth Street. Other yards soon emerged, including Harlan & Hollingsworth, in 1836, and Pusey & Jones, in 1849. Harlan's started as a railroad car manufacturer under Mahlon Betts and Samuel W. Pusey. Thus, the founders of Wilmington's greatest shipyards were relatives.

*W. Whillden* was built by Harlan & Hollingsworth, and other Delaware shipyards began to turn out iron and wooden steamships in record numbers. Other industries were also getting underway. In Wilmington, Jackson & Sharp became a major builder of railroad locomotives and the E. I. du Pont explosives works, begun in 1802, was becoming a great industry—how great only future generations would know.

Railroad competition hurt steamboat traffic on the Philadelphia-Wilmington route, but the railroad found itself at a disadvantage on the overland route to Baltimore. That weakness was capitalized on by a new steamboat line organized in 1844—the Baltimore and Philadelphia Steamboat Company. It was to operate steamboats between Baltimore and Philadelphia via the new Chesapeake and Delaware Canal, using narrow propeller steamers instead of broad sidewheelers. Since the line used the "Ericsson screw" it chose Ericsson Line as its trade name in honor of the Swedish-born inventor. Ericsson, himself had not gained much recognition for his efforts and had failed to impress the British Admiralty with the value of the propeller. He came to the United States in 1839 and found a welcome on the Delaware. The propeller steamer had arrived and the Delaware had set the pace.

Beginning in the 1850s Captain Jonathan Cone acquired a large fleet of passenger and cargo steamers and his operations became the new pride of the Upper Delaware, succeeding the Union Line. One of his first acquisitions was the steamer *Thomas A. Morgan.* She was followed in 1857 by *John A. Warner.* Both were operated by Cone's Upper Delaware River Transportation Company. *Edwin Forrest,* built in 1858, was also acquired. In 1868, Captain Henry Crawford built *Twilight* for the Philadelphia-Trenton route. In 1876 Captain Cone built the 220-foot *Columbia.* His crowning glory, however, was the magnificent 284-foot sidewheeler *Republic* of 1878. Capable of traveling over 20 miles per hour and of carrying up to 4,000 passengers, *Republic* was one of the nation's most beautiful steamboats.

During Captain Cone's halcyon years in the north only a few relatively ordinary steamers were built for the Lower Delaware. One of the more important acquisitions was *Zephyr,* operated by Wilmington Steamboat Company between 1847 and 1863. Activity on the Lower Delaware grew slowly and in 1865 Wilmington Steamboat Company built another *Wilmington* for the Philadelphia-Wilmington line. She was matched the same year by the Pennsylvania Railroad's *Samuel M. Felton.* The latter was named after one of the directors of the Pennsylvania Railroad and she apparently managed to drive *Wilmington* out of the trade shortly after her debut. Thereafter, the railroad clearly controlled the Wilmington route, beginning one of the nation's oldest steamboat-railroad rivalries.

The Reybold steamer *Thomas Clyde,* shown at Philadelphia, was built in 1878 to carry peaches and excursionists. William King Covell

During this period another important steamboat operator had joined the ranks of Lower Delaware steamboating—The Reybold Line. Major Reybold, America's pioneer in peach culture, had amassed a fortune, and it was chiefly for transporting peaches to Philadelphia's markets that Major Reybold and his sons built *Major Reybold* in 1853 and acquired the steamer *Delaware. Delaware* came to be called "The Peach State." The Reybold line was officially known as the Delaware City, Salem and Philadelphia Steam Navigation Company, a name which identified all of its ports of call except Chester, Penn's Grove and New Castle. The company carried its own freight and local passenger traffic, generally non-competitive to Pennsylvania Railroad services.

People were now noticing the aesthetics of steamboating and the differences in the "personalities" of the various steamboats. *Major Reybold* was known for the rich tones of her beautiful silver bell. The Major had directed a slave to carry 500 silver dollars to the foundry which melted the coins that formed that bell, and for the next 30 years its tones echoed across the Delaware. Everyone knew her singular sound.

In 1878 the Reybolds built the steamer *Thomas Clyde.* She specialized in the growing excursion trade, carrying big crowds from Philadelphia and Wilmington to Bombay Hook, where the Reybolds had peach farms and picnic grounds. *Thomas Clyde's* excursions became the talk of the Delaware Valley.

For many years *Major Reybold* sailed under jovial Captain Eugene Reybold who, according to Frederick K. Reybold, his nephew, "was fond of

Jonathan Cone's 284-foot *Republic* was "Queen of the Delaware" when new in 1878. Renamed *Dreamland,* she appears above at New York, circa 1904. Courtesy: The Mariners Museum, Newport News, Va.

everything fast—fast horses and fast boats." Frederick Reybold, a great-grandson of the Major, told the author stories in 1967 of nineteenth century Delaware River steamboating, the excursions of *Thomas Clyde,* the illustrious bell of *Major Reybold* and the beginnings of the Wilson Line. He spoke of his early newspaper career, interviews with President Grover Cleveland and of how he went into steamboating himself, later becoming "public relations manager of the Wilson Line and all of our companies."

When Frederick Reybold was born, J. Shields Wilson, a young Philadelphian, was becoming known as another Delaware River pioneer. However, Wilson belonged to the shipbuilding world in the 1870s, not to steamboating.

Ever since the fast *Samuel M. Felton* made her appearance on the Wilmington-Philadelphia line, the Pennsylvania Railroad had dominated Lower Delaware steamboating. A spurt of opposition came in 1870 from the New York-owned *Eliza Hancox* and *John Sylvester* but that, too, was short-lived. No one, it seemed in 1880, could or would successfully challenge the railroad's hold on the Wilmington-Philadelphia line. No one did until Wilmington Steamboat Company (W.S.C.) re-emerged

J. Shields Wilson, like the pioneering company he re-established in 1882, was considered one of the Delaware's greatest innovators in marine engineering and design. Mrs. Frances W. Richardson

Cramp's shipyard acclaimed the compound engine built for the Clyde Line's *George W. Clyde* of 1872 as "The World's First." The Steamship Historical Society of America, Inc.

on the scene under the guidance of J. Shields Wilson.

J. Shields Wilson would have been the last to imagine his destiny as one of the Delaware's great steamboatmen. This capable young man was born in Washington, D.C. in 1834 of Scottish and Irish background. His paternal ancestor had come to America from Scotland in the 1790s, landing with a brother at New Castle, Delaware. President Woodrow Wilson's paternal ancestor arrived in America about the same time, hailing from Ireland. When America's capital was relocated to Washington, D.C., Shields' family moved there from Philadelphia. His father was a lawyer who once served on President Lincoln's staff. Shields, however, had career aspirations of his own.

The younger Wilson was highly individualistic and felt the call of ships. He sought a career in shipbuilding and turned to the Delaware Valley—"the American Clyde." "Shields," as he was known, received his education in Wilmington, a town he loved. However, Philadelphia offered more opportunities and it was there in the mid-1800s that he served his apprenticeship at I. P. Morris & Company and then at the noted Reaney & Levy shipyard (later Neafie & Levy), which had pioneered with iron-hulled ships and in propeller technology. During the 1860s Shields obtained a post at the William Cramp & Sons Ship & Engine Building Company, one of the nation's largest yards.

By 1870, William Cramp recognized Shields Wilson's ability and made him the yard's chief engineer. In 1872, J. Shields Wilson designed a compound engine for the Clyde Line's new ocean-going steamer *George W. Clyde,* a feat which received considerable attention. In that design, low pressure steam exhausted from the primary cylinder was re-used to power a second piston driving the same propeller shaft, offering greater fuel economy. It was a major breakthrough in an era of rudimentary steam engineering, and Cramp's hailed the *Clyde's* machinery as "The First Compound Engine in America." Actually, there had been a few earlier compound engines, but Wilson's was the first with a receiver between the two cylinders.

The graceful *Taurus* was one of four famed Coney Island steamers built in 1881 under J. Shields Wilson's supervision at Cramp's shipyard. William King Covell

About the same time a new effort was being made to re-establish the Stars and Stripes on the Atlantic and a new entity, the American Line, forerunner of the United States Lines, was organized for that purpose. The line was sponsored by the Pennsylvania Railroad in hopes of making Philadelphia, its headquarters, a hub of transatlantic and domestic passenger traffic. Four iron-hulled liners were being planned but officials were unsure of the best type of propulsion to select.

Accordingly, in 1872, the railroad's subsidiary

sponsored a European trip for Charles Cramp, William's son, and Shields Wilson. Their task was to review engineering trends and to recommend engines for the new liners. On their return they recommended compound reciprocating engines; Cramp's won the contract and Shields was made the yard's superintendent in charge of construction and engine design. *Pennsylvania* and *Ohio* were the first American-flag liners on the Atlantic since before the Civil War and there was great fanfare and several cruisers and corvettes for the Imperial Russian Navy.

The roster of commercial vessels constructed by Cramp's under Shields' direction included the Merchants and Miners' liner *Allegheny* (1881); the Oregon Railway and Navigation Company's *State of California* (1879), *City of Pueblo* (1881), *Queen of the Pacific* (1882); the Oceanic Steamship Company's *Mariposa* (1883) and the Central Pacific Railway's *Tacoma* of 1882.

"Little *Wilmington*" of 1882 successfully revived Wilmington Steamboat Company's services between Wilmington and Philadelphia despite competition from the Pennsylvania Railroad. C. Bradford Mitchell Collection

at their launchings in 1872. Two additional sister ships, *Illinois* and *Indiana,* followed in 1873.

At this time Shields also began to operate tugboats out of Philadelphia. The exact date of this operation and the names of his earliest tugs are lost to history but 1876 has been recorded as the earliest date and may be called the beginning of what later became the Wilson Line. However, Shields Wilson was deeply engrossed in marine engineering and really had no intention of operating a steamboat line.

Many naval and commercial steamers were built at Cramp's during Wilson's superintendency. Noted naval craft built included the U.S. Navy's *Terror* of 1874, powered by compound engines,

Shields Wilson also played a role in designing steamboats, yachts and tugs. The river steamer *Wilmington* of 1882 was built under his aegis, also four steamers for New York's Iron Steamboat Company. In 1880, the steam yachts *Corsair* and *Stranger* were built by Cramp's and in all probability Wilson influenced the engineering of the 1885-built yacht *Peerless,* the machinery for which Cramp's acclaimed as the "First Triple Expansion Engine in America." Wilson left Cramp's shipyard about 1884.

In the popular history of Wilmington Steamboat Company, it has been universally accepted that J. Shields Wilson founded the company in 1882. Actually, this is an over-simplification, as a line of that name had been operating since 1820. Although it has long been assumed that Shields founded Wilmington Steamboat Company and had purchased the steamer *Wilmington* in 1882, members of the Wilson family long believed that he had purchased an already existing company, as well as the steamer, at that time.

Red-haired Captain Horace Wilson became master of *Brandywine* at the age of 23. In his youth he grew a beard to hide his years but he became one of the Delaware's greatest steamboatmen. Mrs. Frances W. Richardson

Moreover, the predecessor company does not appear to have been incorporated. There is an overlapping of two traditions in the evolution of the Wilson Line. "Little *Wilmington,*" as the diminutive steamer was affectionately called, may have been ordered by the predecessor line but she was never owned by anyone earlier than Shields Wilson. In any event, Shields Wilson may well be called the founder of Wilmington Steamboat Company of 1882 as well as founder of Wilson Line.

The new *Wilmington* was first registered in 1882 as owned by J. Shields Wilson, William Fredericks, William, Theodore and E. H. Cramp, J. C. Elrige, and Captains Peter and Joseph Bloomsburg. The Cramp family and its shipyard personnel held a majority interest in the line which might have easily become known as the "Cramp Line" had the Cramp family not soon after sold its interests, leaving Shields and his son, Horace Wilson, in control.

Wilmington Steamboat Company of 1882 was not organized because Shields Wilson personally wanted to operate a steamboat line. Shields' motivation was to find a way to encourage one of his teenage sons to remain in the Delaware Valley—his oldest boy, Horace, born in Philadelphia in 1862. Like other youths, Horace had ideas of heading west as another Horace, Horace Greeley, had so often advised in his famous saying, "Go West, Young Man."

Horace Wilson entered steamboating in 1878, serving as a deckhand on *Blanche,* his father's new tug. The boat had been named for Horace's sister who had died in infancy. When the tug was sold, Horace became interested in railroading and the Reading Railroad offered him a position farther west.

Shields was determined to provide a position for his son in steamboating, his first interest, and at the same time, Shields saw a need for year-round steamboat service between Philadelphia and Wilmington. It was against this background that J. Shields Wilson and his associates organized the new Wilmington line on April 17, 1882.

Captain Henry Crawford was the most experienced steamboatman of the founding group. He once served aboard Stevens' "Old Sal" and had operated *Twilight* since 1868. Horace Wilson started out as purser on *Wilmington* and later, at 22, became master, one of the youngest in Delaware River annals.

Captain Peter Bloomsburg was *Wilmington's* first master. He had a shipbuilding background and it is said that for a brief period he served as superintendent at Harlan's. A pioneer type with a flair for adventure, Captain Bloomsburg once went west during the Alaska gold rush and had commanded steamboats on the Yukon. He was the first man to navigate a steamboat between St. Michael and Dawson City, Alaska. Returning to the Delaware, he had a long career with Wilmington Steamboat Company, serving as captain and later as superintendent of construction.

Initially, *Wilmington* provided two round trips daily between Fourth Street Wharf, Wilmington and Philadelphia, stopping at Chester and Marcus Hook. The Wilmington wharf was subsequently given to the line by the town in perpetuity. Although she was smaller than the Pennsylvania

Railroad's steamers she survived by operating all year round while the railroad boats ran only during the summer months. In 1883, the New York steamers *Morrisania* and *Shadyside,* owned by M. Green & Wright & Co. of New York, entered the trade but lost out in the competition.

*Wilmington's* operations were so successful that plans were made to construct a larger steamer of 1000-horsepower and a 1,000-passenger capacity. Shields Wilson designed the steamer's compound engine and Harlan & Hollingsworth constructed the vessel on the banks of the Christiana River a short distance from Fourth Street Wharf. The keel of the new steamer was laid in mid-March, 1885 and she was named *Brandywine.* Samuel Ward Stanton, in the *Nautical Gazette,* noted that she was "intended to be the fastest steamer on the Delaware."

*Brandywine* was launched on May 9, 1885 and later achieved a speed of over 22 miles per hour on her trials. She entered service on June 15, under the command of 23-year-old Horace Wilson, and she proved to be the fastest propeller steamer on the river. In fact, *Brandywine* was just about the fastest propeller steamer in the world, faster even than Cunard Line's liner *Oregon,* the fastest liner on the Atlantic. *Brandywine* easily beat the Pennsylvania's *Samuel M. Felton* and for the first time since 1865 Wilmington Steamboat Company had the upper hand over the railroad.

*Brandywine* was pioneering excellence but had one problem—at certain speeds, she had an unusual vibration causing her bow and stern to bounce considerably. To reduce the vibration two extra heavy masts were installed and linked by cables to both ends for rigidity. The cables frequently snapped and the masts were later removed. Regardless of the problem to which "everyone grew accustomed," *Brandywine* proved to be one of the river's favorites.

Ill fortune struck the Pennsylvania's *Samuel M. Felton* in 1885 when an unthinking laborer left explosive material near her boiler and the steamer blew up at her pier. The explosion and the Wilmington line's strength finally led the railroad to withdraw from the Wilmington-Philadelphia steamboat trade. (The *Felton* was later rebuilt and sold for excursion service on Chesapeake Bay.)

Having won out over the Pennsylvania's river competition, Wilmington Steamboat Company became the major passenger carrier on the Lower Delaware. People came to prefer "Wilson's line" over travel by horse and carriage on dusty roads or the cindery railroad. Boat travel was cleaner and more interesting. Nevertheless, freight was always the Wilmington line's main source of income, and its two steamers carried freight on their main decks forward. One of their most interesting service features was the carriage of cargo wagons which were hitched to horses and hauled off for inland

Coal-burning *Brandywine* was traveling too fast for the cameraman in this 1885 view. When new she ranked among the world's fastest propeller steamers. The Society for the Preservation of New England Antiquities

delivery on arrival at terminal ports. In this, the line was practicing an early form of intermodal transportation, a concept which revolutionized ocean shipping in the 1960s.

Both Wilmington steamers were safe when the cyclone of October 3, 1885 struck the Delaware but the steamer *Major Reybold* was virtually destroyed. Captain Reybold and his pilot were blown overboard with the steamer's pilothouse. Pilot Emery Townsend was drowned but no passengers lost their lives. The *Major* was later rebuilt but her famous silver bell was never found, a misfortune that saddened many.

*Brandywine* presents a serene picture at Wilmington about 1900, shortly before sailing to Marcus Hook, Chester and Philadelphia. Courtesy: The Mariners Museum, Newport News, Va.

*Brandywine* was the winter boat and although she appeared frail, she enjoyed an enviable reputation for her strength. *International Marine Engineering* once called her "an acknowledged wonder at ice-breaking."

Captain Horace Wilson was fond of a story about *Brandywine* which came to him by way of England. It seems there was a conversation between two English sea captains at a pub. One of them spoke of the heavy ice he had encountered on a trip up the Delaware and of the "best little ice breaker I've ever seen" plowing through the river with ease. "She was *only* a river steamer," he added. When asked her name, the captain replied "Oh, I don't recall exactly, some sort of 'Wine' or something." To that, the second captain exclaimed "Oh, that was '*Brandy*'-*wine*! She's the best little ice breaker in the world!"

By 1887, the Wilmington line needed a larger running mate for *Brandywine.* This new boat, capable of carrying 1,200 passengers, was to be named *City of Chester,* in keeping with the line's policy of naming steamers after historic Delaware cities and towns. Once again Shields Wilson designed the engines and Harlan & Hollingsworth was awarded the building contract.

May 2, 1888 was "City of Chester Day" at Wilmington and Chester. According to the Wilmington *Every Evening's* detailed story:

"The launch of the new steamship *City of Chester* was attended by the largest gathering of citizens and visitors that has been seen since the notable launch of the *Alva* (W. K. Vanderbilt's

285-foot yacht) in October, 1886. Festoons of flags fluttered from every ship along the wharf, from the big *City of Worcester* to the diminutive *Sea Fox*. . . .

"Mayor Coates (of Chester) made the presentation, handing three flags to the care of Captain Wilson, who replied in a few appropriate words. A little before 6 o'clock workmen commenced knocking away the blocks. A bottle of Chester wine, the gift of Mrs. George Abbott of South Chester, was placed in the hands of Miss Agnes Wilson, daughter of J. Shields Wilson (and) precisely at 6 o'clock the boat commenced to glide almost imperceptibly. . . . The next moment the *City of Chester* was smoothly sliding down the ways amid cheers of spectators, eked out by the shouts of a dozen of *Alva's* sailors perched aloft along the yacht's bowsprit, who waved their blue caps frantically as the new boat passed almost underneath them out into the stream."

Although she bore all the overt "gingerbread" of her era, *City of Chester* was technologically a pacesetter for 1888. Here, the "Propeller Queen of the Delaware" is off for Philadelphia on a summer morning in her youth. Courtesy: The Mariners Museum, Newport News, Va.

Following the launch, the Chester delegation was taken by horse-drawn carriages to Wilmington Steamboat Company's Fourth Street Wharf. There guests boarded *Brandywine* for a return sail to Chester. During the trip they were lavishly entertained by "Captain" Shields Wilson in the steamer's dining room. Shields was greeted by rousing cheers and Chester's former mayor Forwood extolled the Wilmington line's enterprise.

Sleek *City of Chester* makes another fast passage between Philadelphia and Wilmington. Her one-hour and 40-minute passage in 1888 was a record. The Steamship Historical Society of America, Inc.

The *Chester* made her trials on June 13, 1888 and received a royal reception everywhere along the river. Commented the *Every Evening:* "The *City of Chester* is the result of the fullest experience of her owners, who have made steamboating a study, and no expense has been spared to make her a first class boat in every particular. . . . The Ladies saloon, main deck aft, and the main saloon will be upholstered in Brussels carpet in which red will predominate and with red plush seats. . . . The managers, with the new craft, deem their equipment complete and will continue to merit the patronage which they have always received."

*City of Chester* was fast, beautiful and a pioneer in her own right. She was the first Delaware River steamer with electric lights and was probably the first American riverboat powered by triple expansion steam engines. She came out a few weeks before the Jersey Central's *Monmouth.*

Three weeks after entering service *City of Chester* established herself as the new "Queen of the Delaware," when, on July 7, 1888 she made the run from Wilmington to Philadelphia in 1 hour and 46 minutes, allowing 6 minutes for a stop at Chester. "This," commented the *Marine Journal* "is the best time ever made on the river." At points, she probably sped at over 23 miles per hour. Other highlights of 1888 were Wilmington Steamboat Company's incorporation under New Jersey law and J. Shields Wilson's designs for the engines of the world's first double propeller ferryboat, the Hoboken Ferry's *Bergen.*

Hoboken ferry *Bergen* of 1888 was hailed as "The World's First Double Propeller Ferryboat." J. Shields Wilson designed her engines. Courtesy: The New York Historical Society, New York City

Under Captain Peter Bloomsburg, "Little *Wilmington*" was assigned to excursion runs from Wilmington to Augustine Park and Delaware Bay, leaving Wilmington twice daily. An 1888 ad pointed out that she offered "Forty miles for 30 cents. Fine fishing and good bathing, an elegant grove with tables at Augustine Park." On Sundays, she also made a trip to New Castle and Delaware City. The New Castle trip cost ten cents. *Wilmington* also did relief work on the Philadelphia line and in 1890 ran excursions from Philadelphia to Lincoln Park.

Proud officers of *City of Chester* pose for their portrait on the steamer's top deck, circa 1900. Wilmington Steamboat Company Collection, Wilson Line, Inc.

"Little *Ulrica*" of 1893, built for year-round ferry service between Wilmington and Penn's Grove, frequently grounded during winter fog in that pre-radar era. Courtesy: The Mariners Museum, Newport News, Va.

However, by 1891 *Wilmington's* services were no longer required and she was offered for sale. Her status came to the attention of Captain John W. Harper, a notable steamboatman from North Carolina's Cape Fear River. He journeyed to Philadelphia and reputedly purchased her "on sight." He sailed her to Wilmington, North Carolina, where, nicknamed "The River Queen," she became the most loved steamboat in Cape Fear River history. She proved so reliable that people set their clocks when they heard her arrival and sailing whistles.

On the Delaware, *Brandywine* and *City of Chester* were acclaimed as the most reliable flyers that river had ever seen, running year round service through sunshine and rain, snow and ice. Recognition of their performance also came from distant points, including the proud Hudson River region where George W. Murdock, dean of Hudson River steamboat historians of the early 1900s, held them in high regard. In one of his unpublished volumes now in the possession of the New York Historical Society, Murdock noted: "These steamers are among the most remarkable in point of record of performance of any vessels in the world of their size. They run between the cities of Philadelphia and Wilmington covering each year more miles than any other vessels of like character afloat."

Running year round, *Brandywine* and *City of Chester* logged almost 800 miles daily on six round trips each, or over a quarter-million miles yearly between Philadelphia and Wilmington. This was a far greater performance than that achieved by any pair of Hudson River steamers.

As Wilmington Steamboat Company approached the twentieth century, it had become the Delaware's most important line and it enjoyed an enviable reputation for fast, reliable transportation. Hundreds of thousands of Delaware Valley people enjoyed river cruises on its flyers each year. One of them was Howard Pyle, the noted artist-writer, who wrote many of his books while making trips on *Brandywine* and *City of Chester*. Philadelphians took the Wilson boats for picnics at Penn's Grove or along Wilmington's idyllic Brandywine Creek. Wilmingtonians traveled to Philadelphia's Independence Hall, Leary's book store and the big city's leading department stores.

However, at the turn of the century, Captain Cone's syndicate in the north came to an end and was reorganized by interests allegedly linked to the railroads. The *Republic* was sold to New York interests and renamed *Dreamland,* after the Coney Island amusement park extravaganza she was to serve. Her place was taken by "Big *Columbia,*" which became the Delaware's largest steamboat. She ran excursions from Philadelphia to Augustine Beach under William J. Thompson. Thompson was nicknamed the "Duke of Gloucester" because of his power in Gloucester, New Jersey, politics and his widespread resort, steamboat, and fishing enterprises. Now, with Delaware River steamboating in a state of change, Wilmington Steamboat Company became more concerned about activities on the Upper Delaware.

*Columbia* was the Delaware's largest passenger steamer in the early 1900's and was nicknamed "The Big *Columbia*" in opposition to the Upper Delaware's *Columbia* of 1876. "The Big *Columbia*" is shown above, new in 1877, under the banner of New York's Knickerbocker Steamboat Company. Courtesy: The Mariners Museum, Newport News, Va.

## Chapter II

# New Lines to Wilmington and Trenton

WILMINGTON Steamboat Company entered the twentieth century with an outstanding record. It had endured the vicissitudes of the national economy and remained independent of the railroads. Remaining outside of railroad control was no minor feat in that era. Rails were still powerful in business and politics—so much so that it had not been in jest that New Jersey was called "the State of Camden and Amboy."

By 1900 Captain Horace Wilson was vice president and general manager of Wilmington Steamboat Company. The line had survived several traffic "wars," and continued to prosper. For more than a decade conditions had been relatively serene and the company looked forward to an even brighter future. That picture, however, was soon clouded by prospects of new competition.

Heretofore, Wilmington Steamboat Company had concentrated solely on the Philadelphia-Wilmington trade. It had not ventured north and the Upper Delaware lines had not come south. That understanding ceased to exist shortly after the reorganization of Delaware River Navigation Company. That line allegedly worked closely with the railroads and it was interested in starting a new line to Wilmington. Apparently reacting to a challenge, real or imagined, Wilmington Steamboat Company moved to build two new steamboats for a northern service to Trenton.

Exactly what had happened to upset the previous balance, or which company first formulated its plans, is not clear. However, public and private announcements are entirely different matters in highly competitive trades and a public announcement per se would be an unreliable indicator. It was certain that the opposition's home waters were considered areas for expansion.

Although not much was made public other than the fact that new lines were being established, a war was on between the Delaware's two steamboat powers. This was to be short and bitter, bearing all of the consequences of such events.

Little has been recorded of the Delaware's steamboat war of 1901. Dayton, in *Steamboat Days* (1924), made only one passing reference to the affair, stating that the Wilmington line had ". . . started competitive service on the Upper Delaware . . ." He might have mentioned also that Delaware River Navigation Company had simultaneously invaded the Lower Delaware! This was an important oversight for there was much more to this clash than has been written and, perhaps, may ever be known.

Yet, while everyone on the Delaware knew that the two lines were on a collision course, there are no recorded explanations for this development. People realized the seriousness of the confrontation as there was really only enough business for one major line on each route. They knew too that in the impending traffic battle both carriers were bound to lose money. The situation was packed with possibilities of dire consequences.

The *Nautical Gazette* commented at some length about the matter and in its March 14, 1901 issue, noted: "There promises to be a lively war between two steamboat lines on the Delaware this coming summer. . . ." That there had been a change in the relationship between the two lines was clear, and that change came after the Upper Delaware line changed hands. Previously the southern and northern lines had cooperated very closely. As for how closely, the same journal added: "For many years the steamers of both lines landed alongside each other, sometimes three deep, and passengers passed across the forward decks of each line's boats as they went to and fro between the respective steamers.

"Freight also was transferred from one boat to another, and the best of good feelings existed on all sides. Since Philadelphia has taken a notion to build some decent piers along her waterfront, the old steamboat landing below the foot of Market Street has been done away with and the two lines now operate from terminuses that are some distance apart. . . ." Transfer distance may have been a factor but that alone fails to explain why both lines took such drastic steps to compete. These were strange times on the Delaware.

Shortly, both lines announced new services for 1901. Delaware River Navigation Company let it be known that its new line would link Philadelphia, Chester and Wilmington. Connections were to be offered to Bristol, Florence, Trenton and way landings. The modernized *John A. Warner* and the newer *Diamond State,* built in 1894 as *Unique* for the Great Lakes, were assigned to the southern line, while *Columbia, John Sylvester, Pokanoket* and *Twilight* were to serve their regular northern leg. It will be recalled that *Twilight* had formerly been operated by Captain Henry Crawford, one of Wilmington Steamboat Company's founders. *Diamond State* of the opposition's fleet, was as unique as her former name. When new she was the nation's first quadruple-expansion steamboat and it was claimed that she was capable of 25 miles per hour and "astonished all rivers."

*Unique* was once hailed as the "Astonishment of All Rivers." Delaware River Navigation Company purchased her in 1901 to compete against Wilson Line. R. Loren Graham

The Upper Delaware line had a fleet of six vessels while Wilmington Steamboat Company had only *Brandywine* and *City of Chester,* both of which were needed on the regular Wilmington-Philadelphia line. In this respect, Wilmington Steamboat Company was not well prepared to launch a competitive service to the north since it lacked the boats to do so. It is far more likely that its new operation represented a reaction to challenge. To overcome its handicapped position, the Wilmington line hurried to construct two new boats especially designed for the Trenton route—the fastest steamboats ever on that line. They too would offer connections at Philadelphia for through service to Wilmington. They would call at Burlington, New Jersey and Bristol, Pennsylvania, making between two to five sailings daily.

The brand new boats were expected to attract a larger traffic than the older steamers used by the Upper Delaware line. Following in the Wilson tradition, they would have a number of pacesetting features. Measuring 162 feet, they were ideal for the service. They were named *City of Trenton* and *Quaker City* after the terminal cities they would serve.

The new boats were Neafie & Levy's Hulls 942 and 943. Owing to the narrowness of the Upper Delaware, Shields Wilson designed them with twin screws for faster turning and better maneuverability. They were of shallow draft for high speed o'clock and just five minutes after that time the boat glided from the ways. . . . As the pretty boat began to move she was christened by Miss Edna May, daughter of Charles May, president of the Board of Water Commissioners of Trenton, N.J. Miss May is one of the belles of the New Jersey capital and she performed the pleasant duty with becoming grace. . . .

"A large delegation of officials and citizens of Trenton and Philadelphia were guests of Wilmington Steamboat Company and Neafie & Levy at the launch and many in the crowd of spectators congratulated the projectors upon the initial step in their undertaking.

*John Sylvester,* veteran of New York service, was chartered by Delaware River Navigation Company in 1901 for its Upper Delaware line. The Steamship Historical Society of America, Inc.

and independence of tides. Although shorter than *Brandywine,* the new boats exceeded her in gross tonnage. They were highly powered for their size as high speed was a design essential. In fact, the two boats were equipped with one horsepower for each of the 1,000 passengers they could carry. Even prior to their completion the local press labeled the duo as the "best equipped boats in this part of the country." They came to be called the "pretty boats."

Enthusiasm abounded at the Neafie & Levy shipyard on March 19, 1901 when the new *City of Trenton* was launched. Few noted, however, that "*Trenton*" was considered an unlucky name owing to the misfortunes which had befallen other steamers bearing it. After the *Trenton's* launching, the party regrouped for a keel laying ceremony for her identical sister ship, *Quaker City.*

The Wilmington *Every Evening* noted that: "The launch was a decided success. Announcements stated that it was to take place at 1:30

"The *City of Trenton,* which is built along the lines of *City of Chester,* running on the company's Wilmington line, was favorably commented upon as she rested gracefully on the Delaware. . . . She is to be finished very much like the *City of Chester* and will provide all of the comforts and conveniences for passengers, which will make her one of the finest of river boats. . . ."

After the launch, Wilmington Steamboat Company entertained guests in the shipyard's mold department which became a banquet hall for the occasion, decorated with American flags and potted palms. After dinner, Mathias Seddinger, president of Neafie & Levy, extended best wishes to the new boat and the new line. Others too, joined in making glowing speeches, predicting that the new service "would have the hearty support of the people of Trenton, Philadelphia and the Upper Delaware." Captain W. F. P. Jacobs of Camden, formerly on *Republic,* was named *City of Trenton's* first master.

*Quaker City* was launched at the same yards on May 18, christened by Miss Mabel Wilson, one of Shields Wilson's daughters. *Quaker City* made her trials on June 12, the same day *City of Trenton* sailed north on her maiden voyage.

In the meanwhile, Delaware River Navigation Company began to publicize its "New Steamboat Line to Philadelphia, Chester and Wilmington with continuous service all the way to Trenton." *Diamond State* made the line's first sailing to Wilmington on June 19 but her voyage was marred by the bad luck that came to typify the rivalry between the lines.

Shortly before *Quaker City* entered service, the Upper Delaware line was publicly censured when its steamer *Pokanoket*, said to be trailing astern *City of Trenton*, failed to assist young victims of an overturned sailboat. *Pokanoket's* officers reportedly mocked their passengers who had implored them to turn the boat around and help the youngsters. Officers suggested that their passengers wait until they reached the city and had had something to drink. As a result, one of the youngsters drowned, and the public was incensed.

*Pokanoket's* personnel also behaved in a haughty manner when called before Philadelphia's Coroner

Wilson's former flyer *Quaker City* knifes her way through New York's East River during the early 1900's. Courtesy: The Mariners Museum, Newport News, Va.

Under Captain M. S. Tucker, *Diamond State* attempted to make a fast run to support her owners' boastful ads. A speed record would have helped their cause immeasurably. Unfortunately, during the trip *Diamond State* lost two blades of a propeller after striking a log. The speed record was abandoned and she limped into Wilmington an hour late with a group of dignitaries on board.

However, the northern line was first to launch a fully competitive service which began on June 21 with *John A. Warner* sailing from Philadelphia 15 minutes after *Diamond State* departed from Wilmington. They were pitted in direct competition with the Wilmington boats—at this point, *City of Trenton* served alone on the Upper Delaware while *Quaker City* neared completion.

Dugan. One passenger pointed out the steamer's mate as the man who had denied that he had been approached by concerned passengers. Others also testified that *Pokanoket's* men had refused to help the boys, "as the boat had to make time." Further, it was discovered that the steamer had been speeding with a damaged propeller.

Addressing the jurors, Coroner Dugan stated that *Pokanoket's* "desire to compete with a rival boat had been held greater by the captain and crew than the desire for the welfare of the passengers, and that it was a most inhuman act not to make an effort to rescue and relieve the young men who were on the overturned sailboat." The coroner then added that "it would be an extreme pleasure to me to commit the captain, pilot and the entire crew of *Pokanoket* to prison for their inhumanity. . . ."

The superintendent of Delaware River Navigation Company stated that his company was satisfied that *Pokanoket's* men could have done nothing to save the lads since it would have taken 15 minutes to turn the boat around, aside from time to lower and row a boat to the craft. Even in these pre-public relations days, the Upper Delaware line won few friends with its public-be-damned attitude. The incident, however, indicated the caliber of the competition with which the Wilmington line had become involved. The same calculated approach to avoiding assistance would again be employed by the Upper Delaware line.

*Quaker City* made her maiden trip to Trenton on July 15, when Wilmington Steamboat Company at last had full service in the north. From the moment that the two new vessels teamed up, enthusiastic reports filled the press in praise of "the pretty boats." Of *City of Trenton,* one Philadelphia journal exclaimed: "The new boat on the line to Trenton is much admired by all who have seen her." Another newspaper commented that "*City of Trenton* has no difficulty in walking away from *John Sylvester.*" The *Sylvester* herself was capable of 18 miles per hour. To the chagrin of Delaware River Navigation personnel, the new Wilson flyers had become "Queens of the Upper Delaware" immediately after their debut. Their reigns, however, were to be shockingly brief.

Delaware River Navigation Company's steamers departed from Philadelphia for Trenton at 8 A.M., 1:30 and 5 P.M. Steamers for Bristol and way landings left at 7:30 A.M., 2, 3:30 and 6 P.M. Connections were provided by trolley at Bristol for Newton, Langhorne and intermediate points. Burlington Island Park was one of the leading attractions to the north. Excursions or round trips to Trenton cost 50 cents.

Wilmington Steamboat Company advertised itself as the "New Fast Line to Trenton" and called its boats "by far the most elegantly furnished steamers on the Delaware." Its schedule called for sailings from Pier 8, above Arch Street, Philadelphia, at 7:30 and 10:30 A.M.; 1:30 and 4:45 P.M. Calls at Bristol also offered trolley connections to Holmesville, Langhorne, Newton and Doylestown, Pennsylvania. It charged exactly the same fare as its competitor. In addition, the Wilmington line operated the small freighter *Fannie* to Burlington, Bristol and Florence.

To the south, *Diamond State* and *John A. Warner* ran their "New Fast Line to Wilmington" with sailings from Chestnut Street Wharf at 7:30 and 10:30 A.M.; 1:30, 4:15 and 9:30 P.M. Probably feeling a bit ridiculous, Wilmington Steamboat Company eventually felt compelled to style itself the "New Fast Line to Wilmington" even though that had been its traditional route! Nothing was "old" in 1901 Delaware steamboating.

*Brandywine* and *City of Chester* departed from Philadelphia's Pier 8 at 7:30 and 10:30 A.M.; 1:30, 4:15 and 7 P.M. The two lines now made

At the height of the steamboat war of 1901, Delaware River Navigation Company's *Pokanoket* refused to aid victims of an overturned sailboat. C. Bradford Mitchell Collection

many simultaneous sailings on both routes and competition in speed was inevitable. By August, the traffic war raged on both fronts and, as the smaller Wilson flyers gained in the north, the older *Brandywine* and *City of Chester* held the loyalty of Wilmingtonians. They were "Wilmington boats" and that meant something special in Delaware.

Shortly before the turn of the century Wilmington Steamboat Company had begun making occasional novelty trips known as "moonlight sails." Heretofore, "moonlights" had not been deemed important by a line which took pride in what were purely transportation services to match the railroads. Moonlights had been held infrequently but in this summer of competition the opposition launched a series of night pleasure cruises from Wilmington. They proved very popular and, following suit, *City of Chester* and *Brandywine* soon made sailings from opposite terminal ports labeled "Extra Trips . . . offering an excellent opportunity for a moonlight ride on the river." Publicly, the Wilmington line stated "these trips are in answer to a demand for moonlight sails." Privately, this new service meant that something had to be done to prevent the opposition from stealing local patronage. (These may have been billed as "romantic" trips but the line's policy was: "No liquor or dancing.") *City of Trenton* also began making moonlights from Trenton and by the end of the summer Wilmington Steamboat Company had survived the worst of the traffic war. Then, calamity struck a lethal blow.

The worst accident in the Wilmington line's history took place about 40 minutes after *City of Trenton* sailed on her afternoon trip to Trenton on August 28. Without the slightest warning, while opposite Torresdale, Pennsylvania, about 16 miles north of Philadelphia, the *Trenton* was wracked by the violent explosion of her port boiler. Whole sections of the steamer blew into the air.

Initially, only seven persons were known dead, four were missing and scores were injured. There were 24 fatalities. The toll conceivably could have been higher but the *Trenton* had only 117 passengers on board during the ill-fated sailing. On the day of the accident, an "Extra" edition of the Trenton *Times* prematurely heralded that "All Lives (were) Saved by the *Twilight,*" and, reassuringly, that *Columbia* was passing near *City of Trenton* when the explosion occurred. However, it was soon learned that neither *Twilight* nor *Columbia* had saved a solitary soul! Still worse was the news that they had not even tried to provide assistance.

Hearing of the explosion, Shields Wilson suffered traumatic shock and hysterically told his son "everyone was lost." An equally stunned Captain Horace Wilson advised the press that: "As near as we can ascertain at this time, the accident to the steamboat *City of Trenton* was due to the explosion of her port boiler, setting fire to the vessel . . . These boilers were built to carry 175 pounds of steam, and passed inspection for same by the United States inspectors in June last, when they were subjected to a water pressure of 263 pounds. Just what caused the explosion we are unable to determine at this time."

Captain William A. Worrell, in reply to accusations that his *City of Trenton* was racing, declared that the boat was on scheduled time. "We were 15 minutes late in starting," he told reporters, and "it was 1:45 o'clock when we pulled out from the dock, with about 100 passengers on board. Forty minutes later the explosion occurred. I was in my office at the time, and First Mate Edward Curry was at the wheel . . . The explosion stunned everybody and for a few minutes there was not a sign of excitement. It was the port boiler that burst, and as near as we can judge, the end blew aft, tearing the entire after part of the boat out." True to tradition Captain Worrell was the last man to leave the boat.

Many passengers praised Pilot Curry's levelheadedness. One of them said that Curry demonstrated "great coolness in steering towards the shore while the pilothouse was ready to topple over at any minute." Curry was blown through the pilothouse window and if his arm had not been caught in the awning frame, would have gone overboard.

*City of Trenton* burst into flames shortly after touching the Pennsylvania shore. The fire proved even more harmful than the explosion and almost everyone jumped into the shallow water and waded ashore. The injured were rushed to the nearby House of Correction which served as an emergency hospital. Only moments before some of the casualties had been singing happily beside the ship's piano. One shoreside observer saw the piano catapulted into the air.

The conduct of *City of Trenton's* men was a credit in the face of disaster. Many passengers praised their behavior. The Trenton *Times* noted that "The crowd was panic stricken, and but for the dauntless courage and masterly tact of Captain Worrell, the number of deaths and serious injuries would have been greatly multiplied. He counseled everybody to keep cool, directed his men in their rescue work and inspired hope in everybody on board."

Survivors also volunteered their "explanations" for the accident. Some became immediate experts. One passenger commented on the steamer's late start and added "It was clear that an effort was being made to make up the time." Some women claimed that the boat was going so fast that they could barely remain on their feet! However, if *City of Trenton* covered the 16 miles from Philadelphia to Torresdale within 45 minutes, her average speed was just over 21 miles per hour—fast, but not her top speed. Obviously, the boilers should have withstood the steaming demands or the safety relief device should have operated.

It was clear that casualties could have been reduced had more help been rushed to the scene. The Wilmington line had always been known for its safety consciousness and its personnel had performed creditably in face of adversity. People tended to forgive the accident but not the competitor's willful inaction. *Twilight* was only about a mile ahead of the *Trenton* while *Columbia* was nearby. However, *Twilight* in particular became a target of disgust, if not hatred. Any effort she might have made could have possibly saved lives.

The August 29 Trenton *Times* carried the following description of *Twilight's* inaction: "Criticism for *Twilight*—Captain Ward Censured—His explanation of Failure to Go Back—Whenever the accident to the *City of Trenton* is being discussed today around the city and in neighboring towns, Captain Ward of the steamer *Twilight*, is being harshly criticized for not turning back when he knew the *Trenton* was burning.

"The *Fannie* turned back, and it is being asked why did not Captain Ward follow her example. Captain Ward's own explanation of why he did not turn back was furnished in the *Times* last night, and is as follows:

" 'I knew nothing of the accident further than that the *Trenton* was ashore near Torresdale when my attention was first called to her by the Trenton freight boat *Fannie*. I was sitting in my office when the *Fannie* notified me of the affair. Looking out my window I saw either steam or smoke coming from the spot where the *Trenton* was ashore. Which it was I am unable to tell. At the time my attention was called to the accident I was two miles and a half ahead of the *Trenton*. The *Fannie* signaled that she was turning back, and with that I concluded that I could be of no assistance. At the point of the river I was in at the time it would have taken me at least half an hour to turn around. Adding this time to that which I must have necessarily consumed had I gone back, the *Trenton*, if she was afire, would have burned to the water's edge before I could have reached her.' "

His was virtually the same explanation *Pokanoket's* men had given in the case of the drowning boy.

*Twilight's* passengers had become very anxious for *City of Trenton's* people soon after her trouble was known. One man, William Wells of Philadelphia, protested that several passengers had implored Captain Ward to help the *Trenton*. The captain, Wells told reporters, simply refused, saying it was too late to go back. "The officers of the *Twilight*," said Wells, remarked that "it's just what they get for racing."

A few days afterward, the *Trenton's* hulk was towed to the Neafie & Levy yards for complete inspection, and Captain Horace Wilson ordered a search for the port boiler. The parts were located and examined by the U.S. Steamboat Inspection Service. A coroner's inquest was scheduled. Many questions were posed as to why the boiler had failed.

The official investigation was completed on October 7, 1901. Had *Trenton's* engineers on watch survived, they might have provided information about what happened just prior to the explosion. However, during the inquiry the government inspector who had granted a certificate for the boiler admitted that he did not know the position of the safety plug until after the accident. Perhaps the most crucial finding was that "the safety plug in the boiler, which should have melted at 463 degrees Fahrenheit, did not melt below 695 degrees." In other words, the fusible safety plug was inherently defective. Had it performed properly the explosion would not have occurred. Evidently, both boats had been built with inadequate boiler safety equipment, and that equipment had been approved by a government inspector before the boats were delivered to their owners who naturally assumed they were accepting safe, new steamers. The coroner's jury also noted that "the requirements of the United States government rules concerning fusible plugs were not complied with by the government . . ."

The traffic war between the leading Delaware River lines was finally brought under control and schedules were revised to avoid direct competition.

*City of Trenton* never returned to service under the Wilmington line. Only four months after her first trip, her wreck was sold at a U.S. Marshall's sale. The hulk was purchased by two men from Fall River, Massachusetts, for $8,500, a fraction of her cost. Reboilered and rebuilt in her original form, she was again sold in 1902 to the Long Island Rail Road, in which the Pennsylvania Railroad then held a controlling interest.

Returning to the Delaware in 1916, *Princeton,* ex-*City of Trenton,* sails for Trenton again, for successors to her erstwhile competitors. The Steamship Historical Society of America, Inc.

The Long Island renamed her *Sagamore,* after President Theodore Roosevelt's Oyster Bay home and she saw several years' service on the railroad's Glen Cove-New York route and its East River Annex run from Wall Street to Long Island City. She brought honor to herself on July 15, 1907 by rescuing 200 passengers from the grounded *Shinnecock.*

As *Princeton* in 1916 she again sailed the Delaware. Ironically she was operated by the successors of Delaware River Navigation Company and found herself running with her former rivals. On October 17, 1923, *Princeton, Columbia* and *Twilight* caught fire at Camden Shipbuilding Company's yards. *Princeton* was damaged but *Twilight* was entirely destroyed, an unusual twist to their earlier situations.

Again salvaged, *Princeton* eventually sailed for Cuba in 1926 where she entered service between southern Cuba and the Isle of Pines. She had been dieselized prior to her departure and sailed with great credit for her new owners, the New York-based Isle of Pines Steamship Company, under the name of *Pinero.* As late as 1969 she was still operating out of Cuba.

*Quaker City* likewise had a long and checkered career. After the *Trenton's* accident she was withdrawn immediately and following a period of idleness was reboilered by Harlan and Hollingsworth. She later resumed the Trenton route with *Brandywine,* but the northern line had ceased to be important.

Alternate employment was sought for *Quaker City* and in early February, 1903 she set sail for Florida under Captain Hettrick. There she ran from Miami to Key West for the next half year

The 22-mile-per-hour *City of Trenton* of 1901 reigned briefly as "Queen of the Upper Delaware." Here, renamed *Sagamore,* she speeds up New York's East River for the Long Island Rail Road in 1902. Courtesy: The Mariners Museum, Newport News, Va.

under charter. Afterwards she was replaced by the bigger *Satellite,* the former *Diamond State.*

Rather incredibly, when *Quaker City* returned to the Delaware she was chartered to Delaware River Navigation Company as a relief for *Columbia* on the Bristol line. The rival line eventually purchased and resold her on the same day, November 3, 1903. Thereafter she was operated at New York by the River & Harbor Transportation Company and the Long Island Rail Road.

The Long Island found *Quaker City* expensive to operate and resold her in 1905 to the Maine Central which renamed her *Sieur de Monts,* running her for many years between Mount Desert, Dark Harbor and Castine. There she was again praised for her beauty and, in *Steamboat Lore of the Penobscot* (1941), author John Richardson noted that "*Sieur de Monts,* a name of dignity . . . seems to admirably suit the steamer of that name . . . She was fast and powerful, driven smoothly . . . Her engine room was a thing of beauty and a joy forever to the engine room crew." She really was everything Shields Wilson had hoped she would be.

In World War I she was taken over by the U.S. Government and received her first "promotion" when renamed *Major l'Enfant.* She was later renamed *General Mathews* and after the war was acquired by the Norfolk and Mobjack Bay Steamboat Company for Chesapeake Bay service. She caught fire on March 22, 1930 at the Norfolk Shipbuilding and Dry Dock Company's yards. Her hull was subsequently converted into an oil barge which lasted until 1949. Her whistle signaled shifts at the Norfolk yards for decades. Like her sister she had lived longer than anyone ever expected.

Wilmington Steamboat Company finally abandoned the Trenton route in 1905 and the northern competitors also retreated to their pre-1900 position. J. Shields Wilson, who had designed the engines but not the boilers of the twins of 1901, grieved continuously after the accident to *City of Trenton.* The event had broken his spirit and is believed to have contributed to his death in 1903. During his father's despondency, Captain Horace Wilson increasingly took over fuller responsibility for the line.

*Quaker City* was renamed *Sieur de Monts* by the Maine Central Railroad in 1905 and operated from Bar Harbor, Maine. Hugh C. Leighton Co.

While the Wilmington line forged a strong comeback, bad luck haunted the steamers of Delaware River Navigation Company. On September 8, 1901, only a week after *City of Trenton's* accident, *Twilight* struck a rock near Morris Island when en route to Trenton. A hole was torn in her bottom and she began to sink while her 350 passengers went into panic. Fortunately, all were rescued. *Bristol* was badly damaged by fire during the winter of 1902 and *John A. Warner,* later converted into a propeller steamer and renamed *Burlington,* sank after striking a rock near Bordentown in 1911. The Upper Delaware lines had passed their prime and Wilson Line ultimately operated the last steamers in the area.

With the return to normalcy on the Delaware, Captain Horace Wilson increasingly turned to professional and civic affairs. In 1904, Wilmington's solidly Democratic City Council elected him (a staunch Republican) Port Warden, and Delaware's

Governor Preston Lea made him an aide-de-camp. In 1905 he was elected second vice president of Wilmington's Board of Trade and began the first of three terms as second vice president of the National Board of Steam Navigation.

Governor Lea appointed him Pilot Commissioner of the State of Delaware in 1906, the year in which he campaigned for the office of Mayor of Wilmington. Captain Wilson became one of the first Republican mayors of that city. At that time Wilmington Steamboat Company formally adopted "Wilson Line" as its trade name, recognizing the public's longstanding informal name for it. This title also helped to avoid possible future confusion among "Wilmington lines."

Captain Wilson was reelected in 1907, at which time he was made second vice president of the League of American Municipalities. A year later he became second vice president of the National Rivers and Harbors Congress. He was considered a colorful mayor and many stories were later told of his days in office. One of them involved payment for his services for a wedding ceremony of a wealthy suburban couple. When the groom asked what the fee was for the marriage ceremony, the mayor explained that there was no set amount. At that, the man turned to him, handed him a dime and said "Here you are, my good man, buy yourself a cigar!"

The Wilson boats also played colorful roles in civic ceremonies. One of these affairs was Philadelphia's "Founder's Week," held during the first week of October, 1908, to mark the 225th anniversary of the city's founding. There was a great naval parade on October 8, and a large part of the United States Navy's fleet, including the battleship *North Carolina,* lined the Delaware off Philadelphia.

Over a million spectators converged on the Camden-Philadelphia waterfronts for the occasion and riverboats bedecked with flags from stem to stern were jammed with sightseers. It was the biggest turnout on the Delaware since the reception for the Navy following the Spanish-American War of 1898, and, for the first time in U.S. naval history, a 21-gun salute was fired for the Mayor of Philadelphia. President Theodore Roosevelt had directed that the exception be made in honor of the Quaker

Gaily bedecked in red, white and blue bunting, *City of Chester* carries a throng to the Naval Parade of Philadelphia's Founders' Week Celebration, 1909. Edward O. Clark Collection

City. The naval parade began with a signal from *Sunflower*.

Leading off was *Samuel H. Ashbridge*, serving as police boat. She was followed by *Burlington* carrying official Philadelphians. *Columbia* came next with members of the city council, then *Thomas Clyde* with the River Display Committee, Wilson Line's *Brandywine* carrying the Founders' Week Executive Committee and *Bristol*, with members of the National Board of Steam Navigation. Notably absent was the venerable *Major Reybold* which had retired in 1906 after 59 years of service.

Everyone cheered as each steamer passed one warship after another, the Navy's new submarine *Plunger* capturing the most attention. On river and shore steam whistles roared in jubilation as only steam whistles can, and one Camden factory held its whistle wide open for over an hour. As the flotilla rounded the battleship *North Carolina* the scene became a frenzied spectacular the like of which the Delaware had never seen before.

Anticipating the public's enthusiasm, Wilson Line adjusted its schedule to meet sightseeing needs. While *Brandywine* took part in the parade, *City of Chester* maintained the Philadelphia line, and her schedule was rearranged so that her trip coincided with the big event, leaving Chestnut Street Wharf at 12:15 "to see the great show of large and small warships of the American Navy."

Wilson Line had always been known for rendering aid to those in distress and *City of Chester* won new respect on July 7, 1909 when, according to government records, "at 3:40 P.M., while steaming down the Delaware, Captain Jacobs of the steamer *City of Chester*, discovered two men clinging to an up-turned canoe. The steamer was stopped. The working boat was launched and cleared the steamer in two minutes. The time from when the steamer was stopped until the men and their canoe were on board the *City of Chester* was fourteen minutes.

"In a letter to the Supervising Inspector, the Supervising Inspector General of the U.S. Steamboat Inspection Service said '. . . the splendid rescue work of the crew of the steamer *City of Chester* is sustaining and encouraging to the Bureau and the Service, and the commendable report of Captain Jacobs is entitled to more than passing notice. Won't you please extend the congratulations of the Department for the maintenance of an efficient and splendid discipline.' "

Owing to his position with the National Board of Steam Navigation, Captain Horace Wilson was honored to play a key role in the greatest marine spectacle ever to take place at New York—the Inaugural Naval Parade of the Hudson-Fulton Celebration of 1909. Some 1,595 steamships, steamboats, coastwise steamers, ferries, tugs, warships and other vessels took part in an extraordinary salute to Henry Hudson and Robert Fulton. The celebration marked the 300th anniversary of Hudson's discovery of the Hudson River and the 100th anniversary of Fulton's *North River Steam Boat*.

The graceful *City of Chester* prepares for a landing at Philadelphia. Wilmington Steamboat Company Collection, Wilson Line, Inc.

Millions lined the New York-New Jersey waterfront to witness replicas of Hudson's *Half Moon* and Fulton's *Clermont* pass in review. Each squadron of steamers was placed under the management of leading steamboat personalities. The mammoth First Squadron comprised 12 divisions and 108 steamboats, the most colorful and appealing of them all, and the man selected to oversee this impressive flotilla was Captain Horace Wilson. His honorary title was "Fleet Captain" and his staff included Richard Van Santvoord of the Hudson's noted steamboat family, Samuel Ward Stanton, the famed marine artist, and Walter Millard, one of New York's best known marine architects.

The First Squadron included New York's greatest passenger steamers ranging in size from the huge Fall River liner *Providence* to more modest riverboats such as *Sagamore* and *John Sylvester*. Captain Wilson remembered *Sagamore*, his former *City of Trenton*, well, also her rival, *John Sylvester*. At the time, Captain Wilson was again having two unique new steamers built for his Wilmington line and, of all the steamboats under his honorary or corporate charge in 1909, only his seemingly luckless *City of Trenton* and his new steamers under construction were to be still in existence some 60 years later.

## Chapter III

# Tales of Three *Cities*

By THE EARLY 1900s Wilmington Steamboat Company's traditional Philadelphia-Wilmington line had enjoyed unprecedented growth. *Sylvan Dell,* the erstwhile "Queen of New York Harbor" and *Pleasant Valley* were chartered from the Gloucester Line in 1908 to relieve Wilson's veteran flyers during overhauls. Until this time Wilson Line had been able to handle all of its winter traffic with one boat, usually *Brandywine,* the Delaware's own "Ice Monarch." It was now necessary to maintain two boats during the winters and a larger fleet during the rest of the year.

This led to the construction of two new steamers and for the first time four express boats were to maintain the Philadelphia line. The new boats were named for the line's historic port terminals—*City of Wilmington* and *City of Philadelphia.*

November 27, 1909 was the date set for the double launching of the new steamers. It was one of the banner days of Wilmington's long shipbuilding history and Harlan & Hollingsworth's yards were the stage for the extraordinary intercity event when the two boats were launched at noon from adjoining ways before crowds of officials and inter-

*Pleasant Valley,* shown at Gloucester, New Jersey, operated from Philadelphia for nearly 40 years. Wilson Line chartered her in 1908. Courtesy: The Mariners Museum, Newport News, Va.

ested people from Wilmington and Philadelphia. The turnout was exceptionally large as the shipyard had complied with Wilson's Line's request to open the gates to the public, a practice which had been discontinued at Harlan's many years before.

To Miss Elizabeth Engelman Wilson, daughter of Captain Horace Wilson, went the honor of christening *City of Wilmington* while Miss Eleanor C. Reyburn, daughter of Mayor John E. Reyburn of Philadelphia, christened *City of Philadelphia.* Both young ladies were given bouquets of roses and held bottles of champagne decorated with red, white and blue ribbons. *City of Wilmington* was launched first, going down the ways at 11:45 A.M. The launching party then walked to the adjoining stand to witness the christening of *City of Philadelphia.* The latter glided into Wilmington's Christiana River 14 minutes after *City of Wilmington.*

According to the Wilmington *Every Evening:* "Whistles were blown, flags and handkerchiefs were waved and cheers went up from the throng of persons present when the two boats were launched. Each was successful in every detail, and the balmy air added to the pleasure of the occasion.

"Following the launchings, the guests, including the sponsors and their parties and officers of the steamboat and shipbuilding companies, were entertained at luncheon in the shipyard offices. The event was one of the most notable of its kind in the history of Wilmington. It is seldom that two boats are launched at one time anywhere."

The launching parties were a veritable "Who's Who" of Delaware Valley government, society, and steamboating. Among them were Mayors Reyburn of Philadelphia and J. Harvey Spruance of Wilmington, Congressman William Heald, General George H. Uhler, Supervising Inspector of the Steamboat Inspection Service; Joseph E. Borden, representing the American Bureau of Shipping (Wilson Line was one of the few East Coast fleets classed by and rated with the highest classification of the bureau); Robert Haig, representative of Lloyd's of London, and Henry T. Bush of the Bush Line.

At the reception, speeches were made praising the "world-renowned" Harlan & Hollingsworth shipyard. Wilson Line itself was lauded by the mayors of Wilmington and Philadelphia for its unifying role in the commercial growth of the entire Delaware Valley region.

Wilson's new twin *City* boats were unlike any others on the East Coast. Two years later the West Coast steamer *Tacoma* of the Black Ball Line resembled a two-stacked version, but in 1910, *City of Wilmington* and *City of Philadelphia* were precedent-shattering. Technologically, they were at least 20 years ahead of their time.

Until the appearance of the *Cities,* J. Shields Wilson had designed all the new Wilson liners. Although a progressive in engineering, Shields was

*Sylvan Dell* was long operated by William J. Thompson's Philadelphia and Gloucester Ferry Company. She ran for Wilson Line in 1908. Courtesy: The Mariners Museum, Newport News, Va.

very conservative in exterior designing and all of the previous boats appeared quite contemporary. With Shields' passing, his son turned to the Harlan & Hollingsworth shipyard. One of the yard's leading naval architects was George G. Sharp, a close family friend who came to America from his native Scotland to pursue his calling. He was known for the originality of his designs and was considered an apostle of modern functionalism. He worked closely with line officials to produce two unique, rather *avant garde* steamboats that would best meet Wilson Line's needs on the Philadelphia service.

Once again, turning diameter in the narrow Christiana imposed limitations on length. Therefore, the new boats were only 204-feet overall and 31 feet wide (41 feet over guards). The horror of New York's *General Slocum* tragedy in which 1,021 lives were lost when the steamer caught fire in 1904, and the burning of its own *City of Trenton* had left an indelible impression. Thereafter, Wilson Line eliminated wood in construction wherever possible. An exceptional amount of steel was used in the new *Cities* in comparison with new vessels being built by other lines. Some traditionalists objected to the sacrifice of "gingerbread" but the line was more than justified in maintaining its safety policy.

While the upper decks of the new *Cities* were wood, they did not rest on any combustible structure. Steel girders and frames carried directly to the hull, being essentially early uni-body construction to enhance safety and minimize vibration. Wilson Line had on its own actually exceeded contemporary government standards. A rarity for 1909, the new Wilson boats were about 60 per cent steel. Following are but a few of the other innovations incorporated in the new boats.

Important architecturally was the construction of a "terraced" or raised deck on the hurricane deck. Later considered a "Wilson Line feature," the terrace permitted those seated inboard to view the scenery as well as those located near deck railings. The terrace also served safety by discouraging sudden shifts of passengers to one side, thereby reducing the likelihood of capsizing. Another bold

*City of Wilmington* (left) and *City of Philadelphia* enter final stages of construction at Harlan and Hollingsworth yards, Wilmington, 1909. Courtesy: The Mariners Museum, Newport News, Va.

departure was a raised second deck on the bow. This was cleverly carried out to maintain symmetry of line while allowing extra height in the forward freight space. Bow stanchions were widely separated for handling large furniture vans.

Power was provided by single-screw triple-expansion steam engines developing about 1,500 horsepower. This was enough to economically propel the coal-burning steamers at 18 miles per hour. High speed was no longer as important as capacity, and fast service was to be achieved by an increased number of daily sailings. The stacks of the new boats were fitted with a steam jet of the then new "Bloomsburg type," designed by Captain Peter Bloomsburg. The jet increased boiler efficiency.

Although freight remained the principal source of income, the new steamers were designed to carry 1,800 passengers. Passenger accommodations as well received special attention. They were unpretentious but very pleasant. On the main deck a social hall extended full width and featured an impressive stairway in baronial style. Commuters particularly relished the Oyster Bar and children enjoyed a candy stand. Accommodations for the sexes were still partially segregated in 1910 and the ladies' saloon was comfortably equipped with leather upholstered chairs on carpeted deck. Shades of the railroad car type were fitted to large windows which were designed to allow passengers seated in the saloon to view the river panorama en route. Separate ports were provided for passengers, who no longer had to weave their way through freight spaces.

The main saloon occupied most of the second deck. Samuel Ward Stanton, in the *Nautical Gazette,* described this space as "commodious and handsomely fitted." This too was carpeted and had Pullman benches running athwartships to the windows. Writing desks and chairs, book stalls and a news-stationery stand were also provided. Steam heat was available throughout, since the boats were intended for year round operations. In short, the new Wilson Liners were ideal commuter boats for their two-hour route. Wilson's "public-be-pleased" policy made the new boats very popular.

*City of Philadelphia* was the first to enter service. Typically Wilson, the *Philadelphia* became a pacesetter on March 19, 1910 when the "wireless telegraph" was tried out for the first time on a Delaware River steamer. This took place during her trial trip. Recognizing the value of this new form of communication, Wilmington Steamboat Company pioneered its application among riverboat operators. The U. S. Navy had tried out the system in 1905 but popular recognition of the value of wireless did not come until the *Titanic* disaster in 1912.

Few lines anywhere enjoyed the type of enthusiasm that Wilmingtonians showered on "their" new boats, and the Christiana waterfront was a scene of intense excitement when *City of Philadelphia* departed Harlan's on her trials. Capturing the feeling, the Wilmington *Every Evening* noted:

The handsome all-white *City of Philadelphia* entered service in 1910. She and her sister ship offered new comforts and attracted record traffic. William H. Rau Photo: Author's Collection

"Gaily bedecked with flags, the new steamboat *City of Philadelphia* of the Wilson Line, just completed by Harlan & Hollingsworth, left the wharves of the builders at 10:30 o'clock this morning, with superintendent William G. Coxe in charge for the builders. Vice President Persifor Frazer, Jr., and other officers of the company were aboard, with Captain Horace Wilson . . . The boat, after leaving the yards, was saluted by craft of all kinds and over 1,000 persons were on Market Street bridge and its approaches for the purpose of wishing well to the new boat and waving congratulations to those on board.

"On reaching the mouth of the Christiana River, the boat, being equipped with wireless telegraph, the wireless operator on board, Norman E. Albee, night operator of the United Wireless Telegraph Co., here, got into communication with Allen F. Curlett, the day operator of the United Co. at the du Pont Building, and eight messages were sent from this city within an hour and eight received. Of these, one was sent to *Every Evening*, Wilmington, Delaware: 'New boat a great success and a credit to the Wilmington builders. Many thanks for your good wishes. Horace Wilson.' "

While finishing touches were made to the new boats, Wilson Line announced its new schedules between Philadelphia and Wilmington for 1910—fully competitive with the Pennsylvania Railroad. In this, it justly claimed the most thorough schedule ever maintained by boat on the Delaware.

Until April 30, boats left both terminals at 7:30 and 10:30 A.M.; 1:30, 4:15 and 7:00 P.M. The excursion or "big boat" season opened in May with 11 sailings daily in both directions. Boats sailed simultaneously from Wilmington and Philadelphia at 7:30, 9:00 and 10:30 A.M.; 12:00, 1:30, 3:00, 4:15, 6:00, 7:00, 8:30 and 9:30 P.M. No round trip passengers were taken on 9:30 P.M. trips—those who were interested could change at Chester to the up or down boat and return on the last boat from the opposite terminal, Chester enjoyed 22 north- and southbound sailings daily.

The fall schedule began in September and was similar to spring operations, while the winter schedule, stretching from November through the end of April, called for four round trips daily and one extra on Saturdays, Sundays, holidays and December 26. Like the rails, Wilson's schedules were so complicated and qualified that they had to be read very carefully. However, if one missed a boat, there was nearly always another arriving shortly thereafter. Lower Delaware steamboating had become an almost unending series of Wilson liners arriving, departing and passing en route. There were few river services which could match the performance of Wilmington Steamboat Company in number of sailings or miles steamed daily.

*City of Philadelphia* made her maiden sailing on March 30, 1910, taking over *City of Chester's* 22-year role as "first boat from Wilmington." Despite chilly weather and the earliness of the hour, a

*City of Philadelphia*, first Delaware River steamer with wireless, off the Quaker City in 1910. A. N. Sanborn, George G. Sharp, Inc.

large crowd appeared at Fourth Street Wharf for her 7:30 A.M. departure. The Delaware Valley's pride in the new Wilson liner was even more apparent upriver where the *Philadelphia* received a warm ovation of "pleasing and cordial salutes" from other river craft. Even the railroad joined in the continuous din of whistles. Large crowds greeted her on arrival at both Chester and Philadelphia.

Arriving at Philadelphia, employees made an extra effort to unload and reload the new boat in record time. At Wilmington, Captain Wilson kept in touch by wireless. Once again, Captain W. F. P. Jacobs was master. His staff included Truston Cain as first mate, John Emering, second mate, George W. Greer, purser, Alexander Craig, chief engineer, and H. B. Hutchins, wireless operator.

After *City of Wilmington* entered service a new surge of business developed, and by mid-April the new boats were equalling that of mid-summer, the normal peak period. Summarizing reasons for their popularity, *Every Evening* commented: "The very appearance of everything about the boats gives assurance to the passenger of their safety and stability . . . They present an appearance of cleanliness at all times . . . everything is inviting, homelike and comfortable, all of which is so noticeable that a person seldom takes a trip on one of the boats without planning at the time for another. The result is that the line has made many new friends in Wilmington, Chester and Philadelphia since the new equipment was added." Press comment such as this was significant, since Wilson Line had historically been publicity-shy, in contrast to other lines which hired publicists to promote their more glamorous steamers.

The veterans *Brandywine* and *City of Chester* were temporarily withdrawn for general up-dating once the new *Cities* maintained the line. *City of Chester* had a major overhaul, including the extension of her second deck to the bow in somewhat the same style as the newest boats. Despite their years, the older Wilson liners were still the fastest on the river. They were still royalty among the nation's passenger-cargo steamers.

While the new Wilson boats basked in pre-season popularity, the New Jersey & Wilmington Ferry Company's little *Ulrica* received but footnote press coverage. She deserved more, as she too was pioneering on the Delaware. At this time the automobile was beginning to capture widespread interest, and *Ulrica* was altered to "carry as many as four machines on a trip across the river." Although few realized the significance of her novel alterations, *Ulrica* had become the first auto ferry across the Lower Delaware. The idea of providing autoists with a new route to the Jersey Shore, as well as attracting north-south traffic via Wilmington to by-pass Philadelphia, was timely and bound to become more important.

By this time the third generation of Wilson men had come into steamboating. Joseph S. Wilson, Captain Horace Wilson's only son, graduated from Cornell University in 1909. His career paralleled those of his father and grandfather, for whom he had been named. An engineer, he first went to New York and worked for the Manhattan Traction Company and Bethlehem Steel Company. He later became a marine engineer and spent two years at sea.

Like his father before him, Captain Wilson desired to develop a position for his son in steamboating. When Joseph recommended purchase of the old New Jersey & Wilmington Ferry Company in 1912, the captain reacted favorably, and Joseph was made vice president in charge of operations.

As a safety precaution, Captain Wilson insisted that passengers leave their cars once aboard *Ulrica*. It was a good rule but on one occasion a passenger refused to get out of his car. The captain, fortunately, had persuaded the man's wife and children to comply. Before *Ulrica* departed from Penn's Grove, the man accidentally reversed his car, crashed through the gunwale and plunged into the river. The driver was rescued by *Ulrica's* crew, but instead of being grateful, he initiated an unsuccessful lawsuit. The safety rule remained in force.

Since its earliest years Wilmington Steamboat Company had provided pickup and delivery service from markets to its steamboats at Fourth Street Wharf, Wilmington. All the line's shoreside deliveries were made by its own fleet of horses and carriages, and large stables adjoined its wharves. However, the line suffered a tragic stable fire in 1913 in which some 40 horses died. Instead of replenishing its stock, Wilson Line acquired eight electric motor trucks, then a very advanced mode for delivery services.

Nothing spurred industrial expansion on the Lower Delaware as much as the impact of World War I, and no Delaware Valley industry boomed more than the du Pont powderworks. Existing plants near Wilmington were no longer adequate to meet the enormous war orders that arrived almost daily from European belligerents. This key Wilmington industry and thousands of Wilmingtonians literally migrated en masse to new sites on the New Jersey side of the Delaware.

The Carney's Point du Pont works had been established prior to the European hostilities but great expansion came during 1914. Population followed the new factories, and new villages—Rubberoid and nearby Riverview—rose almost overnight near Deepwater Point and Carney's Point. Salem, Pennsville and Penn's Grove also felt the changing conditions. By 1915, war-related contracts were valued at some $400 million.

Powderworkers from the tri-state region came by the thousands daily to the bustling new plants in New Jersey. Most of the Pennsylvanians and Delawareans took Wilson Line's ferries to Penn's Grove. New wharves were built at Deepwater Point and Carney's Point to accommodate passenger steamers.

Overwhelmed by the new traffic, Wilson Line had to acquire several additional ferryboats for the Penn's Grove service. The beam-engined *Long Beach* was purchased in 1913 from the Long Island Rail Road for the New Jersey & Wilmington Ferry Co. In addition, two separate ferry entities, Christiana Ferry Company and the Wilmington & Penn's Grove Transportation Company, were established. The ancient sidewheeler *Arctic* was acquired in 1915 from the Pennsylvania Railroad's Camden Ferry Co. Later, *Cape May, Peerless* and *City of Reading* were also acquired. The ferries sailed from Fourth Street Wharf, Wilmington, and side-loading was the rule. Steamboats and ferries made well over 30 Wilson sailings daily. Wilmington became a beehive of steamboating. Wilson services, however, were soon to become phenomenal.

To improve land transport, work began in March, 1916 on the new Salem & Penn's Grove Traction Company line along the Jersey shoreline. Services commenced in April, extending from the Penn's Grove ferry slip to Carney's Point. The trolley was later extended to Deepwater and Pennsville before terminating at Salem. Captain Wilson

"Old Powdermakers" of du Pont Company's Brandywine Mills pose on *City of Wilmington,* June 12, 1921. Alfred I. du Pont appears to the right of gentleman holding crutch. The Hagley Museum

became interested in this development and purchased a large number of the traction company's bonds.

Ferry traffic soon boomed beyond anything imaginable. By 1916, the Penn's Grove ferries were making sixteen sailings daily, from Wilmington. Ferries also departed Penn's Grove on the same schedule. The last ferry for Wilmington departed at 12:45 A.M.

As retired du Pont employee Frank Gentieu later noted in the *Carney's Pointer:* "The main transportation across the river was by the Wilson Line which operated their large steamers between Fourth Street Wharf and Deepwater Point carrying some eight hundred to one thousand on each of the eight-hour shifts with regular shift trains of passenger coaches transporting the men to the various plants where they were employed." *Brandywine* was transferred from the Philadelphia line to a new service between Wilmington, Deepwater Point and Carney's Point.

However, as traffic continued to climb and the steamers on the Philadelphia line could not be spared, Wilson Line sought steamers from other sources. To this end, in 1915 Captain Wilson went to New York to acquire the cargo-passenger steamer *John P. Wilson.* She was renamed *Merchant* and placed under the New Jersey & Wilmington Ferry Co. In March, 1916, Wilson Line also began a charter of the Upper Delaware steamer *Springfield.* She sailed between Orange Street Wharf and Deepwater Point, relieving *Brandywine* to return temporarily to the similarly hard-pressed Philadelphia service. After 23 years on the Penn's Grove ferry, little *Ulrica* was sold to movie interests. (She later burned at New York during the filming of a motion picture.)

While World War I raged in Europe, there was increasing uneasiness within the nation and a growing demand for America's intervention. When former President Theodore Roosevelt accused President Wilson of "cowardice" for his stand on the war, Delaware Valley shipbuilding and explosives industries had achieved unprecedented wartime production. This was the atmosphere in which Wilson Line proceeded with its plans for another express steamer for the Philadelphia line. The steamer was virtually a sister ship to the 1910 *City* class. The Battle of Verdun was underway in France on March 4, 1916, the day the new boat, *City of Camden,* was launched.

Christening honors went to Miss Frances Wilson, another young daughter of Captain Horace Wilson. Clutching a bouquet of American Beauty roses, Miss Wilson broke a bottle of champagne across the steamer's bow at 12:15 P.M. and, as the clean-lined steel steamboat slowly moved down the ways, cheers arose from hundreds of spectators who had gathered at the shipyard and across the Christiana. Steamboat line and shipbuilder alike were very proud.

Launchings of Wilson liners were important

Miss R. Frances Wilson (second from left) prepares to christen *City of Camden,* March 4, 1916. William G. Coxe, Harlan's president, and Miss Wilson's father, Captain Horace Wilson (wearing derbys) are at far right. Mrs. Frances W. Richardson

events on the Delaware and *City of Camden's* was no exception. Interest was aroused not because the Wilson boats were so spectacular to view, but because their services were valued so much by the region's population. In this period people still said "no one took the train if he could help it," since the boats were the favorite way to travel. The Wilson service remained economical, in no small measure due to direct railroad competition. Fares were still less than a penny a mile, a charge that was less than in "the good old days." One way to Chester was only 10 cents; to Philadelphia, 15 cents. Round trips were 15 and 25 cents, respectively—much less than the railroad.

In addition to the steamboat families, the launching party included Mayor and Mrs. James F. Price of Wilmington, Delaware; Mayor and Mrs. Charles H. Ellis of Camden, New Jersey and William Ward, Mayor of Chester, Pennsylvania, representing the three states then served by Wilson Line. Also present were Col. John Biddle, Robert Haig, Lloyd's representative, and William G. Coxe, president of Harlan & Hollingsworth. Following the launching, Wilmington's Mayor Price said a few words, excused himself, and rushed off to attend a woman's suffrage meeting. (After all, he was a busy politician and suffragettes were future voters.)

Speaking at the reception, Robert Haig praised the way *City of Camden* was launched and the workmanship of Harlan & Hollingsworth. Captains Wilson and Bloomsburg also paid tribute to the builders. Captain Wilson remarked that the most he could say in praise of the shipyard was to note that "every boat built by the yard had given satisfaction and that Wilson Line returned to Harlan & Hollingsworth each time it needed a new boat."

William G. Coxe, president of Harlan's, cited the longstanding "good feeling" that existed between the Wilson Line and his shipyard and noted that all the boats then on the Philadelphia line were built at Harlan's. Hailing from another Delaware shipbuilding town, Mayor Ellis of Camden had a touchy diplomatic problem as he took his turn at the rostrum. The mayor commented that "Camden thinks it can launch vessels better than any other place in the world," but, he added, he was "compelled to admit that Wilmington does just as well."

*City of Camden* was the first Wilson boat named for a city not directly served by the company. Her name was selected to salute the many residents of the New Jersey city who were faithful travelers on the line. Having lived in nearby Haddonfield at one time, Captain Wilson was partial to Camden. *City of Camden* made her trials on May 2, 1916

The mayors of Wilmington, Chester and Camden were among those cheering when *City of Camden* glided into the Christiana River on March 4, 1916. Courtesy: The Mariners Museum, Newport News, Va.

and began her busy and well-ordered career a few days later.

The Penn's Grove ferries led less charmed lives. While Wilson Line had become the leading carrier of du Pont workers, it was not alone. Competition came from all types of boats, large and small, and another traffic war was soon underway. Running new competition, among others, were the newly organized "People's Company" and the "Dime Line." The latter's uninspiring name was derived from its fare. The situation between the new lines and Wilson Line soon was described as "The War Between Ferries."

The Dime Line employed the old sidewheeler *Sylvan Dell* and she began running from Wilmington to New Jersey on March 9, 1916. However, bad luck haunted the competitors once again when *Sylvan Dell* nearly sank on one of her first trips. While off Wilmington, ice stove a hole in her side. About 350 passengers were aboard at the time and when she reached the Christiana she had to be beached near Third Street Bridge. The receding tide left her on the mud and gave repairmen a chance to patch her bottom, returning her to service in a few days. That kind of competition did not provoke much ire. After all, who had ever heard of an opposition boat nearly sinking at the competitor's wharf?

Powdermaking continued to set new records, and thousands of workers traveled on Wilson boats. The region had never before dealt with such massive shipments of material or huge numbers of people in daily transit. While the majority of the laborers went about their tasks without incident, it was not rare to hear of men fired for sleeping on the job or of an explosion now and then. There were also many "celebrations" amongst these earthy men who could barely wait to spend their cash on pay days.

Some of the temporary workers were entirely unprepared for the transition from farming to industrial work and some incredible things happened to them. One poor soul somehow ended up in Georgia, suffering from amnesia. He was identified as a Wilmingtonian only through his possession of a Wilmington Steamboat Company ticket! Employing and transporting temporary workers was not an easy task for either the du Pont Company or Wilson Line.

The almost unrealistic conditions attracted some

Spotless and proud, *City of Camden* maneuvers through Wilmington's Third Street drawbridge, May 2, 1916, bound for trials. A. N. Sanborn, George G. Sharp, Inc.

undesirables to the ferries and to the workers' shoreside habitats. The problems they created were symptoms of wartime conditions even prior to America's entry into the fray. Wilson ferries had their hands full with some of the men who made discipline difficult to maintain on occasion. Disorder of any type was simply unknown on the Wilson Line fleet prior to this time and the line took several steps to cope with the "wild ones."

These efforts led to the barring of grafters, who sold, among other things, toothpicks for "ill" husbands or wives. Different couples were apprehended on the ferries fraudulently appealing to decent workers' kindheartedness. One woman was collared after having sold $10 worth of toothpicks on one crossing to support a ficticious sick husband. "Sings," too, were halted, as one line spokesman explained, "since the whiskey and beer tenors did not harmonize!" (Wilson Line had never permitted the sale of liquor on its boats but the men often had a few drinks in New Jersey prior to returning to Wilmington.)

In another attempt to insure order, the line adapted to the ferry service the commuter booklet system that had so long been used on the Philadelphia line. Tickets were not to be removed from the booklets until collected on board the ferryboats. However, the system collapsed when some of the workers would not cooperate. In one instance, a company ticket collector asked local police to arrest several men who refused to comply with the rule. The police did so, and a disturbance ensued. The case was thrown out of court on the grounds that the steamboat operator could not demand compliance with its procedure of ticket collecting.

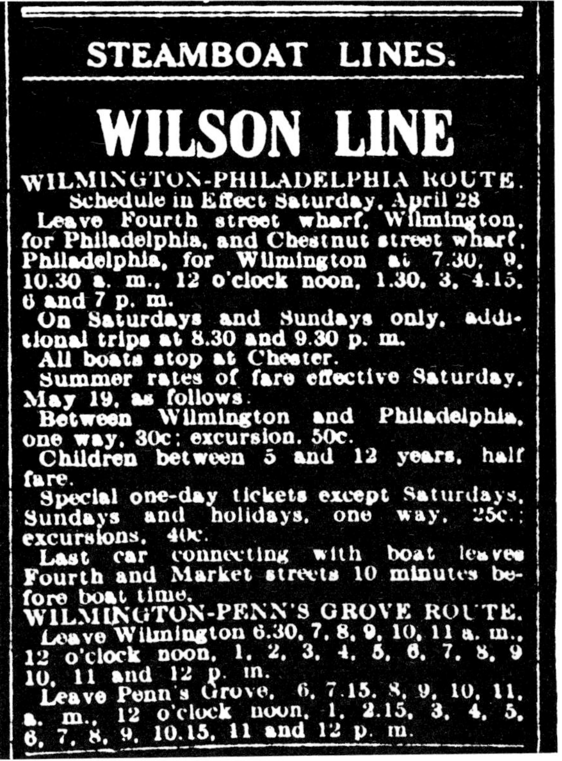


Wilson Line's ad in 1917 announces nine steamboat and 19 ferryboat sailings daily from Wilmington. Wilmington *Every Evening*

The venerable side-wheeler *President,* ex-*Columbia,* is at Wilson Line's Pier 5, Philadelphia, circa 1916. Courtesy: The Mariners Museum, Newport News, Va.

This was a challenging operation for Wilson Line but the workers too had a few complaints. They'd be thankful, some said, if they "could go aboard the ferryboats before the freight is loaded." Others commented that they wished they had "a sheltered waiting room on the Penn's Grove ferry slips." However, these were minor discomforts compared to situations confronting those who took other routes across the Delaware.

On March 15, 1916 the naphtha launch *Hyacinth* carrying nine du Pont employees had to be abandoned in midstream when ice crushed in the boat's sides. A large ocean freighter spotted the men and rescued them from the freezing waters. Others fell victim to collisions with freighters, and women who made trips on the small boats often became hysterical when the boats began to roll.

Despite heavy crowding, Wilson Line maintained order and made mass transportation a remarkably smooth operation. The line and the du Pont organization had successfully met the emergency needs and had provided one of the greatest, if unheralded, records of the war. Indeed, the Allied successes of World War I were in no small measure made possible through the du Pont gunpowder works, and the du Pont performance would not have been possible without the Wilson Line's dependable round-the-clock transportation.

By 1917 Wilson Line was forced to respond to growing demands for excursions. Accordingly, Captain Wilson rehabilitated French's Grove, an old-time resort near Penn's Grove, and the picnic center subsequently gained new popularity, especially after Penn's Grove was made a regular port of call for the Philadelphia steamers. About the same time, Riverview Beach was rediscovered for its sandy beach and attractive grounds. Within the next few years the line became increasingly interested in developing the potentials of that location as an excursion destination, but, in 1917, Wilson's steamboats and ferries landed passengers at Penn's Grove where they transferred to trolleys for Riverview Beach.

To promote the Wilmington-Philadelphia trade, the company advertised in half-page newspaper ads: "Healthful, delightful, hours on the Delaware—on the four most comfortable and elegantly furnished steamers on the river." On day trips, passengers were advised to "bring the little folks along," and, to spur moonlight sails, the firm

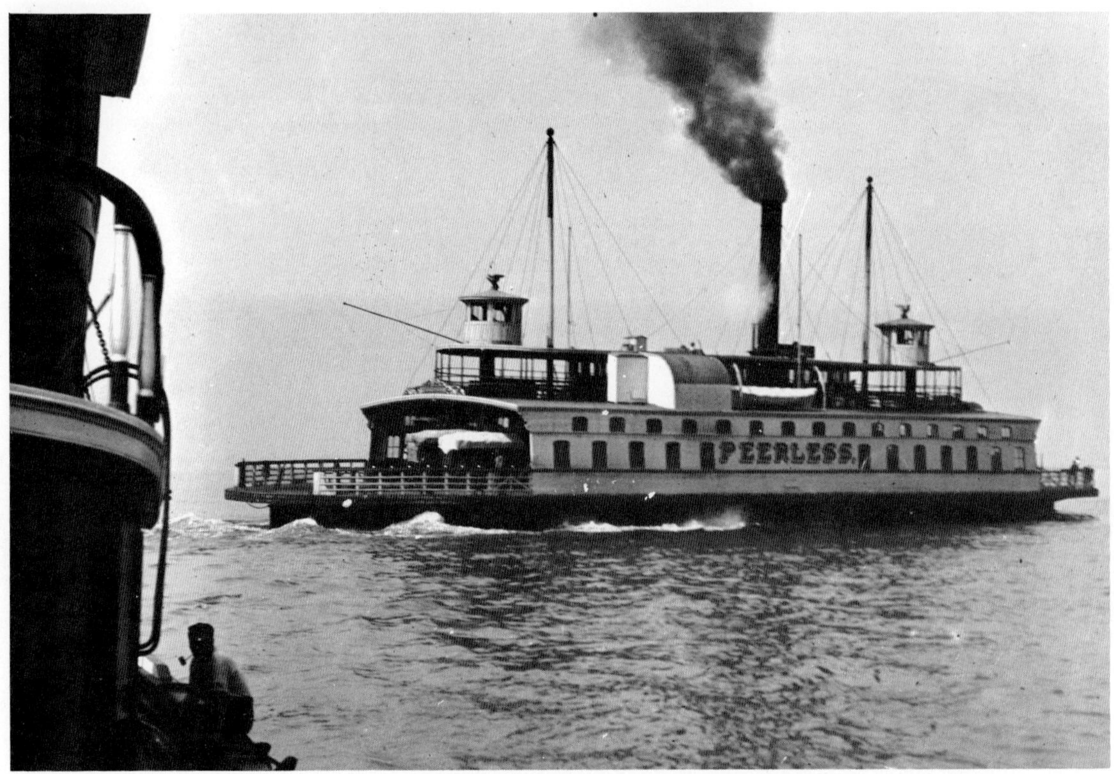


The aged *Peerless* was one of many ferryboats acquired by Wilson Line during the World War I era. Wilson had three ferryboat subsidiaries at the time. Courtesy: The Mariners Museum, Newport News, Va.

claimed that: "the evening trips have solved the problem of summer entertainment."

Passengers taking the Philadelphia steamers could not but notice the extraordinary traffic on the Penn's Grove ferries and the Deepwater boats. At Chester *Cape May*, the "boat that everybody loved" (formerly Captain Cone's splendid *Republic*), had become a "floatel." Her new role was to accommodate 600 shipyard workers of the Sun Shipbuilding Company and a 300-foot restaurant was built near her berth. This project was financed by *Cape May's* owners in cooperation with the shipyard.

Farther north, passengers viewed construction of 50 massive shipways at Hog Island. The U.S. Shipping Board's Emergency Shipbuilding Corporation had developed this yard "to build a bridge of ships to France." Although the armistice had been achieved before the yard fulfilled its potential, Wilson Line itself played an important part in the Hog Island story.

In 1918 the U.S. Government made an agreement with Wilmington Steamboat Company to carry shipyard workers between Hog Island and Philadelphia. In addition to its own fleet, the Long Island Rail Road's steamer *Montauk* was chartered for the Hog Island-Philadelphia run. Wilson's Philadelphia, Penn's Grove and Hog Island services were operating under peak conditions. As if the line was not busy enough, it acquired the neighboring McCullough Iron Works and carried out ship repairs during the war years. It later built a marine railway on the property to do its own maintenance.

Wilmingtonians were kept well-informed on the progress of the war in Europe and the great battles at sea. As a shipbuilding town, Wilmington naturally followed news of ship casualties with intense interest. One report involved a ship identified as *City of Wilmington*. Apparently a few details were overlooked in the rush to print when on April 17, 1918, Associated Press wired news to the local *Every Evening* that "*City of Wilmington* (had) burned at sea." However, according to the story: "The *City of Wilmington*, which hailed from Wilmington, Delaware, had a gross tonnage of 749 . . . was 192 feet long . . . was built at Wilmington in 1910. How large a passenger list was aboard could not be determined here, but because of the size of the vessel it was not thought that it was heavy." That only the local Wilson liner of that name fitted the description was completely

It's sailing time at Penn's Grove, New Jersey, circa 1918, and travelers hurry aboard *Brandywine*. Note bathing beauties in black stockings. Wilmington Steamboat Company Collection, Wilson Line, Inc.

overlooked by the Wilmington press. Nevertheless, the *Wilmington's* crew probably read of their steamer's troubles off Nova Scotia with considerable interest! Moreover, an accident did involve "old *Brandywine*" about three weeks later when the newspaper reported that: "Jetty Rams Steamer." The ferry *Long Beach* went to her assistance and transferred 200 passengers.

Throughout the war, Wilmington, like the rest of the nation, was in a high state of morale and patriotism was at its peak. Parades and Liberty Bond drives "to support our boys over there" were everyday events. The nation's shipyards were in hot competition, keeping production scores and boasting of their records as if a great international football game was being played.

Typical Wilmingtonians, Captain Wilson and his son were in the forefront of local patriotic events. As former mayor, the captain held several civic posts at this time, including membership on Wilmington's Military Draft Board, the Board of Harbor Commissioners, and the Water Commissioners. Joseph Wilson was president of Wilmington's Rotarians and dedicated a Liberty Bond drive for them. Under his novel installment-buying plan more could be raised "until the end of the war, if it is necessary," he said. Captain Wilson was on the reviewing stand for many a long and musical bond parade, including Harlan's, when some 5,000 shipyard workers marched through Wilmington. The captain's daughters also did their civic duty as "Liberty Girls."

By the end of 1918, Wilmington Steamboat Company's fleet had carried over 50 million passengers and over 3,270,000,000 pounds of freight since the line's reorganization in 1882. Its steamers had logged some 3,875,000 miles—equivalent to 155 voyages around the world. It had become one of the nation's leading river carriers.

With its own fleet severely taxed, Wilson Line revived an interesting sideline operation on the Upper Delaware in the summer of 1918. The old sidewheeler *Dolphin* (ex-*Glen*, ex-*Amphion*) and *Trenton* (ex-*Richmond*, ex-*Albion*) offered "Wilson's Select Evening Trips Up the Beautiful Delaware." Both steamers had been acquired from New York's McAllister Navigation Company a few years earlier for the Dolphin Line's Philadelphia-Trenton route. Under McAllister line, *Amphion*, in 1913, was one of the first excursion steamers to operate to Bear Mountain. However, in 1918, it is said that Wilson Line controlled several up-river passenger and freight steamers including *F. W. Brune*, one of the oldest boats on the East Coast. The then 58-year-old *Brune* had seen service during the Civil War.

Trucking was beginning to compete for freight and it did so far more effectively than had the Pennsylvania Railroad. Nonetheless, Wilson Line launched its own trucking operations and its

Wilson's ferries ran dependably in all kinds of weather but occasionally had predicaments such as *Cape May's* shown above at Penn's Grove, 1918. Wilmington Steamboat Company Collection, Wilson Line, Inc.

freight trucks provided the first "ship-to-store" service in the area. Combined steamboat-trucking operations extended the line's services to points far inland from port terminals. Freight transfers and deliveries were accepted at Wilmington and Philadelphia, giving the line a stronger position than other steamboat operators vis-a-vis both trucking and railroads. A Wilson subsidiary, Peninsula Auto Express (PAX), was said to be the pioneer trucking firm in the Delmarva region. As in the past, Wilson continued to adjust to current needs.

During World War I, Wilmington Steamboat Company's staff had been enlarged to handle its expanding fleet. However, peace in 1918 brought a sharp cutback in operations and presented the line with the dilemma of developing new jobs or losing many fine men. One solution was to expand its operations. Captain Wilson regularly spent winters in St. Petersburg, Florida and in 1919 he saw an opportunity to acquire the St. Petersburg Transportation Company. Best known as "The Favorite Line," this company had long provided passenger and freight service between Tampa, St. Petersburg, Palmetto, Bradentown, Manatee and Manavista.

During peak summer operations, upwards of 300 men worked on the Delaware steamers. However, only about half that number could be retained during the winter months. By acquiring the Favorite Line, Captain Wilson hoped to provide year-round employment while expanding operations. It was felt that some of the Delaware steamers, otherwise idle during the winter, might be sent to Tampa for that period and returned to Delaware in the spring when business normally increased.

In 1919, the Favorite Line's fleet included the propeller steamers *Favorite* and *Pokanoket.* The latter, it will be recalled, had been a keen competitor during the steamboat war of 1901. *Favorite* was the type of boat that Wilmington Steamboat Company might have built—a pacesetter which had been hailed as the world's first triple screw commercial steamer when new in 1894. She had been running out of Tampa since 1906. *Pokanoket* had been sold to the Favorite Line in 1912 and had run at various times with *Favorite, Manatee, H. B.*

*City of Philadelphia* steams on tranquil Tampa Bay during the early 1920's. Wilmington Steamboat Company Collection; Wilson Line, Inc.

Side-wheeler *Hanover,* later renamed *Mandeville,* was one of Wilson's "Favorite Line" steamers at Tampa, Florida in 1919. John C. Mills

The unprecedented excursion boom following World War I is evidenced by this view of jam-packed *City of Camden* at Riverview Beach, 1920. Wilmington Steamboat Company Collection, Wilson Line, Inc.

*Plant, Vandalia, City of Jacksonville* and *Fred'k de Bary*.

Under Wilson ownership, the Tampa firm's trade name was retained although its official title was changed to the Tampa and St. Petersburg Transportation Company. The Favorite Line also ran all-year service and its advertisements boasted "Fast and Frequent Passenger and Freight Service." Reflecting its new geographic diversification, Wilmington Steamboat Company restyled itself "The Wilson Lines."

As part of the overall plan, *City of Philadelphia* was assigned to the Favorite Line during the winter of 1919-20 and departed from Wilmington in November, 1919. Inauspiciously enough, she ran aground off Florida Reefs on the final leg of her long ocean voyage, breaking two blades of her propeller. Completing the trip under tow, the *Philadelphia* later entered service but proved too large and was returned to Wilmington in April, 1920. The line subsequently abandoned the "summer-north, winter-south" plan.

*City of Philadelphia's* place at Tampa was taken by the 188-foot sidewheeler *Mandeville* which had been built at Wilmington in 1914 as *Hanover*. She had been intended for service between Cuba and the Isle of Pines but never operated on that route. The Louisiana Steamboat & Ferry Company later acquired her for service on Lake Pontchartrain. In 1916, she was renamed *Mandeville*. Wilson Line employed her for about a year on the Favorite Line. The service was finally abandoned in 1925 when the southern fleet was brought to Wilmington.

Thereafter, the only reminders of the Florida experiment were a 5-foot model of *Favorite* and an oil painting of *City of Jacksonville* which decorated Wilson Line's headquarters at Fourth Street Wharf. However, Tampa came to know another Wilson boat when "Little *Wilmington*" was dieselized, renamed *Pinellas* and converted into a double-ended ferry for the Bee Line's Tampa Bay services.

In 1925, *Mandeville* was transferred to Wilson's Wilmington & Penn's Grove Transportation Co. but was not operated by Wilson on the Delaware. Subsequently she was sold to the Delaware Beach Company for excursions from Philadelphia. In 1928 she was sold to the Trenton and Philadelphia Steamboat Company and renamed *William Penn*. Ultimately she was the last sidewheel steamer on the Upper Delaware. In 1930 she was sold to New York interests and ran excursions from Newark to Coney Island. In 1934 she was destroyed by fire at winter quarters in Perth Amboy, New Jersey.

*Favorite*, too, went to New York via Wilmington. While at Tampa, she was transferred in 1920 to the Christiana Ferry Company and in the following year to the Wilmington & Penn's Grove Transportation Co. In May of 1925 she was sold to Captain Daniel F. McAllister for service to the Statue of Liberty. Sold again in 1939 to the Sutton Line, she was finally abandoned in 1941.

Throughout the initial post-World War I slump, excursions became an increasingly important business for Wilson Line. More and more people looked to the line for recreation rather than for transportation. The company once again adjusted to the times and because of popular demand it was becoming the nation's greatest excursion line.

## Chapter IV

# From *Cities* to *States*

BY THE EARLY 1920s several of the Delaware's once popular excursion steamers had concluded their useful careers. Among them were *Thomas Clyde, Penn,* and *President,* the river's largest steamboat. The last had been operated for many years by William J. Thompson and was long known as "The Big *Columbia.*" On the Upper Delaware the Dolphin Line was about to make its last sailings. In contrast, Wilson Line, which had begun direct sailings to Riverview Beach in 1921, was carrying the biggest crowds ever seen on the Delaware.

Turnouts for Wilson Line cruises were enormous but no publicity campaigns were needed. Indeed, the line's services were so well-known that the company simply posted its schedule in Philadelphia's newspapers with its initials "W" and "L" serving as sufficient identification.

Until this time all Wilson boats had been built for year-round passenger and freight service. From the passenger's point of view they were well enclosed and comfortably heated for fall, winter and spring but rather too enclosed for summer excursions. Nevertheless, it was a rare summer's day when the fleet wasn't jammed with thousands of Delaware Valley families making one-day outings on the river. For Wilson Line, transporting over 20,000 passengers daily had become routine.

New steamers were needed and as Wilmington Steamboat Company planned its first pure excursion vessels, it heeded public comments favoring "open" construction. This was but one of many design criteria considered for the wholly new type of steamboats planned for the Riverview Beach line. Other considerations were moderately high speed for the 35-mile trip, huge passenger capacity with maximum visibility, and entertainment features such as ballrooms. Fireproofing and stability were essential. The overriding challenge was to design the largest boats compatible with the perennial length limits imposed by the narrow Christiana River.

The line probably would have turned again to Harlan & Hollingsworth but, as a Bethlehem Steel subsidiary, Harlan's no longer built steamboats. In the meantime, Captain Wilson's longtime friend, George G. Sharp, had opened a naval architectural office at New York, and he was given the designing task in 1921. It soon became clear that Wilson and Sharp were once again developing pacesetting steamboats. Dwarfing the *City*-class steamers, Wilson chose to name its new twins *State of Delaware* and *State of Pennsylvania.*

As originally planned, the *States* were to have been 275 feet long, accommodating up to 4,300 passengers. Apparently, however, operation from Wilmington was reconsidered and their lengths were subsequently reduced to 225 feet, allowing service on the Christiana River and a capacity of 3,500; 4,000 with special permit. The *State* boats almost became America's first turbine-driven riverboats but costs proved too high. Building contracts went to Wilmington's own Pusey & Jones Corporation and the keels of the new boats were laid on October 25, 1922 with delivery set for the spring of 1923.

Wilson Line had hoped to surpass its memorable launchings of 1909 by having its largest boats also make spectacular simultaneous maiden sailings down the Delaware. However, those plans were abandoned because of continued shipyard delays. Built for approximately $400,000 each, the *State* boats took form about the same time that two other *State* boats were being built for the Old Bay Line at the same yards. While the latter, *State of Maryland* and *State of Virginia,* were rather tra-

# WILSON LINES

**GENERAL OFFICES—Fourth Street Wharf, Wilmington, Del.**

## WILMINGTON STEAMBOAT COMPANY

HORACE WILSON, President, Wilmington, Del.
JOS. S. WILSON, Vice-Prest. and Gen. Mgr., "
W. S. MARTER, Secretary, Philadelphia, Pa.
HARRY CRAWFORD, Traffic Manager, "
J. W. MARTENIS, Purchasing Agent, Wilmington, Del.

**Frequent Fast Passenger and Freight Service**

BETWEEN

**PHILADELPHIA, PA., and WILMINGTON, DEL.**

**Stopping at Chester, Pa.**

BETWEEN

**Wilmington, Del., Pennsgrove and Deepwater Points, N.J.**

*Schedule Effective June,* 1922.

**"Daylight Saving" time.**

| | | | | | | | | | | | | |
|---|---|---|---|---|---|---|---|---|---|---|---|---|
| [LEAVE | A M | A M | A M | A M | Noon | P M | P M | P M | P M | P M | P M | P M |
| **Philadelphia** | *7 30 | *9 00 | •10 30 | ♮11 00 | •12 00 | *1 30 | *3 00 | *4 15 | *6 00 | •7 00 | *8 30 | *9 30 |
| **Chester** ...... | 8 30 | 10 00 | 11 30 | 12 00 | 1 00 | 2 30 | 4 00 | 5 15 | 7 00 | 8 00 | 9 30 | 10 30 |
| **Pennsgrove** . | 9 10 | 10 40 | – – | 12 40 | 1 40 | *b*3 05 | 4 40 | – – | 7 40 | – – | 10 10 | 11 10 |
| **Wilmington** .. | 9 40 | 11 10 | 12 30 | 1 10 | 2 10 | 3 35 | 5 10 | 6 15 | 8 10 | 9 00 | 10 40 | 11 40 |
| [ARRIVE | A M | A M | P M | P M | P M | P M | P M | P M | P M | P M | P M | P M |

| | | | | | | | | | | | | |
|---|---|---|---|---|---|---|---|---|---|---|---|---|
| [LEAVE | A M | A M | A M | Noon | P M | P M | P M | P M | P M | P M | P M | P M |
| **Wilmington** .. | *7 30 | *9 00 | ♮11 00 | •12 00 | *1 30 | *3 00 | •4 15 | *6 00 | *7 00 | •8 30 | †9 00 | •9 30 |
| **Pennsgrove** . | 8 00 | 9 30 | 11 30 | 12 30 | a2 00 | 3 30 | – – | a6 30 | 7 30 | 9 00 | – – | 10 00 |
| **Chester** ...... | 8 40 | 10 10 | 12 10 | 1 10 | 2 35 | 4 10 | 5 15 | 7 10 | 8 10 | 9 40 | 10 00 | 10 40 |
| **Philadelphia** | 9 40 | 11 10 | 1 10 | 2 10 | 3 35 | 5 10 | 6 15 | 8 10 | 9 10 | 10 40 | 11 00 | 11 40 |
| [ARRIVE | A M | A M | P M | P M | P M | P M | P M | P M | P M | P M | P M | P M |

**Additional Boats**—Leaves Wilmington for Philadelphia ▲•10 30 a.m. Leaves Philadelphia for Pennsgrove †7 30 p.m. Leaves Pennsgrove for Philadelphia †9 45 p.m.

* Daily; † daily, except Sunday; *a* stops Saturday, Sunday and holidays; *b* stops Saturday only. ♮ Daily, except Sunday and holidays. • Runs on Sunday and holidays only. ▲ Does not stop at Pennsgrove.

**WILSON LINE FERRY SERVICE**

**Passengers and Vehicles**

BETWEEN

**WILMINGTON, DEL., and PENNSGROVE, N.J.**

**Frequent Service**

**Short Cut for Automobiles from South and West to New Jersey Coast Resorts.**

## TAMPA AND ST. PETERSBURG TRANSP. CO.

HORACE WILSON, President, Wilmington, Del.
JOS. S. WILSON Vice-President and General Manager, "
W. S. MARTER, Secretary, "
HARRY CRAWFORD, Traffic Manager, Philadelphia, Pa.
J. W. MARTENIS, Purchasing Agent, Wilmingon, Del.
HARRY T. CRAWFORD, Superintendent, Tampa, Fla.

**Fast Passenger and Freight Service**

BETWEEN

**TAMPA and ST PETERSBURG, FLA.**

*Schedule in Effect June,* 1922.

Daily, including Sunday.

| | | | | | | | | | | |
|---|---|---|---|---|---|---|---|---|---|---|
| [LEAVE | A M | P M | P M | .... | .... | .... | .... | .... | .... | .... |
| **Tampa** .............. | 8 30 | 2 30 | 4 30 | .... | .... | .... | .... | .... | .... | .... |
| **St. Petersburg** ..... | 10 25 | 4 30 | 6 25 | .... | .... | .... | .... | .... | .... | .... |
| [ARRIVE | A M | P M | P M | .... | .... | .... | .... | .... | .... | .... |

| | | | | | | | | | | |
|---|---|---|---|---|---|---|---|---|---|---|
| [LEAVE | A M | A M | P M | .... | .... | .... | .... | .... | .... | .... |
| **St. Petersburg** ..... | 8 30 | 11 30 | 5 30 | .... | .... | .... | .... | .... | .... | .... |
| **Tampa** .............. | 10 25 | 1 25 | 7 25 | .... | .... | .... | .... | .... | .... | .... |
| [ARRIVE | A M | P M | P M | .... | .... | .... | .... | .... | .... | .... |

**PASS-A-GRILLE on the Gulf of Mexico reached via Wilson Line to St. Petersburg; Trolley and Boat, via Gulf Port.**

STANDARD—*Eastern time*

**Connections.**—At Tampa and St. Petersburg—With Atlantic Coast Line R.R.

Wilson Line's normally detailed schedule became even more extensive with the addition of its southern subsidiary. Official Railway Guide, June 1922.

The 204-foot *City of Philadelphia* pivots in the Christiana after leaving Fourth Street Wharf, 1923. Wilmington maneuvering was considered fascinating. Wilmington Steamboat Company Collection, Wilson Line, Inc.

ditional, Wilson's duo were typically futuristic in concept, being early streamliners with simple exterior lines. Interiors of the Wilson boats were also very conservative but enriched by liberal use of mahoganized wood trim.

Interestingly, however, Wilson's first excursion boats were to become the most powerful, the tallest, the widest and the largest capacity single-screw steamboats ever built on the East Coast. Wilson had come to avoid frills in favor of safety and economy but, with minor changes, the *States* could have been beauties. Even so, they were very impressive and stately.

had anticipated that he could readily maneuver free with the flood tide once visibility improved.

However, the ferry had been rammed ashore harder than he realized and *Long Beach* couldn't get out after the tide came in. As the hours passed some relieved the boredom by playing cards or reading newspapers. Others were cheered by the impromptu entertainment provided by a minister who had expected to appear at a church show that evening. After company personnel found the missing boat with flashlights she was hauled free by the dredge *Minquas* and finally arrived at her Wilmington slip at 12:45 A.M., December 9. Her pas-

Port-side view of *City of Wilmington* after Gloucester Line's *Fearless* sideswiped her in fog, December 15, 1922. Wilmington Steamboat Company Collection, Wilson Line, Inc.

Wilson's services were remarkably dependable, even during inclement winter months, but extremely dense fog caused many problems for the line during the winter of 1922. The line's *Long Beach* had a classic delay on December 8, 1922 when she ran into impenetrable fog during a routine crossing from Penn's Grove to Wilmington. What turned out to be the longest trip in her career had begun at 4:15 P.M. Eight hours later the paddlewheeler landed at Wilmington and her 330 passengers raced ashore, tired, hungry and laughing! It had been far from a routine trip after all.

All had gone well until *Long Beach* entered the Christiana. There, fog veiled all navigation lights and rather than take chances, Captain John Emering decided to beach the boat on a mud flat opposite the new Wilmington Marine Terminal. He

sengers were elated to step ashore but they soon heard that their adventure was mild compared to those of numerous motorists who had driven into ditches along city roads in the same fog.

Poor visibility persisted and eight days later the Gloucester ferry *Fearless* collided with *City of Wilmington* shortly after the latter left her Philadelphia pier. The ferry inflicted a colossal gash in the steamer's side but fortunately no one was injured. Both vessels were severely damaged and were taken out of service for several days for repairs. Wilmington Steamboat Company later filed suit against the Gloucester Line and won the case. The Gloucester Line subsequently went into receivership, climaxing a bad luck year for the erstwhile pride of "Billy" Thompson. Its veteran *Dauntless* had been destroyed by fire only two months earlier.

On December 27 another siege of fog forced Wilson to suspend its New Jersey operations after *Deepwater,* then maintaining the Penn's Grove-Deepwater Point route, was forced to anchor at the mouth of the Christiana overnight while passengers were transferred to small craft. When interviewed by newsmen who sought a dramatic story about the weather's impact on operations, a seasoned employee of the line typically understated that the "siege" which the reporter dramatized was "quite common and part of regular winter storms."

Hundreds cheer as the futuristic *State of Delaware* glides into the Christiana River on April 3, 1923. Pusey & Jones Company

However, the winter of 1922 was atypical since it took virtually impossible conditions to tie up the Wilson fleet. The real news was cancelled sailings.

*State of Delaware's* launching took place on April 3, 1923. At 1:46 P.M. Mrs. Joseph S. Wilson christened the steamboat and a big crowd cheered as the Delaware's newest steamboat personality moved down the ways. Among the dignitaries were members of the Wilson famliy, C. W. Pusey, president of Pusey & Jones, designer George Sharp, A. B. White of the Baltimore & Ohio Railroad, Captain L. H. Cone and Frederick Reybold. A reception followed at the Wilmington Country Club in beautiful suburban Wilmington.

However, neither of the *States* was ready for service by Memorial Day, the original date set for their simultaneous maiden voyages. The *Delaware's* maiden trip was set for Monday, June 11 and it was reported that "scores of men are busy . . . putting finishing touches on the magnificent river steamer *State of Delaware* . . . (and that) . . . Because of the big demand for such a commodious steamer, the boat builders have been utilizing every minute of daylight so that the big boat will be ready. . ."

Her first trip was an unusual event, a moonlight trip with the E-Li-Ki-Ro Clubs (Exchange, Lions, Kiwanis and Rotary) and underscored the changing times. Transportation for travel was giving way to transportation for pleasure. The *Delaware* was the river's first steamer with a ballroom and it gave some 600 people an opportunity to dance in a setting fit for a Rudolph Valentino silent movie. Music was by "Shorter's Celebrated Orchestra."

Radio was a novelty in 1923 and considerable interest was aroused by Wilson's installation of a radio station on board the *Delaware* through which a special concert program was received. An old time community sing was also held on the observation deck and on the ballroom deck prizes were awarded to the couple performing the best waltz. With that happy sendoff, *State of Delaware* became an immediate success.

Meanwhile, the launching of *State of Pennsylvania,* her twin sister, was postponed until May 3. Christened by Miss Elizabeth Marter of Burlington, New Jersey, Captain Wilson's niece, "Pennsy" was to be one of the most loved of Delaware River steamers. She was also the last steamboat built exclusively for the Delaware.

*State of Pennsylvania's* trials were held on July 12, 1923, under the command of Captain Arthur Phillips, formerly of *City of Philadelphia,* with Amos Cascaden, a Mississippian, as chief engineer. Like her sister, she made her debut with a moonlight cruise from Wilmington to Riverview Beach. The fare was 50 cents and Wilson urged: "Do not miss this opportunity of making the first trip on the newest boat on the river." Thousands turned out and the tall-stacked river liner departed with her decks athrong and the music of the Hotel Dupont orchestra drifting from her ballroom. *State of Pennsylvania* made her first trip from Philadelphia on July 15, nearly a month after the *Delaware.*

*State of Pennsylvania* departs on her Delaware River trials. Newspapers reported that "she showed perfection" on them. George G. Sharp, Inc.

*State of Pennsylvania's* christening party at Pusey & Jones yards, May 3, 1923. Miss Elizabeth W. Marter (holding flowers) was sponsor. Her mother, Mrs. Agnes Marter, nee Wilson, who had christened *City of Chester* in 1888, stands highest on the ladder. Miss Frances Wilson, wearing glasses, christened *City of Camden* in 1916. Designer George G. Sharp (fourth from right) and Captain Horace Wilson (far right) had planned the *States*. Pusey & Jones Company

The Mammoth New Steamer

State of Pennsylvania

MOONLIGHT

Down the Delaware

Saturday Evening, July 14, 1923

Leave Fourth Street Wharf at 8 P. M.

A stop will be made at Riverview Beach at 9 P. M. to accommodate those desiring to stop at the Beach. On return trip boat will stop at Beach at 10.30.

FREE PARKING SPACE FOR AUTOS

in our Spacious Yard, Fourth Street Wharf

DANCING

STATE OF PENNSYLVANIA'S DANCE SALOON

Music by Shorter's Celebrated Orchestra

ROUND TRIP 50c

Do not miss this opportunity of taking first trip on the Newest Boat on the River

Full-page ad heralds the maiden sailing of "The Mammoth New Steamer" *State of Pennsylvania,* July 14, 1923. Wilmington *Every Evening*

Both *States* set new passenger records on the Delaware and comments on their design were soon heard from both sides of the Atlantic. In America, *Marine Engineering and Shipping Age* noted that: "Wilson Line's policy is to keep their regular passenger fleet up-to-date by the addition from time to time of new vessels especially adapted to their requirements and embodying the latest developments in the field of naval architecture. Their steamers have invariably been in advance of their time, and it is already apparent that the latest additions fully maintain the reputation and traditions of the company." The same journal also added that the design of the newest Wilson boats ". . . marks a distinct advance in the economics of operation and structural design . . ." in England, A. C. Hardy, in his *American Ship Types,* also praised the efficiency of the *State* boats.

Riverview Beach now surpassed Penn's Grove as the favorite destination of excursionists and the Wilmington line's 1923 ads hailed Riverview as a site for "Wonderful Midweek Excursions for Family Picnics . . . after a cool, delightful ride, you will find awaiting you a hard, sandy beach just like the actual seashore! This is the nearest place to Philadelphia where you can plunge into real salt water—the most refreshing and stimulating of all baths—simply glorious on a hot day . . . And after your bath and a trip on the water slide—the showers and then amusements galore—a beautiful dance pavilion, an immense roller coaster, carrousel, the whip, etc. . . .

"Take the children for a day on the Beach and a beautiful cool, invigorating River Trip on the mammoth new steel steamers, by far the largest passenger boats on the Delaware." (Over half a million Philadelphians did so each summer during the 1920s.)

The *States* sailed for Riverview twice daily, departing from Philadelphia's Chestnut Street Wharf at 8:30, 10:00 and 11:00 A.M. and 2:00 P.M., calling at Chester en route. Return sailings were at 11:45 A.M., 4:00, 5:00 and 9:30 P.M. The *City* boats also made trips to Riverview but people preferred the more open and spacious *States* with their huge ballrooms and triple-terraced decks.

The *States* were also preferred for moonlight cruises. The *Delaware* sailed from Wilmington on Thursdays throughout the summer season and on other nights she and the *Pennsylvania* sailed from Philadelphia at 8 and 9 P.M. Both featured one of the "Celebrated Wilmington Steamboat Company orchestras" and provided entertainment for thousands of dancers and romancers, the young and young in spirit of the Charleston Era.

Chester, Pennsylvania, Wilmington and Brandywine Springs Park in Delaware and Penn's Grove across the river were destinations for other Philadelphians who made trips aboard the regular Philadelphia steamers. All boats sailed from Chestnut Street Wharf and adult fares were still only 25 cents each way. The regular steamers sailed from both Philadelphia and Wilmington at 7:30, 9:00, 11:00 A.M.; 1:30, 3:00, 4:15, 6:00, 7:00 and 9:30 P.M.

One of the most colorful of the Wilmington charters was the annual excursion of the du Pont Company's "Old Powdermakers" to Riverview Beach. *City of Wilmington*, the favorite for this outing, usually featured "a philharmonic orchestra" to serenade the families of veteran powdermakers who had been with the du Pont organization since the early days of the local industry.

*State of Delaware*'s "mammoth ballroom," showing dancing couples posed by the builders. Pusey & Jones Company

The excursion boom made Wilson Line one of the world's busiest steamboat operations. Every few minutes one of its tall-stacked boats would pass another, riding low on the water with the weight of her human cargo. Steamers exchanged salutes and passengers waved to fellow excursionists. These were happy excursion years.

Wilson's schedule was a maze of details, highlighted by stars, asterisks, etc., to qualify the *special* sailings. The complex schedules indicated only public sailings, not the line's growing number of charter trips. During the summer of 1923, for example, the fleet made over 11 day and 28 moonlight charters during one week alone. Boat rides were the thing for social groups, big and small.

Members of the du Pont family also went along and employees wore colorful badges resembling miniature cans of powder.

Crowded piers and crowded boats were the summer scenes along the Delaware during the 1920s. Yet, Wilson's services were not fancy. There was, moreover, a certain charm and personality in its folksy simplicity. Dinners were not served on the boats but all had refreshment stands where children could buy soda, ice cream cones or popcorn for five cents, a ham or cheese sandwich for a dime. Tea and coffee cost five cents, but even prior to prohibition, Wilmington Steamboat Company refused to sell alcoholic beverages. There were comfortable armchairs, wide sun or shade decks as preferred. There was music and fun, and there were the animated personalities of the steamboats themselves, all of which meant memorable trips for millions of people, especially the children.

The shift to the excursion trade continued and in 1925 Wilson Line announced plans to reconstruct its 37-year-old *City of Chester* into a modern excursion steamer. George G. Sharp was again selected as designer, and the construction bid was won by the Baltimore yards of the Bethlehem Steel Corporation for about $200,000.

Sporting a bold and totally new look, the "new" *City of Chester* re-emerged in the spring of 1926. Her trials were held on June 24 and her return to service coincided with the inauguration of Wilson's new Pennsville-New Castle ferry service. The rebuilt *City of Chester* was a much larger boat and could carry 2,500 passengers, double her original capacity. This was made possible by installation of a larger, wider superstructure and an additional deck. Her hull was sponsoned out to support the new capacity and to increase her stability. A speedy beauty in her youth, *City of Chester* remained a fast and appealing steamer in her new, rather quaint, early "streamliner" guise. She was still the "Sweetheart of the Wilson Line" around Fourth Street Wharf.

But once again, as Wilson Line rode the crest of success, an adverse situation was near at hand. Its excursion line was booming and the regular line held its own. While motor trucks were causing concern, the rise of interstate freight trucking and the use of autos also served to increase traffic on Wilson's Penn's Grove ferry. Competition for this service, one of the line's main sources of income, was a significant development.

The rebuilt *City of Chester* carries a delegation of the Atlantic Deeper Waterways Association on a demonstration cruise through the widened Chesapeake and Delaware Canal in 1926. Wilmington Steamboat Company Collection, Wilson Line, Inc.

The competition began in early 1925, four miles south of Penn's Grove. There, an opposition line, calling itself the New Castle-Pennsville Ferries, Inc., was organized by Captain L. H. Garrison and Pennsville interests who had purchased the stock of the Garlick Transportation Company. Garlick's chief asset was an exclusive ferry franchise provided by the City Council of New Castle. The new line used the innocent-sounding trade name of "White Line," but the battle brewing was far from black and white.

Offering a quicker line than Wilson's Penn's Grove-Wilmington route, White Line soon cut deeply into Wilson's trade, a development Captain Wilson could not overlook. Initially, everything was in White Line's favor. Captain Wilson had long been aware of the merits of the new route and had in fact purchased land for a ferry slip at New Castle years before. However, he had assumed that an interstate bridge would eventually be built to replace his ferries. The bridge he envisioned was to come over thirty years later. Like his boats, his thinking was far ahead of the times.

White Line opened its new operation with *Whitehall* and *Montauk,* two well-worn sidewheelers acquired from the Long Island Rail Road, a subsidiary of the Pennsylvania Railroad. These were subsequently renamed *New Castle* and *Pennsville.* They were joined in 1926 by a third boat, *Baltic,* purchased from the Pennsylvania's Camden ferry. Accustomed to the long struggle between Wilson Line and the Pennsylvania, many Wilmingtonians thought the new competition was the railroad's idea but this was not the case.

The "new" New Castle ferry created considerable interest, especially in New Jersey. No one remembered that the river's first ferry had begun at New Castle over two centuries earlier. New Castle marked its semi-centennial on September 1, 1925

*State of Delaware* rests at Fourth Street Wharf, Wilmington in 1923. She was the first "new" type of excursion boat in many decades. Wilmington Steamboat Company Collection, Wilson Line, Inc.

The women's lounge on *State of Delaware.* Pusey & Jones Company

Side-wheeler *William Penn* ran under the Delaware Beach Line in the mid-1920's after Wilson Line liquidated its Florida subsidiary. Courtesy: The Mariners Museum, Newport News, Va.

*State of Pennsylvania's* 3,000-square-foot ballroom, decorated by John Wanamaker of Philadelphia, was ideal in the Charleston era. Wilson Line, Inc.

and that date was considered a popular one on which to start the new ferry and win local support.

White Line's management had everything set for its gala maiden crossing but *New Castle* ran aground in her insufficiently dredged Pennsville slip on her first trip. It was an embarrassing situation, especially since the line was hosting a delegation of local officials. It was no less embarrassing when assistance came from White Line's chosen adversary.

The forty-year-old Wilson liner *Brandywine* attempted to pull *New Castle* free but she was forced to give up after demolishing part of her own stern section. That "old *Brandywine's*" engines were stronger than her structure was embarrassing to Wilson Line. Finally *State of Delaware*, with her 2,900 horsepower engine, yanked the ferry free. White Line's "Opening Day" had become a steamboatman's tragicomedy, producing the wrong sort of publicity for the Pennsville group.

Wilson Line's announcement of its new New Castle ferry, June 24, 1926, when "The Great New Castle Ferry War" began. Wilmington *Every Evening*

Wilson Line ran a fleet of transfer trucks like these during the 1920's and practiced "door-to-door" shipping. Wilmington Steamboat Company Collection, Wilson Line, Inc.

Wilson's postcard of the late 1920's pictured seven steamboats with a "carrying capacity of 15,000 passengers." Wilmington Steamboat Company Collection, Wilson Line, Inc.

Refreshment-stand crew on *State of Delaware* pose for photograph before hungry thousands return to the boat. Sandwiches cost 10 cents in 1925. Wilmington Steamboat Company Collection, Wilson Line, Inc.

Wilson personnel, however, were not laughing over lost traffic and reluctantly concluded that the challenge could no longer be avoided. In early 1926, the line began construction of head-on slips at New Castle and another was soon underway near its Riverview Beach pier, within a few feet of the opposition's terminal. Wilson was soon ready but could not operate without a franchise. Finally, after some politicking, an elusive franchise was made available by the New Castle City Council. White Line's "exclusive" rights had been circumvented.

Wilson Line's own New Castle ferry began on June 17, 1926 using *City of Reading*, *Cape May* and *Arctic*, all formerly of the Penn's Grove route. In addition, the Long Island Rail Road's *Manhattan Beach* was acquired and renamed *Harding Highway*. The "Great New Castle Ferry War" was underway. The line also offset some of the opposition's advantages in July, when it cut fares from

*State of Delaware* debarks a happy throng at Riverview Beach, New Jersey, Memorial Day, 1925. Historical Society of Delaware

Rival ferry slips at Pennsville, New Jersey, during the summer of 1926. Wilmington Steamboat Company Collection, Wilson Line, Inc.

$1 to 50 cents on the Penn's Grove line and shortened that crossing by shifting its Delaware terminal from Fourth Street Wharf to the new Wilmington Marine Terminal.

Wilson was prepared to pay dearly to win but in this war it faced an opponent whose questionable tactics were overlooked by the Pennsville officials and associates who were investing their cash to take away part of Wilson Line's business. Once again the stakes and emotions ran high as both lines operated side by side offering sailings every 20 minutes. Wilson had won endorsements from the Automobile Association of America and others. Their signs lent prestige at Wilson's terminals but were of little immediate value.

Wilson's handicaps were obvious, particularly at Pennsville, where barkers stood almost side by side at rival slips vying for traffic. "This way to the Wilson Line!" shouted one. "This way to White Line," shouted another. Most drivers did not care which line they used. Both terminals were served by a single road which forked to the separate sets of slips. At Pennsville, a one-sided battle was staged over the Independence Day weekend and local police deliberately lined up traffic at White Line's slips, as Wilson boats sailed virtually empty all weekend long.

Firecrackers and other holiday explosives, innocently or not were tossed at those who drove to the Wilson Line terminal. All of this harassment was overlooked by local law enforcement. To further block Wilson, Pennsville officials permitted a taxi stand and a bus stop to be placed near the entrance to the Wilson slip. This effectively diverted traffic to White Line and there was little Wilson could do in the face of the "fait accompli." Over the weekend White Line naturally carried the field, transporting 1,076 cars as against 183 on the Wilson ferries. Wilson had taken a beating but there was to be another day.

*City of Camden* makes a landing at Penn's Grove during the 1920's. Wilson had painted hulls black during World War I. Wilmington Steamboat Company Collection, Wilson Line, Inc.

By Labor Day, Wilson Line had obtained an injunction against the blatantly unfair practices at Pennsville, but during 1926 Wilson Line carried only 9,000 vehicles compared to 140,000 on White

Line boats. However, statistics alone did not reflect where the real strength existed. Wilson Line had lost some key battles but not the war. By out-oppositioning its opposition, White Line's fund-raising bonds had been made far less attractive and its backers began to have second thoughts as the war continued.

the life of the Delaware-New Jersey Ferry Company. The "Great New Castle Ferry War" had ended and what came to be known as "that gold mine," was destined to be vital to the growth of north-south traffic.

The reorganized fleet consisted of nine once splendid ferryboats, including *Cape May, City of Reading, Peerless, Long Beach, Arctic, Baltic, Pennsville, New Castle* and *Harding Highway.* Ironically, while Wilson Line long prided itself on operating ultra-modern steamers, it had in this fleet one of the rarest collections of 19th century sidewheelers found on the east coast. The veterans, however, were as reliable and serviceable as they were old-fashioned.

"Old *Brandywine*" attempts to haul White Line's *New Castle* out of mud at Pennsville, September 1, 1925. Moments later *Brandywine* damaged her stern. Historical Society of Delaware

In early 1927 Wilson offered to purchase its opposition for $400,000 but White Line flatly rejected the offer. Nevertheless, some of White Line's stockholders began to sell their holdings to Wilson Line and shortly afterward White Line agreed to a merger. Thus, on March 28, the Delaware-New Jersey Ferry Company, a new subsidiary of Wilmington Steamboat Company, was formed. The new company took in the ferry fleets of both lines, even though Wilson chose to keep the Penn's Grove ferry in operation.

Captain Wilson became the new company's president and Captain Garrison, his astute competitor, was general manager, a post he held throughout

For 72 per cent of the new firm's stock, Wilson paid but $20,655. However, Wilson had really spent a great deal more, considering its terminal construction and operating losses during the pre-merger period. Wilson had won the war it had tried to avoid and, owing to the success of the new ferry system, construction of the Delaware River bridge at New Castle was postponed indefinitely.

White Line had ultimately lost its independence but it had gained a share of the successful Delaware crossing. Gaining a share was its primary intention from the start. However, years later, Captain Garrison insisted: "We were not licked. On the contrary, Wilson Line, losing $200 daily, was licked, but they could afford the licking, while we could not afford the victory!"

Captain Clarence J. Turner makes a log entry on *City of Chester.* Wilson Line, Inc.

Within a few years time the Delaware-New Jersey Ferry Company's annual traffic grew from hundreds of thousands to millions of passengers and vehicles and it became a regionally important transportation system. Having phased out its St. Petersburg subsidiary Wilson Line once again concentrated all services on the Delaware. Its fleet stood at nine passenger-cargo steamers and nine ferryboats with a combined passenger capacity of nearly 20,000. In summers, the fleet made over 200 sailings daily from Delaware River ports. The company never looked more formidable.

By 1927, Wilson operations included the Philadelphia-Chester-Penn's Grove-Wilmington year-round passenger-freight line, the Philadelphia-Chester-Riverview summer line, a Wilmington-Riverview summer service, a Wilmington-Penn's Grove-Deepwater Point year-round passenger-freight line, two separate ferry operations, a tug and barge operation, and shoreside trucking services. Yet, contemporary trends posed eventual threats to continuation.

With prospects of increased labor costs for freight handling, the line's chief business, the future looked bleak to Captain Wilson by 1928. Trucks were taking more and more freight and more off-season travelers were using the trains since the Pennsylvania electrified the line to Wilmington.

Although few had believed it could happen, Wilson Line in late 1928 sold the entire company to a Philadelphia syndicate headed by Kansas-born George B. Junkin. In the sale Captain Wilson realized over $1,000,000. (Less than a year later business collapsed en masse following the Wall Street debacle.)

Although there was widespread interest in the disposition of the Delaware's greatest steamboat line little information was made public about its sale. On February 6, 1929, the Wilmington *Every Evening* reported only that: "An application for a charter to Wilson Line, Inc., having been granted, the organization of the company is nearly completed . . . The amount of capital mentioned is $1,000,000, and there will be 75,000 shares of stock with no par value. George B. Junkin of Bryn Mawr, Pa., is named as the incorporator." Total purchase price was not revealed. Ownership of the steamboats passed to the syndicate on February 25 and Wilson Line, Inc. assumed full control on March 12.

After more than a century there was no longer a Wilmington Steamboat Company on the Delaware. The Wilmington Steamboat Company of 1882—"Wilson's line"—had been one of the nation's great water carriers, safely transporting over 70 million passengers and consistently pioneering more in steamboat design and operation than virtually any other operator. However, the new management carried on the line's traditions and the distinctive spirit of the old line transcended the change in ownership. Wilson Line was more than a steamboat line. It was an institution.

*City of Chester* steams serenely through the Chesapeake and Delaware Canal during the late 1920's. Wilmington Steamboat Company Collection, Wilson Line, Inc.

It's sailing time at Riverview Beach and *State of Pennsylvania's* passengers line the long pier which stretches to deeper waters in the Delaware. This mid-1920's aerial view captures all of the key elements of the traditional excursion appeal—scenery, steamboat, pier, beach and the classic amusement park. At the time, "Pennsy" made one evening and two daytime round trips daily from Philadelphia to Riverview. Photo: Wilson Line, Inc.

## Chapter V

# A Steamboat Empire Is Formed

THE TRANSITION from Wilmington Steamboat Company, a New Jersey corporation, to Wilson Line, Inc., a Delaware corporation, brought few immediate changes. The new entity retained its predecessor's trade name, added new steering wheel stack insignias to the fleet and continued all services as before. However, the new management had far-reaching ideas of its own and various plans to adapt Wilson Line to the changing and precarious times.

George B. Junkin, the line's new president, was not well-known on the Delaware but he had an impressive background in ship operations, A Naval Academy graduate, his naval career spanned from 1913 to 1924, when he resigned his commission following the Disarmament Conference which reduced American naval strength. His active duty included service on a variety of vessels from submarines to battleships. Junkin brought the "can-do" spirit of the Navy to a depressed business.

Throughout the nation steamboat companies faced a gloomy future, possibly no future at all. The Great Depression spurred the inevitable and many lines fell by the wayside. However, Wilson Line had two bright service areas. Its ferry operations were enjoying growth and continued to provide substantial income. The excursion business was also strong. The depression dampened sales of autos, a situation which helped to assure the continued popularity of summer excursions. The line further reduced fares, thus assuring continued patronage for its steamers.

Plans were also formulated to convert the line's passenger-freight steamers into excursion boats, to decentralize operations, and to begin new services far from the Delaware. However, all of its traditional services continued until those plans could be implemented. As Lynn Groh later commented in "Pleasure Is Their Business," a concise history of the line appearing in the summer, 1956, issue of *Ships and the Sea* magazine: ". . . One cannot help but admire the foresight and initiative of the men who came up with a new idea that not only saved a company from what appeared to be certain death, but also launched that company on a completely new career . . ." In effect, Wilson Line, Inc. had begun a steamboat empire never before attempted. It was determined to survive.

However, not everyone liked the changing personality of the staid old line or the new roles slated for its veteran steamers. Yet, companies, like individuals, seem to have definite personalities and, in the following years, although something of the old line passed, something survived. The old line's charm had been its utter unpretentiousness. It was proud but generally avoided publicity and, it had not been aggressively commercial. Its boats were simply there, morning and night, all year round. The service sold itself. There is no evidence that the line had ever issued promotion booklets and apparently the line never felt it needed them.

The new line continued its predecessor's interest in advanced and original design, and it was to add considerably to the number of "firsts" already established by Wilson Line. Entering steamboating when others were giving up, the new line had no choice but to be far more promotional. To this end, Frederick Reybold, scion of one of the Delaware Valley's first families, was made director of public relations for Wilson Line and all of its subsidiaries.

Wilson Line proceeded with plans for conversion of its combination steamers into excursion boats but local traffic was insufficient to support eight boats on the Delaware. Some of them, it was felt, would have to be placed in service elsewhere and since other lines were ending operations at various ports there would be opportunities for diversification, and for the establishment of the "Wilson System."

Not one American steamboat line built a new boat during the depression. New construction was neither justifiable nor, in many cases, financially possible. Wilson could afford to build one or two new excursion boats or rebuild four passenger-cargo steamers. It chose the latter course and planned to spend a million dollars on reconstruction. Millions more were earmarked for development of new ferry systems, all of which was considered wildly speculative by contemporary steamboat people.

Geographic diversification began in the spring of 1930 when *City of Chester* was prepared to start the new line's first non-Delaware service. On April 24, 1930 she was re-christened *City of Washington* and on May 30 began sailing daily from the nation's capital to Chapel Point, Maryland and Colonial Beach, Virginia. Wilson's second oldest steamer was soon considered one of the finest and fastest boats that had ever sailed the Potomac. A fine steamboat and a scenic river trip were perfectly matched and in its first attempt Wilson Line had established a very popular and profitable branch operation. The Washington Division served local patronage and the capital's big tourist trade as well.

In the line's annual report, George Junkin ad-

Wilson liners and children were a happy combination for nearly a century. Above, *City of Washington*, ex-*City of Chester*, hosts the younger set. Wilson Line, Inc.

vised stockholders that: "The *S/S City of Washington* produced revenues of substantial proportions which largely offset declines in passenger revenues in the Philadelphia District." This good news pointed to continued diversification. Another beneficial move came in 1931 when Wilson Line acquired the 155-year-old Bush Line, one of the nation's oldest transportation firms. Thereafter, Bush and Wilson freight operations were merged to provide additional savings for both lines. In the merger, Bush Line's freighters *Christiana* and *West River,* the tug *J. C. Reichert* and the barge *Foote* joined the Wilson fleet.

Wilson employees pose with *State of Pennsylvania* in 1931. Note rail spur connecting Wilson's Wilmington wharf with the Pennsylvania Railroad. Wilson Line, Inc.

Henry T. Bush joined Wilson's board of directors, thus adding to Wilson Line's historical human ingredients, the name of Bush to those of the Wilsons, Crawfords and Reybolds. Wilson Line had become the last survivor of the native Delaware River lines and a virtual "home" to descendants of many Delaware River steamboating people of yesteryear, with the ironic exception of the Wilsons themselves.

"Acquisition of Bush Line," Mr. Junkin added in his stockholders' report, "has served to increase gross freight revenues over those enjoyed in any previous year of your company's existence and, upon any return to normal business conditions, the net profits of your company should expand materially . . . Business originating through coordinated Motor Truck Lines (another Wilson subsidiary) shows promise of development."

Lastly, the new president advised: "Your management has recently concluded negotiations for operation of the *S/S State of Delaware* at Baltimore, Maryland, during the summer of 1931. This operation will cover a passenger and excursion business between Baltimore and Seaside Park, on Chesapeake Bay. In view of the success of your Washington operation, it is expected that this move will be a beneficial one."

Despite the depression, Wilson Line continued to earn its way. In 1929, its operations grossed $821,777 and netted $235,610. By 1931, these figures had risen to $922,492 and $237,705, respectively. Many other lines operated in the red, went bankrupt or, like the Ericsson Line, continued under receivership.

Freight boat *Christiana* became a Wilson liner after Wilson purchased the 155-year-old Bush Line in 1931. Wilson Line, Inc.

Changes were also in store for the Delaware-New Jersey Ferry Company. Shortly after reorganization, *City of Reading* was sold to New York interests and was replaced by the former Pennsylvania Railroad ferry *Cincinnati*. When new in 1891 *Cincinnati* had been considered one of the world's most beautiful ferry boats. She was no longer in that class but still proved a valued addition to the fleet.

In 1930, 57-year-old *Peerless* was abandoned and 49-year-old *Baltic* was renamed *Brigantine*. The old *Peerless* was replaced later by the ultra-modern new propeller boat *Jersey Shore*, built for $250,000 by Pusey & Jones in 1931. *Jersey Shore* was the first boat built for Wilson Line, Inc. and the first diesel powered ferry boat on the Delaware. She could carry twice as many autos as the older sidewheelers.

At this time auto fares were 75 cents a crossing, while passengers paid 10 or 20 cents on the Penn's Grove and Pennsville ferries. In the mid-1930s Wilson Line introduced ship-to-shore telephone service by which motorists could reach any location in the United States.

However, in the spring of 1931, as Wilson Line planned its second non-Delaware service, it was dealt a tragic setback. On the afternoon of April 19, 1931, a fire broke out aboard *West River* at Wilson's Fourth Street Wharf. Fanned by high winds, the fire ignited the nearby *City of Washington* and both steamers were soon engulfed by flames. The fire was out of control long before firemen reached the scene and several thousand spectators gathered to view the waterfront inferno. For-

Aerial view of broad-beamed *State of Delaware* on Chesapeake Bay, 1931. Wilson Line, Inc.

## A Steamboat Empire Is Formed

Aftermath view of the tragic fire which swept Wilson's Fourth Street Wharf on April 20, 1931, shows the twisted hulk of *City of Washington*. Wilson Line, Inc.

Rebuilt *City of Washington* gleams under warm June sun at Pusey & Jones shipyard, Wilmington, just prior to returning to service. A. N. Sanborn

tunately, *City of Camden* had departed for Philadelphia at 4:15 P.M., moments before the fire erupted.

Although *City of Washington's* framing was steel, her decks were wood and these burned completely. *West River's* fire was finally extinguished only after she filled with water and foundered in the Christiana outboard from the *Washington.* During the four-hour blaze flames also ignited some of *State of Delaware's* canvas deck covers. Firemen placed highest priority on saving the *Delaware* and towed her away from her berth where her fires were isolated and contained successfully. The steamer's damage was limited to blistered paint and burnt canvas. The *Foote* also survived with but little damage. At one point, Jack Smith, the watchman on *West River,* was forced to leap overboard by the flames consuming his boat. Another Wilson employee, Albert McCormick, dove into the frigid waters to rescue him.

Relief Captain Wharton keeps his alert eyes ahead as he guides *City of Washington* down the Potomac during the early 1930's. Wilson Line, Inc.

At the time of her loss *West River* was loaded with a consignment of a sugar extract used in manufacturing dynamite. It was bound for a du Pont Company plant at Gibbstown, New Jersey. After *West River* sank, some of her cargo, still burning, floated to the surface and continued to pose a serious fire hazard along the Christiana waterfront. Men in rowboats beat out scattered patches of burning material with oars and brooms. A fire watch was stationed overnight at the smolder-

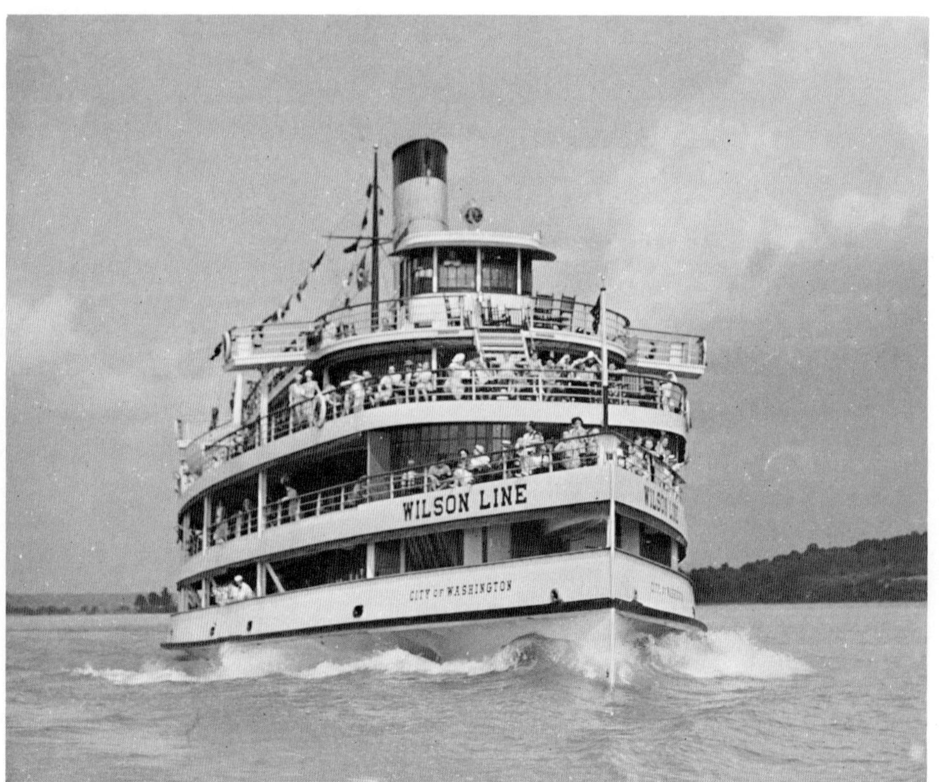


With "a bone in her teeth," all-white *City of Washington* speeds down the Potomac in 1935. She still made 20 miles per hour. Wilson Line, Inc.

ing wreckage and wharves of Wilson Line and the nearby American Car and Foundry Company. The fire had been one of Wilmington's worst.

Losses were estimated at $300,000 and it was not known whether the *Washington* could be salvaged. Without her the line also stood to lose earnings from its new Potomac River service. Accordingly, *City of Camden* was reserved as a possible replacement at Washington.

Wilson personnel were strongly identified with their line and many of them raced back to Wilmington as soon as they heard the news. No one was more disturbed than Captain John Emering, *City of Washington's* master for 20 years. Typical of the line's senior captains, he was fiercely proud of his boat.

He was one of the line's oldest employees at the time, having begun his career in 1896 as a mess boy on the same boat when she was the new *City of Chester*. News of her burning was a personal tragedy for him. On reaching Fourth Street Wharf he stood helpless in the throng and wept openly as his boat became a twisted skeleton.

Captain Emering and his crew had just been ordered to return to work in preparation for the coming season but his sad task instead was to direct salvage operations. Workmen said that he was often observed gazing at the *Washington's* wreck as though he was looking upon an old and wounded friend. He could not have been happier later to receive news that the line had decided to take bids for her reconstruction.

Wilmington's Pusey & Jones yards submitted the winning bid at $150,000 and under the contract the steamer's reconstruction was to be completed

Captain John Emering beams with pride in front of *City of Washington's* pilothouse as "his" boat returns to service in 1931. Wilson Line, Inc.

With her whistle roaring and a capacity crowd, *City of Washington* passes through Wilmington's Third Street drawbridge on June 19, 1931. Wilson Line, Inc.

*Arctic* loads vehicles at New Castle, Delaware, in 1934. She was the oldest unit of Wilson's Delaware-New Jersey Ferry Company fleet. C. Bradford Mitchell

Gaily bedecked with signal flags, the jammed *State of Delaware* backs from Pier 8, Light Street, Baltimore, July 17, 1933, bound for Seaside Park. R. Loren Graham

Wilson Line had become many things to many people by the 1930's, but it was still a source of leisure trips on the Delaware. Above, *City of Camden* is at Philadelphia, July 19, 1933. R. Loren Graham

*Deepwater* is at Wilmington in 1934. Wilson Line operated her for the du Pont Company for many years after World War I. C. Bradford Mitchell

Clean wide decks, comfortable armchairs and the scenic Potomac trip made *City of Washington* one of the Potomac's most popular steamboats. Wilson Line, Inc.

within two months. Exactly 60 days later *City of Washington* stood proudly on the banks of the Christiana, almost in her previous form, ready to return to Washington. Amazingly, she had "replaced" herself and was back on the Potomac by June 21.

Wilson's twin flagships parted company in 1931 when *State of Delaware* launched Baltimore operations. Following another Wilson tradition, her maiden Chesapeake sailing was a gala moonlight cruise on May 27, sailing from Pier 8, Light Street. She was under the command of Captain William T. Hunton, an expert shiphandler who had been with Wilson Line since 1918.

In a public relations effort, the line invited important state, city and local officials to the *Delaware's* debut and during the sail guests were entertained by motion pictures on the steamer's open boat deck. This was another Wilson innovation on riverboats and presaged later outdoor movies. The novelty was very popular on moonlights until "talkies" became more common.

The *Delaware* began running to Seaside Park on May 28 and soon reestablished this line. The park, formerly known as Chesapeake Beach, was located

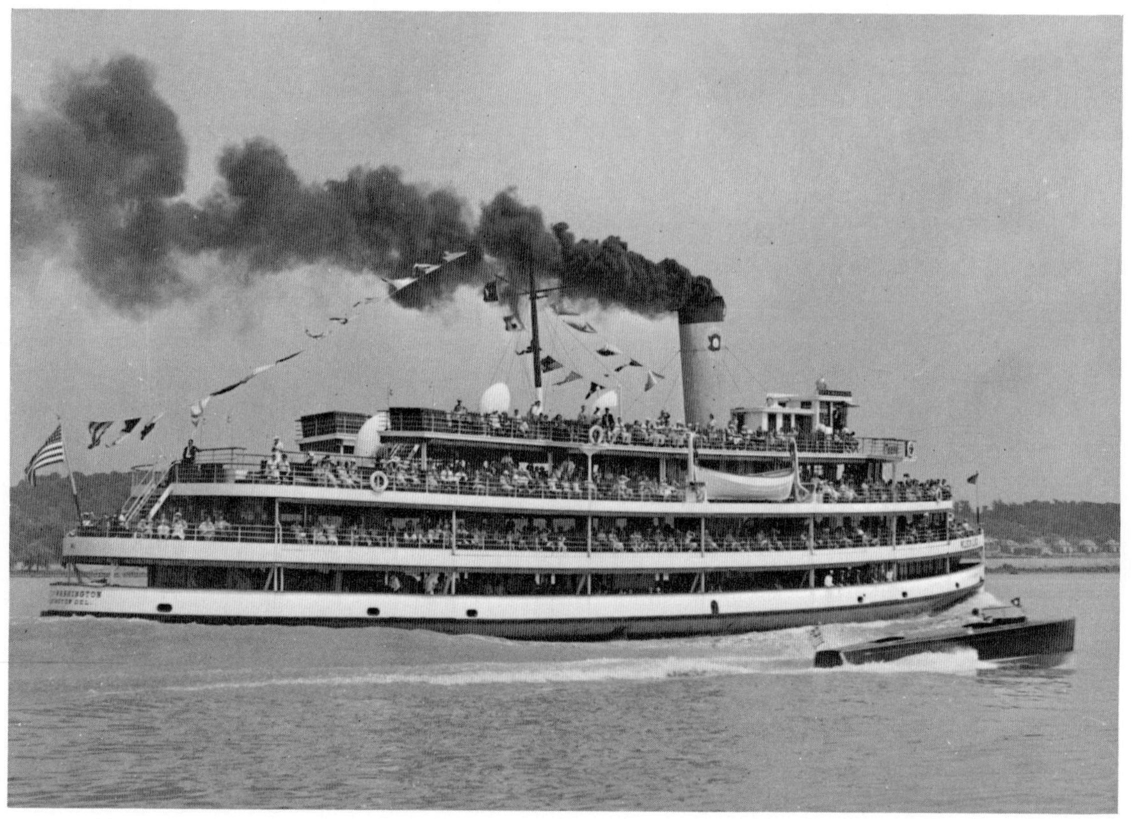

*City of Washington* is paced by a motorboat enthusiast on the Potomac. Small boat operators often would tease a steamboat by crossing her bow. Wilson Line, Inc.

about 55 miles from Baltimore on the beautiful western shore of Chesapeake Bay. The route had last been served by the aged sidewheeler *Dreamland*, which, like the *Delaware*, hailed from the Delaware River. As Captain Cone's *Republic* she had engaged Wilson's *Brandywine* and *City of Chester* in many a spirited race.

While the Chesapeake sail was filled with beautiful views, it was somewhat long for youngsters who were eager for swimming and other amusements. In addition, the Seaside pier, a quarter-mile in length, was sometimes discouragingly long for those who walked to the beach weighted down with picnic baskets, beach gear and straggling children. However, youngsters loved the pier's miniature railroad which carried them to and from the boat.

*State of Delaware* at Seaside Park, formerly Chesapeake Beach, August, 1935. Note tracks of the pier's miniature railroad. Roland R. Klages

In 1933 the beam-engined *Tolchester* began running to Tolchester Beach, an old favorite resort on the Chesapeake's Eastern Shore. B. B. Wills subsequently acquired control of the Tolchester Line and advertised the big sidewheeler as "The Biggest Steamboat on Chesapeake Bay," in competition with Wilson's claim for *State of Delaware*, which had the biggest capacity. Wilson's problems were worsened when a hurricane damaged the Seaside Park pier that same year. Incidentally, competition from the Tolchester Line could have been avoided had Captain Wilson pursued his idea of purchasing the line in the 1920s.

Wilson also revised its Washington operations in 1933, shifting *City of Washington* to a new service to Mount Vernon, Virginia, the plantation home of the nation's first president, and to Marshall Hall Amusement Park. The new service appealed to both tourists and local patronage alike. Marshall Hall, Inc., a wholly owned subsidiary of Wilson Line, had been developed by the line to cater to the young. It was located in Maryland about 17 miles from Washington and comprised over 377 acres of what was once an original colonial tract owned by the famed Marshall family.

Despite its excellent situation in Washington, Wilson soon faced new competition there as well as in Baltimore. In 1933 B. B. Wills acquired the former Albany Day Liner *Albany*, renamed her *Potomac* and began opposition with his own Potomac River Line. The old *Potomac* was also billed as a "streamliner" and she assumed the cruise run to Chapel Point which had been abandoned by *City of Washington*.

B. B. Wills was also building a system of his own along the East Coast and for decades the Wilson-Wills competition served chiefly to depress already low fares. Nevertheless, the Wilson System carried the biggest crowds on the coast and offered the nation's most modern riverboats. As one seasoned Wilson employee phrased it: "Wilson was the King of American excursion lines."

Veteran side-wheeler *Tolchester,* originally built in 1878, began running to Tolchester Beach in 1933 and vied with *State of Delaware* as "Baltimore's Largest Excursion Steamer." Edward Mueller Collection

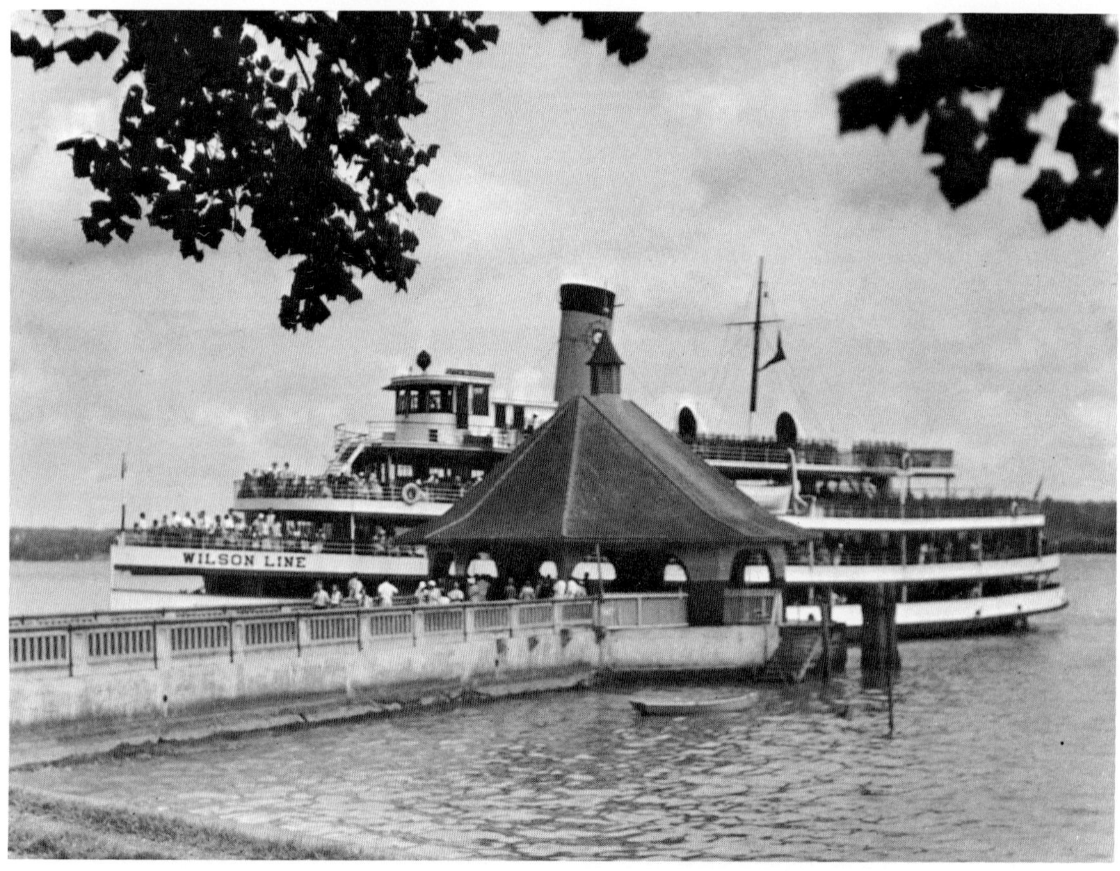


*City of Washington* brings tourists to President George Washington's Mount Vernon plantation during the summer of 1935. The Mount Vernon Ladies' Association of The Union

## Chapter VI

# Giant Boats for the "Ocean Highway"

AFTER Wilson Line's reorganization, rumors persisted that the new line was a subsidiary of the Pennsylvania Railroad. That rumor was widely believed although there was no connection whatsoever between the two corporations. The substance of this belief lay in the fact that George B. Junkin was a son-in-law of Samuel Rea, president of the Pennsylvania Railroad from 1913 to 1925.

Although Rea had retired four years before Wilson Line's reorganization, many held that the close family relationship meant that Wilson Line had become a "subsidiary" of the giant Pennsylvania System. The movement of part of the fleet away from the Delaware also seemed to substantiate the rumor.

But, according to both corporations, Wilson Line, Inc., was never owned by the Pennsylvania Railroad nor by any of its subsidiaries. Neither were any directors of the railroad ever officers of the steamboat line, or vice versa. However, after 1929, the former rivals developed closer cooperation than ever before, and that led to a corporate link in 1933 through the formation of the Virginia Ferry Corporation, an important chapter in the saga of the Wilson Line.

Captain L. H. Garrison had successfully led Wilson's Delaware-New Jersey Ferry Company to an enviable position by the early 1930s. Promotion of the shorter route via the Delaware River ferries brought substantial new year-round income to the line and led to important new highway construction in New Jersey, Delaware and Maryland.

U. S. Route 13 in Delaware and U. S. 40 from Baltimore were rebuilt largely as a consequence of traffic generated by the Delaware-New Jersey Ferry Company's promotion efforts. However, Captain Garrison, the new Wilson Line and the Pennsylvania Railroad Company looked forward to a new ferry service across the Chesapeake Bay, a service which would cater to the passenger autos, buses and motor trucks which were revolutionizing American land transportation. The new ferry was to be geared to growing interstate highway systems along the Eastern Seaboard, particularly in the Delmarva region.

The concept of an "Ocean Highway" was promoted by Captain Garrison, the Wilson Line and the Pennsylvania Railroad. Virginia Ferry Corporation's proposed services were part of that concept in that they were to close a second major water gap in the north-south route. Despite its obvious merits, other operators regarded this new service as an overly ambitious undertaking for the depression era, especially for Wilson Line. Service to the motor vehicle trade was new on the Chesapeake, but there was nothing new about ferry service across the bay.

As early as 1884, the New York, Philadelphia and Norfolk Railroad, a subsidiary of the Pennsylvania Railroad, had operated passenger ferry service between Cape Charles and Norfolk with the chartered steamer *Jane Moseley*. Railroad passenger cars were carried separately by carfloats under tow. Once trains were reassembled at either terminal, passengers reboarded and continued on their trips.

In 1885 the "Nip an' N" built *Cape Charles* for the route. She carried passengers and four Pullman cars for through service, connecting rail services between New York and Jacksonville, Florida. However, the big sidewheeler was unsuccessful and was sold in 1886. She was replaced by *Old Point Comfort,* and in succeeding years several fine steamers were operated by the railroad, including the sleek *New York* and *Pennsylvania* which resembled the Jersey Central's *Sandy Hook* and *Monmouth.* The trim *Maryland* followed in 1907 and the handsome *Virginia Lee* went on the route in 1928. However, the Pennsylvania's steamers were not built to meet the needs of the auto and truck traffic of the early 1930s.

In 1929 the Pennsylvania Railroad decided to shift its southern carfloat terminal from Norfolk to the sheltered waters of Little Creek, Virginia. This move cut the distance across the bay from 36 to 28 miles. The railroad had become increasingly aware of the need to operate steamers to Little Creek and recognized the desirability of serving the auto and truck traffic. Other operators were of like mind. In 1930, Charles Harrison of Norfolk, president of the Peninsula Ferry Company, began an auto-passenger ferry service across the bay with the steamer *Pioneer,* a veteran of Maine and Hudson River services. *Pioneer* made two round trips daily and continued to provide somewhat irregular service until 1931. The franchise held by this company was subsequently granted to the new Virginia Ferry Corporation.

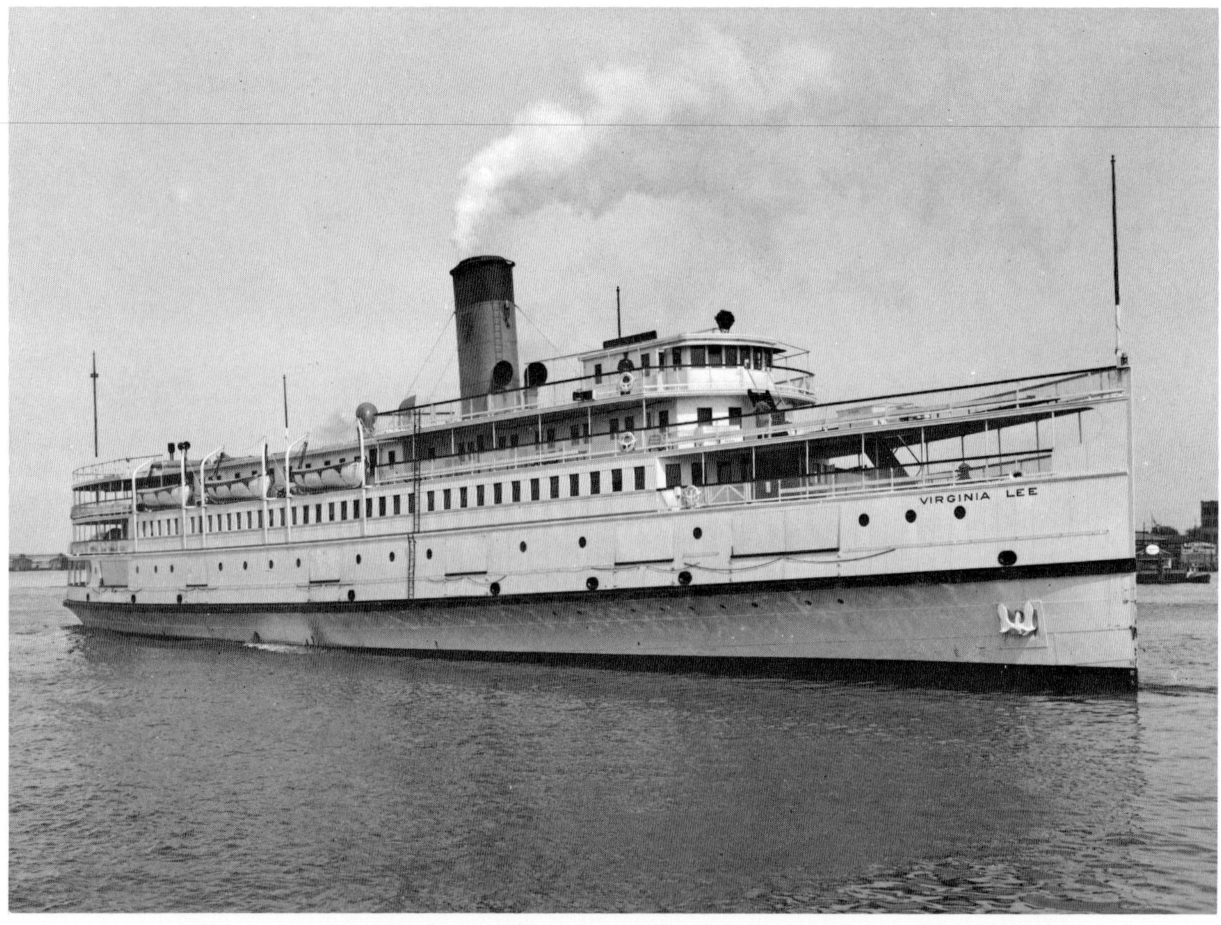

The Pennsylvania Railroad's staunch *Virginia Lee,* built in 1928, was one of several railroad steamers chartered by the new Virginia Ferry Corporation in 1933. Courtesy: The Mariners Museum, Newport News, Va.

Captain Garrison believed that the time was right for full scale development of auto-passenger service on the Chesapeake and he sought and gained support from the Pennsylvania Railroad. Virginia Ferry Corporation came into existence on April 1, 1933, with John F. Deasy as president and George B. Junkin, later his successor, as vice-president and director. Captain L. H. Garrison became general manager, a post he held simultaneously in Wilson Line's Delaware-New Jersey Ferry Company. The new company shared Wilson Line's Wilmington offices and was 50 per cent owned by Wilson's Delaware-New Jersey Ferry Company. The remaining 50 per cent was owned by the Pennsylvania Railroad. The Delaware's longtime rivals were at last effective partners.

adapted to autos and trucks and, although capital was limited, the company promptly contracted with Pusey & Jones Company of Wilmington for the construction of a steamer designed for the route's current needs.

During 1933, the Virginia Ferry Corporation's chartered steamers carried 25,305 vehicles and 94,204 passengers. It was noted, however, that the bulk of traffic came during the warmer months,

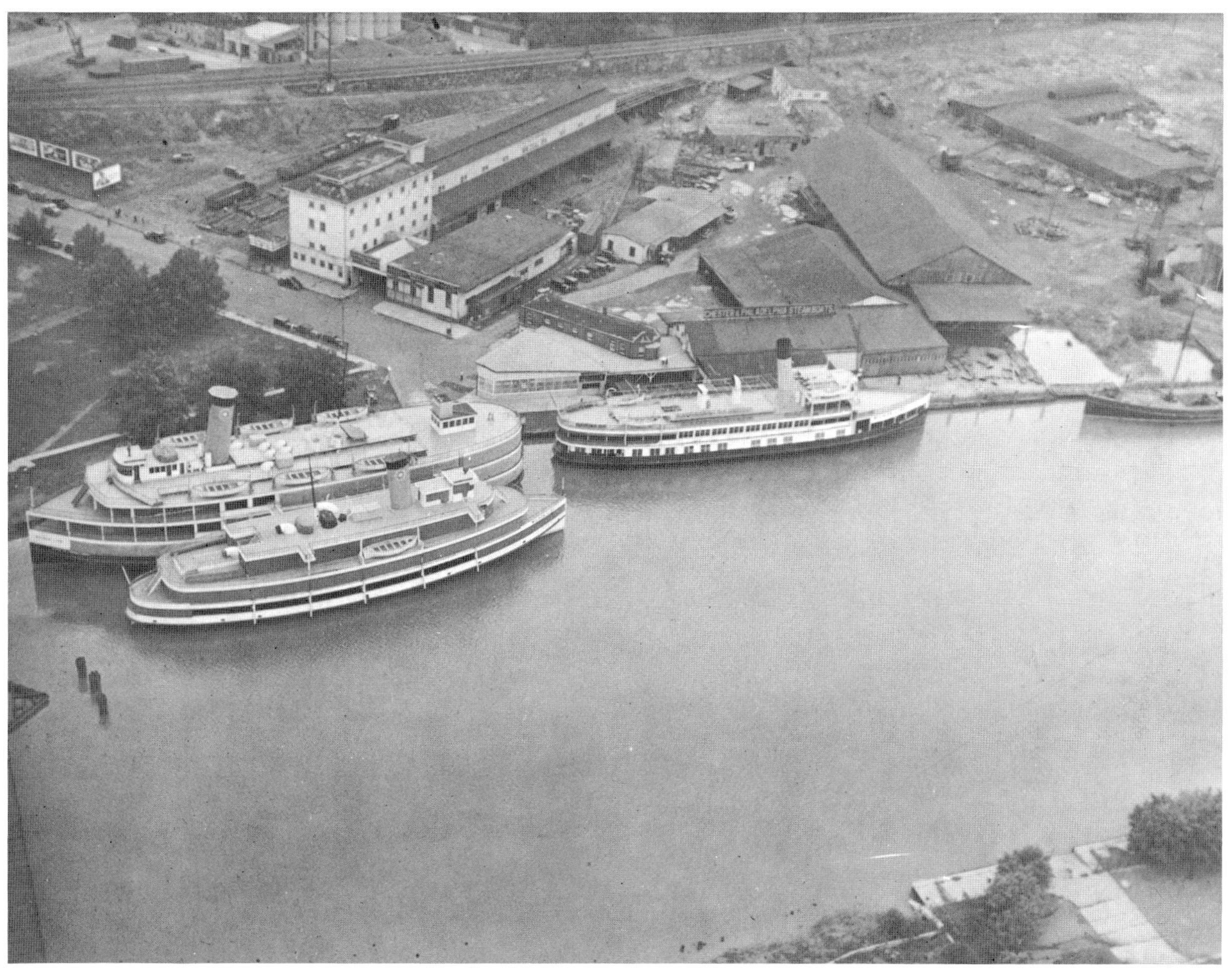

Wilson headquarters in the fall of 1936 shows summer steamers *State of Pennsylvania* and *City of Washington* (left) hibernating while *City of Philadelphia* continues year-round service to Philadelphia. Wilson Line, Inc.

except for an important number of wealthy Yankees being chauffeur-driven to the Florida sunshine during the winter.

Initially, the Pennsylvania Railroad's older steamers *Maryland* and *Pennsylvania* and the new *Virginia Lee,* which normally ran the Norfolk-Cape Charles line, were chartered to Virginia Ferry Corporation for the new Little Creek route. *Pennsylvania* inaugurated the service with three round trips daily carrying passengers and vehicles as best she could. Trucks still had to be carried by carfloats. The Pennsylvania steamers were not well-

Meanwhile, the Virginia Ferry Corporation's first entirely new steamer, the 260-foot *Del-Mar-Va,* took shape at Wilmington and was launched on November 2, 1933, a decade after Wilson's *State* boats came from the same yards. Actually, *Del-Mar-Va* bore a striking resemblance to the *States,*

being an adapted, enclosed version. Built at a cost of over $600,000, *Del-Mar-Va* was named for the states sharing the peninsula on which the line's northern terminal was located. Externally, *Del-Mar-Va* was modern, but not particularly futuristic. Her uniqueness was in her interiors and her engineering plant.

3,100-horsepower steam uniflow engines manufactured by the Skinner Engine Company. She was the first vessel of her class ever equipped with uniflow drive, a particularly smooth and efficient type of steam reciprocating engine. On her Delaware River trials *Del-Mar-Va* achieved 18.22 miles per hour, well above expectations for a vessel of

Virginia Ferry Corporation's pacesetting auto-passenger transport *Del-Mar-Va,* making her maiden crossing of the Chesapeake on January 7, 1934. Wilson Line, Inc.

*Maryland* teamed with *Del-Mar-Va* in 1934 when traffic doubled that of 1933. Wilson Line promoted the "Ocean Hiway" to spur north-south travel. Courtesy: The Mariners Museum, Newport News, Va.

The new steamer's passenger accommodations included comfortable lounges and a dining room with a panoramic view of the sea. They also included a ballroom—the first ever fitted out on a steamer of her class. She could carry 1,200 passengers and up to 90 autos. Autos and trucks were handled through huge bow doors. However, *Del-Mar-Va's* most distinguishing feature was her her beam. Furthermore, she amazed the maritime community by her ability to reverse from full ahead to full astern in 3.5 seconds!

Pacesetting was still the hallmark of the Wilson tradition to which *Del-Mar-Va* belonged. As *Marine Engineering* phrased it: "This ship possesses outstanding features in design and engineering which are marked departures from past standards for this type of craft." A truly new steamer had appeared on America's rivers and bays again and once more the vessel was a product of George G. Sharp, Inc., Wilson Line and a Delaware River shipyard.

Recognizing the value of uniflow drive, Virginia Ferry Corporation later ordered similar engines for other new steamers. As to the performance of steam uniflow drive, Captain George H. Seeth, former president of the New York Sandy Hook Pilots Association, later described the engines of Virginia Ferry Corporation's steamers as "the best in the world for maneuverability." Captain Seeth, it should be noted, had known and handled nearly every major transatlantic liner that arrived at the Port of New York during the twentieth century.

*Del-Mar-Va* made her maiden sailing on the Chesapeake on January 7, 1934 and was immediately acclaimed as the fastest and largest vessel of her class in the United States. Although popularly termed "a ferry," she was correctly classed by her owners as an auto-passenger transport, and so described in her promotional literature distributed to patrons. Functionally designed for the route, *Del-Mar-Va* proved enormously successful.

*Pennsylvania* returned to the Norfolk run and *Maryland* took her place as *Del-Mar-Va's* running mate. By the summer of 1934 the two steamers provided seven round trips daily and by the end of the new line's second year, traffic had doubled to 50,745 vehicles and 183,190 passengers. A new "gold mine" was in the making, and plans went forward to construct a sister ship for *Del-Mar-Va*.

However, while *Del-Mar-Va* and *Maryland* could barely cope with summer traffic, Virginia Ferry Corporation realized the need for a more even flow of traffic if the route was to support two large transports in year-round service. Captain Garrison recognized that the ferry's potential market was in the development of north-south travel and transportation on a scale never before envisioned. Promotional activities of the type planned, however, were beyond the resources of the Pennsylvania-Wilson team alone. Wilson Line provided assistance but it was also investing heavily in its new excursion system and modernization of its Delaware River ferries.

Then in 1934, Charles Russell, one of the pioneer motel operators on the East Coast, launched a modest campaign to promote patronage of his "Whispering Pines Cottages" in Accomac County, Virginia. In his advertisements, Russell urged southern motorists to utilize the convenient new ferry service across the Chesapeake to reach the Delmarva Peninsula. To his surprise, 118 responses came from Floridians. Nearly half of them drove north, used the Virginia Ferry Corporation's ferries, and spent some time at "Whispering Pines." If one proprietor's campaign could help his own business and also promote utilization of the fledgling ferry system, what might a regional organization be able to do, Captain Garrison pondered.

After the "Whispering Pines" success, Captain Garrison developed the idea of a cooperative organization comprising key business interests from New York to Miami. Resorts, cities, and industries stood to gain through greater north-south travel and trade—especially the two Wilson ferry systems.

The first informal meeting of what might be termed an "association" was held in March, 1935, at The Cavalier Hotel, Virginia Beach. Businessmen agreed to send solicitation letters to civic and resort interests on the East Coast and to hold their next meeting farther south on U. S. Route 17. At all subsequent meetings Captain Garrison advised interested groups of his plans and pledged the financial backing of the two Wilson ferry systems. On August 20, 1935, the captain's efforts were climaxed by the organization of the Ocean Highway Association at Myrtle Beach, South Carolina. Substantial new backing came from owners of fine hotels, resorts and industries. L. H. Siau of Georgetown, South Carolina, was elected president of the association.

Advertising committees later shortened the association's name to "Ocean Hiway" and developed the slogan "The Shortest Route from Northern Pines to Southern Palms." This was later reduced to simply "From Pines to Palms," and maps, folders and advertisements soon began to appear along the eastern seaboard describing historic, scenic and business points of interest on the entire route.

Nevertheless, the "Ocean Hiway" ideal was still a long way from fulfillment, and in 1935 there were four toll ferries, three toll bridges and some 200 miles of one-lane "highways" in need of major repairs. Despite these drawbacks, the route soon burgeoned as one of the nation's major arteries. The efforts and high standards of the Ocean Hiway Association were bearing visible results. Although Captain Garrison declined the presidency of the association until 1945 he was regarded as its founder and driving force. He had come a long way since accepting Captain Horace Wilson's proposal to merge the Wilson and White Line ferries on the Delaware.

In 1935 Captain Garrison purchased a parcel of land for Virginia Ferry Corporation at an important intersection near New Brunswick, New

The "Nip 'n N's" sleek *Pennsylvania* made the first sailings of Virginia Ferry Corporation's new Little Creek-Cape Charles operation in 1933. Courtesy: The Mariners Museum, Newport News, Va.

Wilson liners on the Delaware, Patapsco and Potomac rivers featured orchestras for moonlight sails. This group entertained on *State of Pennsylvania* in the mid-1930's. Wilson Line, Inc.

Jersey. On it he erected an illuminated 130-foot sign promoting traffic to the Pennsville-New Castle ferry and the transports of Virginia Ferry Corporation. To further promote the route he often chartered Bellanca aircraft and introduced businessmen to the route's advantages from the air, a novel feature of salesmanship. One of his selling points was the very absence of traffic! Subsequently, the which Little Creek and Virginia Beach are situated. The launching was attended by representatives of Wilson Line, Virginia Ferry Corporation, the Pennsylvania Railroad and some 30 officers of the Ocean Hiway Association from seven states.

Although almost identical to *Del-Mar-Va* in size, *Princess Anne's* appearance was entirely different. She was more streamlined in 1936 than

The superstreamlined *Princess Anne* of 1936, shown on her trials, seemed "revolutionary" when new, as her design was years ahead of her time. The Penn Central Company

Ocean Hiway Association established information bureaus and launched major publicity campaigns which brought nationwide attention to the route.

In the meanwhile, the company's newest transport neared completion at the Sun Shipbuilding and Dry Dock Company's yards in Chester, Pennsylvania. The new "sister ship" to *Del-Mar-Va* was revolutionary in appearance as Wilson Line's streamlining ideas were carried to the ultimate. The bold new steamer was christened by Mrs. John H. Rodgers of Norfolk on May 18, 1936. Her name was *Princess Anne,* after the Virginia county in

most liners in 1970. Built at a cost of over $691,000, the *Princess* took her turn as the most expensive ferry ever constructed in the United States.

Credit for her design went to Raymond Lowery, one of the nation's best-known creative industrial designers. On her debut, she was widely hailed from coast to coast as a stunning example of beautiful streamlining. *The Mutual Magazine* described her as "the ferry transport of tomorrow . . . today . . . the first of its kind . . . its launching inaugurated a new era in water traffic . . . it gives the impression of a fleet, ocean greyhound rather than a vessel engaged in the comparatively staid field of inland ferrying."

*Princess Anne's* spacious sun decks, elegant lounges, ballroom and dining room were similar to facilities found on a contemporary cruise liner and, together with *Del-Mar-Va,* she introduced ship-to-shore radio telephone service to vessels of her class. Quite naturally, *Del-Mar-Va's* racy stepsister caused a small sensation in the maritime industry as the nation's first fully developed streamliner retaining the basic ship profile. *Marine Engineering* predicted that she "paves the way for future developments in ship streamlining."

"Why," some asked, "was she so streamlined?"

The answer, according to the journal, was this: "It is frankly admitted (by officers of the Virginia Ferry Corporation) that the speed of the vessel under normal weather conditions did not warrant the application of streamlining with a view to reducing wind resistance and increasing propulsive efficiency.

"The main objective of the owners in applying this mode of construction to the new vessel was to produce a design that embodied something different and daring which would appeal to the taste and attention of the traveling public already familiar with the application of artistic air-flow design in rail and motor transportation."

This statement reflected the new Wilson Line's preference for contemporary design.

Understandably, some traditionalists objected to Wilson Line's total abandonment of "gingerbread," but the line was in reality merely continuing the pacesetting tradition of the Delaware. Moreover, there was something courageous in the line's continuing search for new expression. It was a rare sign of life in an otherwise increasingly old-fashioned form of transportation.

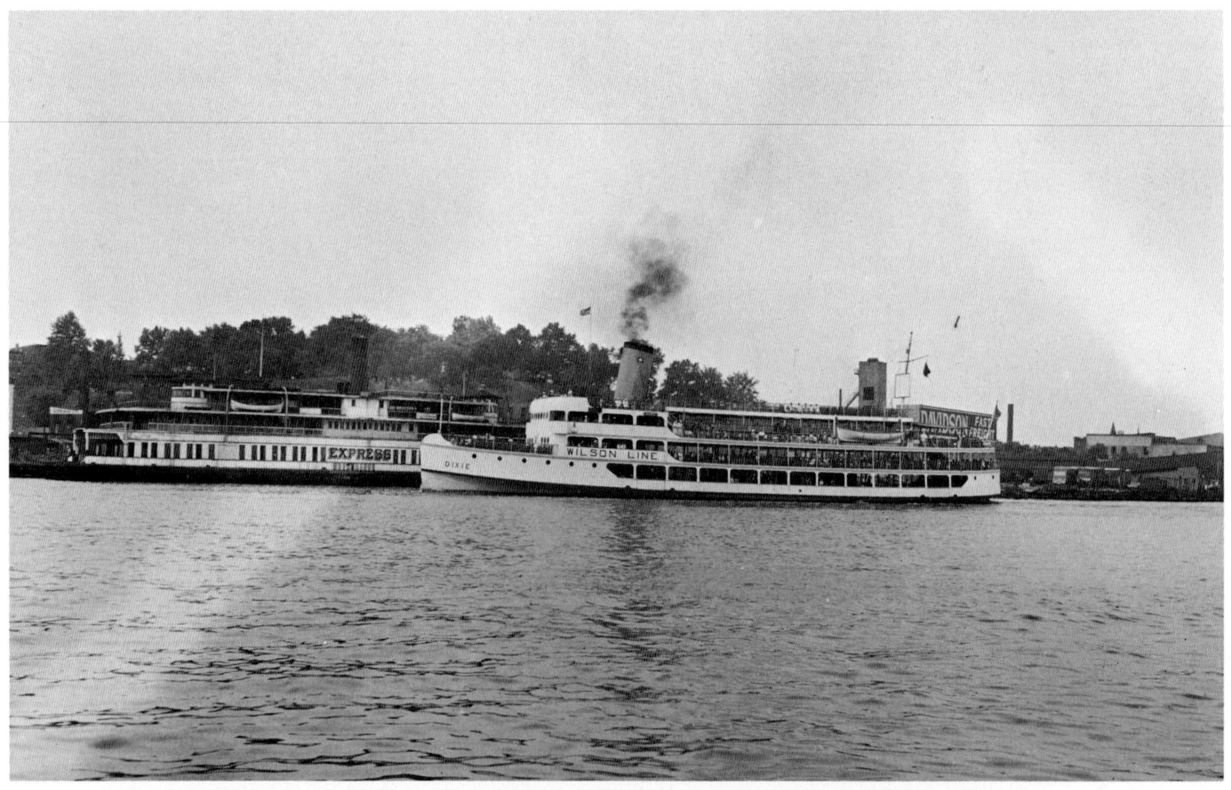


Ultramodern *Dixie* passes the laid-up Tolchester ferry *Express,* July 6, 1936. The streamliner was three years older than "old" *Express.* R. Loren Graham

At the time *Del-Mar-Va* entered service in 1934, Wilson Line was preparing to continue the reconstruction program launched by its predecessor to up-date the passenger fleet. Plans were drawn up in 1934 to reconstruct "old *Brandywine*" into an ultra-modern three-decked excursion steamer. However, her reconstruction was delayed until 1936 owing in part to stringent new government regulations which followed in the wake of the tragic losses of the Ward Line's coastwise steamers *Mohawk* and *Morro Castle.*

One result of the new regulations was to cut—in some cases drastically—the capacities of passenger steamboats throughout the nation. As Wilson Line prepared *Brandywine's* conversion, the number of decks she would require remained an important unanswered question of economics and structural planning. In 1935 the line closed ranks with other operators to protest the new regulations and, in particular, the reductions in capacities.

ranging from 3,500 to 4,000 passengers, while on 30 trips the *City* boats had carried between 1,600 and 1,800 passengers. Pointing out that the steamers were not as crowded as might appear, the line advised that during most trips up to 20 per cent of the passengers had room to walk about the boats. The Coast Guard reconsidered, and increased the capacities of the *State* boats to 3,330.

As for the rest of the fleet, the new regulations

The exuberant sound of "Dixie" was frequently heard on Wilson's *Dixie*. Above, the rebuilt 51-year-old boat departs from Baltimore with 2,000 passengers, August, 2 1936.
Roland R. Klages

In Wilson's case, capacities of the *State* boats were cut from 3,500 (4,000 with special permit) to 3,034. The recently rebuilt *City of Washington's* capacity was cut from 2,250 to 1,900 while the *City* boats' capacities fell from 1,800 to 1,398. In all, the reductions represented the equivalent of the loss of one of the *State* boats. Owing to the number of daily sailings, the reductions represented a serious loss in earnings, especially during the depression era.

Wilson Line accordingly pleaded hardship and advised the Coast Guard that, during 1934 alone, the *State* boats had made 19 trips with capacities

served mainly to spur the line's reconstruction program and it was decided to make each of the steamers into four-deckers to give them capacities which in fact exceeded their original allowances. The boats were also to be safer than any other steamboats in the nation since their extensive alteration plans embodied all contemporary safety requirements for new construction. Wood, for example, was prohibited. The line which had led all others in eliminating wood, now offered the public the first virtually fireproof construction, at the same time vastly expanding the longevity and earning ability of the fleet.

Thus, after a half-century of steaming, "old *Brandywine*" emerged in the spring of 1936 totally transformed as a four-decked streamliner. She was a bold new type and the basic prototype for future Wilson reconstructions. Unlike anything ever attempted in American steamboating, the "new" boat featured an ultramodern profile, a jauntily raked stack, a modified "ocean liner" recessed bridge, a canoe bow, a ballroom deck and a motion picture facility. Wilson Line called her "The Steamer of Tomorrow" and, in her 51st year, the line's oldest unit became the nation's first fireproof excursion steamboat.

During her reconstruction, the basic hull was cut in two and lengthened 21 feet. At the same time her hull was sponsoned out to 45 feet and her ancient compound engine was replaced by a triple expansion engine transferred from the 1897-built U.S. lighthouse tender *Iris* which the line had acquired specifically for this purpose.

As rebuilt, the steamer was allowed to carry more than twice her original capacity. The remarkable transformation was largely done by Wilson Line itself.

What "they" had done to the venerable Delaware steamer horrified some local people but others commended the line's efforts and valiant "old *Brandywine's*" perseverance in starting a new career at an age when most steamboats would have been scrapped. Like the Wilson Line itself, the older she became, the younger she looked. Befitting her exciting new "mod" appearance, the line gave her the rousing southern name of *Dixie*. She had her own personality and proved a favorite on the Chesapeake as she replaced *State of Delaware* on the Seaside Park route out of Baltimore. Thus relieved in 1936, *State of Delaware* was prepared to open a second service for her owners, this time at America's greatest port.

## *Chapter VII*

# *Delaware* on the Hudson

"ENCOURAGED by the excursion outlook in the New York area, the Wilson Line plans to operate its Flagship, the *State of Pennsylvania,* on Hudson River and Long Island Sound cruises . . ." Such was the buoyant public relations phraseology used by Wilson Line to announce its long-awaited operations at the Port of New York, but all hopes for a line at America's greatest port had faded by the time *State of Delaware* began her ocean journey from Wilmington in April 1936.

Wilson had wanted to begin a new service from Jersey City and New York to Bear Mountain, a route for which the *Delaware's* capacity and speed were ideally suited. However, while Wilson was the monarch of the Delaware, the Hudson was Day Line territory. Naturally, the Day Line and McAllister Navigation Company, which handled the Bear Mountain patronage, were against sharing their trade with a third carrier. The I. C. C. denied Wilson operating rights on the Bear Mountain route but did permit unlimited charter operations in the greater New York metropolitan area.

Previous obstacles to Wilson's plans for a national steamboat system were minor compared to those mustered at New York which boasted the nation's largest fleet of inland passenger steamers. To some New York steamboatmen, Wilson's debut represented a threat to the status quo—a status much less profitable than it seemed, even though the local fleet still carried enormous crowds.

New York's largest steamboat fleet, Hudson River Day Line, continued to operate five big steamers in its very fine, traditional style. How-

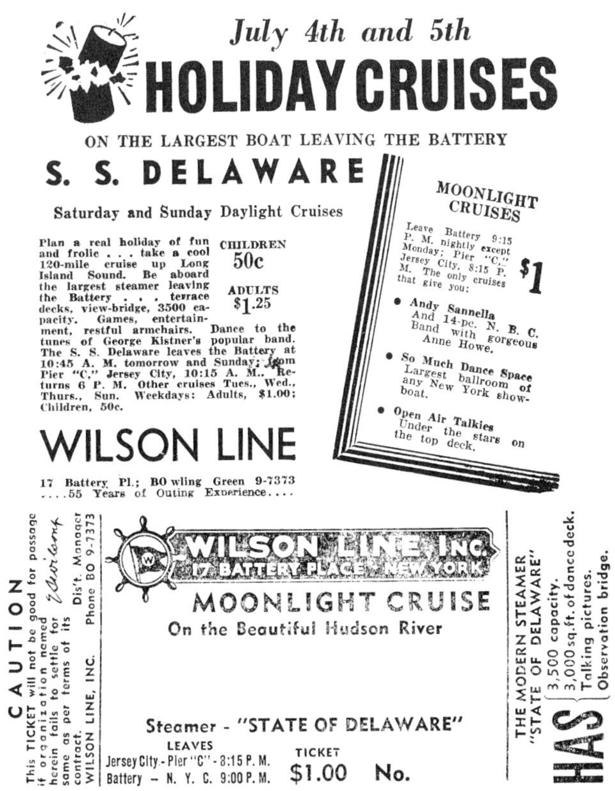


(Top) Wilson's press release announcing *State of Delaware's* new operations at New York. (Bottom) Ticket for a *State of Delaware* cruise, 1936.

ever, the Day Line was operating under self-appointed receivership, and at a loss. The other Hudson giant, Hudson River Night Line, also had gone bankrupt, continuing under various receivers, including the Day Line. The venerable Iron Steamboat Company, another of the nation's great water carriers, had collapsed in the early depression period, and its popular Coney Island steamers were auctioned for pathetically low bids.

In contrast, Wilson profitably operated the nation's largest river fleet, consisting of nineteen passenger and freight steamers, excursion boats, auto-passenger transports and ferries. Even so, the setback to its hopes at New York was a major disappointment and the line reluctantly decided to operate the *Delaware* on a charter basis until a Bear Mountain or equally desirable route became available. Like many a newcomer to the big city, the *Delaware* could not have been placed in a more competitive environment.

Until the *Delaware's* first season was booked, she operated four days weekly on 120-mile, nonstop, Long Island Sound cruises from Jersey City and New York's Battery Park. She also made nightly moonlight sails up the Hudson and was billed as "The Largest Boat Leaving The Battery."

The *Delaware* was starting her new service with handicaps, but she soon attracted the largest excursion parties that had been seen since the days of the memorable *Grand Republic,* the long-time queen of New York's excursion steamers. She was now the largest steamer operated at New York on a charter basis, and her new master was Captain George H. Stenken, the last master of *Grand Republic.* He had left McAllister's *Bear Mountain* to work for Wilson Line, and it was partly through his acquaintanceships that many of the groups which had once enjoyed *Grand Republic* cruises now turned to the big boat from Delaware.

Bear Mountain's popularity for excursions is evidenced by this typical view in the 1930's. Shown (l. to r.) are *Wauketa, Westchester, Americana, State of Delaware, Mayflower* and *Clermont.* Courtesy: The Mariners Museum, Newport News, Va.

Although some were cool to the *Delaware's* lack of gingerbread, many came to consider her one of the port's most exciting boats. She was the "new" boat of the "new" company, but few realized that Wilson's own traditions actually predated most of the local lines. Since Wilson usually introduced new developments in steamboating, it enjoyed a perennially modern image.

However, it was the ultraconservative Day Line

which introduced "showboat" cruises at New York. That novelty, a glorified moonlight cruise, was begun in 1932 by Day Line as a means of bolstering its declining income. In addition to its regular Hudson service, the line now operated evening trips up the Hudson to the showboat *Buccaneer,* a converted sailing craft anchored in the Hudson's broad Tappan Zee. On board were Bobby Sanford's "Showboat Revue" and a cast of fifty entertainers, including thirty-five "Sanfordolls." "Not a snob in a boatload," said the line's more commercial new ads. Other lines followed Day Line's example.

Meseck Line's *Americana,* dubbed "The Showboat of America," offered nightly sailings up the Hudson complete with a chorus line, "Free" dancing and a "Broadway Revue" that resembled old-style vaudeville. McAllister's *Bear Mountain* featured "Captain" Kay Parsons, a jovial female master of ceremonies, a "Gorgeous Girl Revue . . . Zippy Music . . . and a Marine Rathskeller." To suit the whim of a wealthy New York socialite on one occasion, McAllister had *Bear Mountain's* stack painted bright pink! The steamer's crew was furious over that nonsense and they bitterly resented the "Mississippi Showboat" concept as being both non-Mississippian and non-Hudson. They were right.

Another time, McAllister's *Clermont* featured an "all-girl orchestra" and "girl boxers." *Mandalay* ("The Mandalay Waltz" was composed in her honor), and other steamers also offered "thrills galore" for thousands of New Yorkers who turned out nightly for fun under summer night skies. Wilson neither painted its boats pink nor operated showboats converted from sailing vessels, but the new line knew that people wanted more entertainment and its policy was more liberal in this regard than its staid predecessor. *State of Delaware's* moonlights also provided "Broadway Revues" plus the novelty of motion pictures and live radio broadcasts on the National Broadcasting Company's network. In fact, the steamer was billed as "The N.B.C. Dance Boat," featuring Andy Sannella's fourteen-piece band with "gorgeous Anne Howe," vocalist.

Andy Sannella led his 14-piece NBC dance band on *State of Delaware* moonlight cruises in 1936. Movies also were provided. Wilson Line, Inc.

It was the era of the "Big Band Sound" and the new "Bops," Lindys and Brazilian sambas were the rage. One of the Marx brothers and other nationally known entertainers made appearances on the *Delaware's* shipboard shows. In effect, she was one of the many zany "floating night clubs" which sailed up the Hudson every summer night. It was,

Steamboats paraded up the Hudson every summer day in the 1930's. Above, in 1939, are (l. to r.): *Americana, DeWitt Clinton, Alexander Hamilton,* the Dodge yacht *Delphine* and *State of Delaware.* Donald C. Ringwald

(Top) The Yonkers Kilty Band with bagpipes and tartans joins *State of Delaware's* welcoming entourage for *Queen Mary.* (Bottom) Boxing world champion Jack Dempsey and "Little Johnnie," who chanted Philip Morris commercials, are on *State of Delaware,* June 1, 1936. Maurice Childs

however, the June 1, 1936, maiden voyage reception for Britain's *Queen Mary* that really introduced *State of Delaware* to New York.

As part of the welcoming flotilla, *State of Delaware* carried nearly 3,000 members of the British-American War Veterans and related clubs, and for the occasion she flew Union Jacks from each of her flagstaffs to welcome the huge ship. On board were Jack Dempsey, the Wilmingtonian who had become the World's Heavyweight Champion, and little Johnnie, whose "Call for Philip Morris" chanting cigarette commercials were a part of the contemporary radio world. The colorful Yonkers Kilty Band, with bagpipes and 14 satin-clad showgirls with three-foot trumpets, were also on board.

At about 11:40 A.M., the *Delaware* swung alongside the superliner, and the female trumpeters blared "God Save the King," while a military color guard in full regalia formed near the steamer's pilothouse. *State of Delaware* then sounded three gusty-throated blasts on her triple-chambered whistle and was, in turn, saluted by the *Queen's* quivering roars. The welcome continued for hours, and the *Delaware's* passengers literally shouted themselves hoarse in their enthusiasm. The *Queen Mary's* reception was a high point in the *Delaware's* career, and through her participation she enjoyed extensive publicity in journals, radio and newsreels. Audiences at Wilmington, Baltimore and Philadelphia theaters could easily spot the familiar Wilson boat in newsreels depicting the event.

The 814-ton *State of Delaware,* with 3,000 British-Americans on board, welcomes the 81,000-ton *Queen Mary* to New York, June 1, 1936. Typically, there were more passengers on the riverboat than on the superliner. The Port of New York Authority

From that time on, whenever there were exciting events at New York, *State of Delaware* was usually on hand. Shortly after greeting the *Queen Mary,* she was jammed with Polish-Americans greeting the liner *Batory.* She often went to the Poughkeepsie regattas and was on hand for the harbor reception for Britain's King George VI and Queen Elizabeth in 1939.

people were represented. Witnessing one of the *Delaware's* excursions was to see a happy version of humanity at play. Excursion boats probably were the most social of all craft, providing an opportunity for huge old-fashioned group outings on a scale never before witnessed afloat!

Although boat rides were often exhausting, people were rarely deterred from making other trips.

Arriving at Bear Mountain in June, 1936, *State of Delaware* shows off her clean lines. Anthony's Nose Mountain is in background. William G. Muller Collection

Her excursions took her to different places almost every day—to Bear Mountain, West Point and Poughkeepsie, New York; The Bronx, Staten Island, Yonkers, Bayonne, Jersey City, Hoboken; Norwalk and Bridgeport, Connecticut; Rye Beach, Rockaway, and the Jersey Shore. These were not the big events but they were no less colorful. There were luncheons, dances and community sings. There were thousands singing in reasonable unison on her decks, strolling minstrels with violins and accordions, excited youngsters making discoveries en route, children playing games and mothers searching for their strayed little ones. All types of

Few parents could refuse children the excitement of a river or bay trip and, having made one, refuse another, even when it rained. As one perceptive newspaperman commented after experiencing a *Delaware* trip: "When the people of this country cease to endure all-day outings such as these on Long Island Sound or up the Hudson, then, and only then, will there be cause to worry about the physical future of the Americans . . ." There was no doubt about the stamina of excursionists in the 1930s.

Cruises for Soap Box Derby contestants, police outings for youngsters, excursions with the Bowery's "society," a "Crazy Cruise for the 'Stoopnocrats'," a cruise to raise books for the Joseph Conrad Library of the Seamen's Church Institute, and jaunts for political groups generated as much publicity for the single Wilson liner as the rest of New York's steamboats put together. Unlike its predecessors, the new Wilson Line fully utilized publicity, and the press soon dubbed the *Delaware* "the *State of Fun*," a "swell boat," "the *City of Delaware*," "a handsome, modern steamer," "the *State of Confusion*," and, to be sure, "an old tub." The last, however, was regularly used by steamboatmen, usually affectionately. They just resented anyone from another boat passing the remark.

One of the latter-day captains of Day Line's *Alexander Hamilton*, the late Captain DeWitt Robinson, once told the writer his recollections of *State of Delaware*, and one of his stories related how Captain Stenken had once admonished *Empire State's* officers for tying up alongside "his" boat at Bear Mountain without using guard bumpers (logs placed between the boats to prevent rubbing or other damage). "Until you put out the bumpers," Captain Stenken remarked, "you can take that 'old tub' away from my boat." As Captain Robinson smilingly recalled, "I couldn't blame Stenken . . . *Empire State* really *was* an old tub at that time . . . I think she was faster when backing than when going ahead . . . someone said her sidewheels had been put on backwards!"

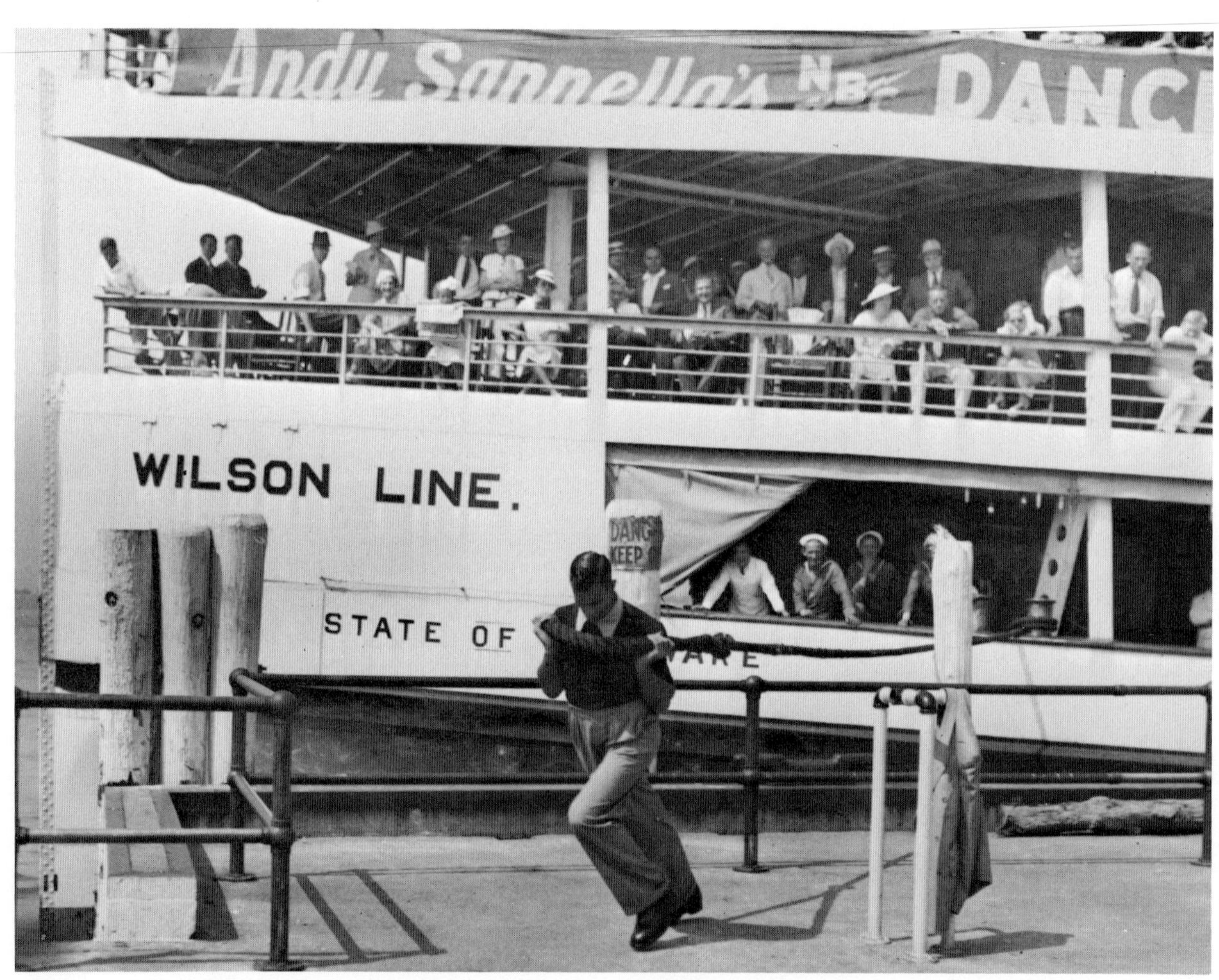


A clowning stroller at Battery Park pretends to pull *State of Delaware* to her berth as passengers enjoy a laugh. Frank Weber Collection

*State of Delaware* was known as one of New York's friendliest boats, and she soon had more business than she could handle. The New York management had received quick support from local charterers and wished to reciprocate by taking ads in company journals. To do so, however, permission from headquarters was needed, and "Wilmington," as employees called headquarters, was not too enthused over any new expenses. Lawrence C. Campbell, the line's vice-president, advised: "A very definite policy, established by our Executive Committee, makes it impossible to contribute to publications (or dances) sponsored by organizations. You and your customers will understand why this stand has been taken when you know that each year more than 4,000 organizations take outings on the Wilson Line and, as you can see, a contribution for even so small a sum as $5.00 would amount to $20,000 or 50 per cent of the entire annual advertising appropriation. . . .

"As you know, we make it a practice to treat all groups, large or small, in the same fashion, and you also know that neither time nor expense is spared in helping to plan and promote all phases of any day or moonlight outing. This is the contribution we make to organizations, and we hope you will agree that this policy is reasonable and equally fair to all."

Generosity to children, however, was also Wilson policy, and its management almost always took

The Central Railroad of New Jersey's *Sandy Hook* resembled a Wilson liner after George G. Sharp redesigned her in 1931. R. Scozzafava

Handling Father Divine's excursionists at New York's West 132nd Street are (l. to r.): *Ossining, State of Delaware, City of Keansburg, Clermont, Calvert* and *Susquehanna.* At far left, *Peter Stuyvesant* waits. Donald C. Ringwald Collection

time to answer inquiries from youngsters, providing photos of the boats and any other available material. Wilson's management liked children and the children appreciated this. The line also sponsored free boat trips for disadvantaged or handicapped young people, usually avoiding publicity on such occasions.

the summer season. We also diversified and developed new, year-round services while reinvesting a large part of our earnings to up-date the fleet."

In addition to the operation of its Delaware River and Chesapeake Bay ferry systems, Wilson's seven passenger steamers made about 2,300 day and night cruises each summer during the 1930s. In that

Aerial view of 1937 captures four types of Wilson liners at Wilmington. Shown (l. to r.) are *Christiana, Washington, J. C. Reichert* and *Dixie*. Wilson Line, Inc.

Careful financial management helped to assure the line's continuation, but while its success amazed other lines, no single characteristic could explain the "magic formula" some ascribed to it. Frank Weber, the line's general manager in the 1950s, who had begun his career with Wilmington Steamboat Company as a youth in 1918, told the writer that "plain hard work" was the key to Wilson Line's success. He added: "We succeeded while others failed because we worked harder. We found that the only way we could earn enough to survive was by working nearly all day throughout

period, Mr. Weber recalled: "the *States* were our big income makers." *State of Delaware* was invited to run daily service from New York to Pleasure Beach Park at Bridgeport, Connecticut, in 1937 and 1938 because of her value as a feeder for an amusement center, but Wilson declined, preferring to wait for a more convenient run which could at least match the *Delaware's* nearly $200,000 summer earnings from the excursion trade.

The steamer's excursion services were far more complex than a line operation, but the organizations which chartered her did most of the promotion work involved, including the preparation of excursion booklets, some of which were very elaborate. One company, Wright Aeronautical Corporation, issued a twelve-page brochure including a schedule of events on the boat and at Bear Mountain, a sightseeing "log" of the Hudson and statements of corporate personnel policies. Employees traveled, especially those hailing from inland points. Some accidentally went home on the wrong boat, which did not always return to the New York pier from which they had sailed in the morning. At Roton Point, Connecticut or Bear Mountain, New York, the *Delaware* often found herself crowded in nests of four to 10 boats, and when they

*Susquehanna* and *State of Delaware* are at Rye Beach, New York, in the summer of 1938. At sailing time whistles roared, bands played and people waved goodbyes. Playland Park Commission

were advised to "Leave your hat at home as a Wright Aeronautical yachting cap will be provided on boarding ship," and to "have your vocal cords in tune for singing old time songs." Besides caps, badges and other paraphernalia, the boats themselves often flew charterers' house flags from a flagstaff or over one of the steamer's railings. The flags advertised the company and helped employees to identify their boat at sailing time, sometimes a difficult chore when many were nested together at Bear Mountain.

It was not rare to find people making trips without knowing the name of the boat on which they sounded their whistles almost simultaneously at departure time, confusion carried the day!

Charterers' ads customarily noted that their cruise would be on an "outstanding," "new," or "favorite" steamer. However, one organization once skipped the usual adjectives and presented a cartoon depicting the completely overloaded Wilson liner towing a crowded rowboat with one of its passengers protesting that the steamer "ought to be the *State of Texas!*" In the 1930s, a riverboat needed a capacity which matched the population of many an American town.

Although *State of Delaware* had become a favorite at New York, she posed a special "recognition" problem at Yonkers. While few in Yonkers recall how the local "first to spy" custom began, generations of that Hudson River city's youngsters were so fascinated by the animated steamboats that paraded past the city each summer day that they competed with one another for first identification. In many instances no more than a white dot appeared in the distance but children were so familiar with the steamers' profiles that they could identify them many miles away. Once they knew the boat, they would call out: "First to spy *Hendrick Hudson* . . . *Peter Stuyvesant* . . . *Americana* . . . *City of Keansburg*," or whatever steamer they thought was approaching. Win or not, many children continued this ritual year after year.

Day Line's *Robert Fulton* was probably the easiest to recognize. As hundreds of youngsters phrased it: "She's the one with the three stacks 'stuck' together." From shore, the *Fulton's* three closely spaced stacks running athwartships did appear that way. Ironically, although the *Fulton* was the most old-fashioned steamer at New York, she was the most admired by Wilson personnel. Unlike the local boats, the *Delaware* carried her company's name on her sides and her own name in small letters on her bow. Until she became better known at Yonkers, many children called out "first to spy the 'Wilson Line'!" (Yonkers' youths were also very adept at identification without sight, relying solely on the sound of steamboat whistles. They were amazingly accurate.)

There were fancier steamers at New York than the *Delaware* but few evoked more enthusiasm than the unpretentious Wilson liner and no location enjoyed her more than Yonkers, where, like the venerable *Grand Republic* of bygone days, she gave visible understanding to the meaning of the word "popular." Although the *Delaware* only made about six to ten trips each season from Yonkers, the size of her crowds on any single trip exceeded the total turnout of a whole week's twice-daily sailings of the entire Day Line fleet at Yonkers.

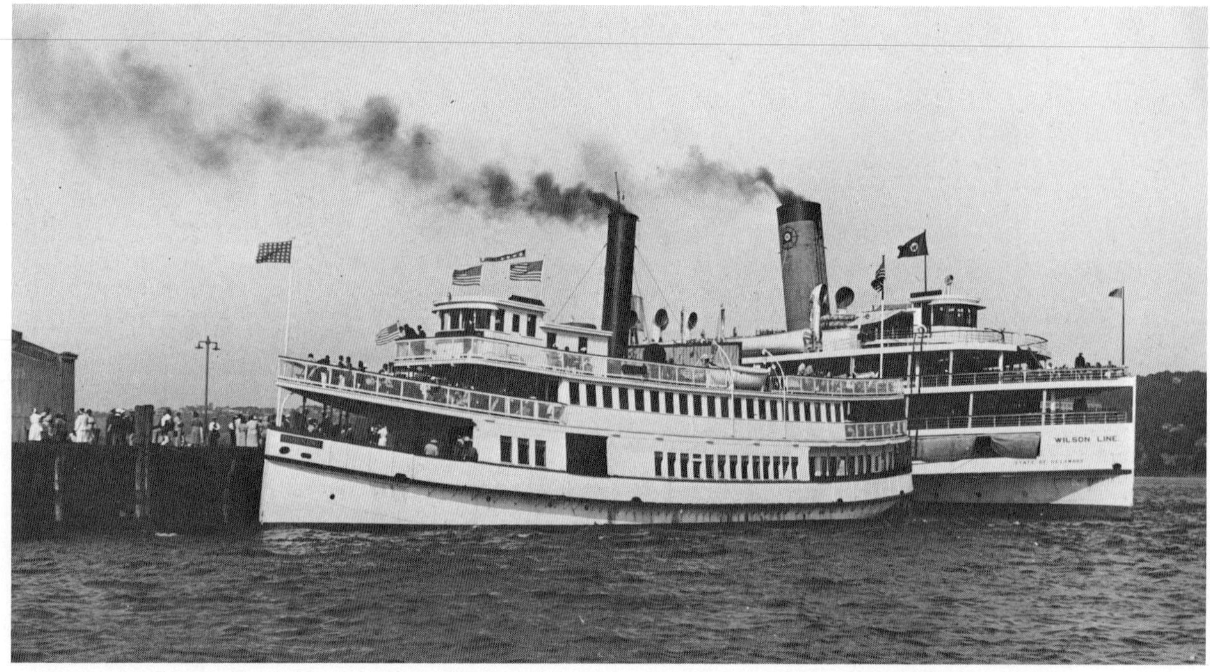


Steamers *Ossining* and *State of Delaware* take excursion parties from New York's West 132nd Street pier, June 25, 1939. R. Loren Graham

Yonkers crowds liked the *Delaware's* breezy, open decks and her downriver excursions on the route they had so long enjoyed with *Grand Republic*. The scenic northern route was always available but the southern journey was always more attractive, especially for families with youngsters. Going south, the steamer would pass the most colorful stretch of the Palisades, steam under the majestic George Washington Bridge, and past New York's incomparable skyline before weaving through harbor traffic, usually running close to the world's greatest ocean liners.

Passengers viewed the Statue of Liberty, Ellis Island and Coney Island, then enjoyed a bit of salt air while steaming briefly along the Atlantic coast before entering Jamaica Bay en route to Rockaway. Few short trips anywhere offered a more interesting sail than "going down the bay to Rockaway."

Yonkers' "Newspaper Day" excursion was another of the *Delaware's* favorite trips, traversing the Hudson, Upper New York Harbor, the East River and Long Island Sound before arriving at Rye Beach on Westchester's eastern shore. To take the free trip from Yonkers all one needed was a "Newspaper Day Coupon" clipped from the Yonkers *Herald-Statesman*. In 1939, the August 2nd edition exclaimed: "'Member the *Delaware*—that joy-craft on which you had such a fine cruise to Rye last year? More than 2,500 persons took the ride from Yonkers to Rye and return. It was one of the real highlights of the free party the *Herald-Statesman* puts on every year for its readers. And we're going to have the same fun medicine for you again—only in a larger dose than ever—There will be music, dancing, games and—if last year's ride is repeated—community singing on the return trip."

"Newspaper Day" excursions were always successful but nothing quite surpassed the *Delaware's* political excursions in sheer numbers and "good times." She'd be the "Democratic boat" one week and the "Republican boat" a few days or weeks later, often with many of the same people on board. These excursions were paid for by the ward treasuries and neighborhood families rode free or for a nominal cost. The trips took on a convention-like atmosphere with speeches, hoopla and colorful badges. The question of President Roosevelt's third term, and the likelihood of America's going to war during the next season, dominated discussions in 1940.

In July, 1941, the Democrats chartered the *Delaware* for a Rockaway trip for 3,000 mothers and children and, breaking tradition, no one missed the boat. This was so unusual that it made front page news in the local press. As usual, however, the party chiefs bemoaned all their work. Sighs of "never again" were immediate reactions to each of the almost legendary Democratic excursions. The 1941 adventure, moreover, had been the subject of an "exposé" in the New York *Daily News* which contrasted the prosperity of the Yonkers crowd with the Democratic Party's avowed support of "the poor."

As the *News* noted: "The steamboat *Delaware* early yesterday sailed as usual for the long day's outing to Rockaway . . . It was loaded to the gunnels with 3,100 well-dressed women and children. (But) Because there were so few of the poor from down near the railroad tracks and so many families of Yonkers merchants, city employees and politicians, sponsors said yesterday's jaunt would be the last . . . The transition from soda pop to champagne crowds has occurred during the ten years in which the excursions have become a Yonkers institution . . ."

There was really little "news" in the report since Yonkers charterers traditionally had paid little attention to social status and backgrounds, and just about anyone who wanted to take an excursion could find a welcome. Excursions of one ethnic, religious or political group were often well attended by those of dissimilar backgrounds.

A few days later, the *Delaware* took 3,000 "Republicans" on that party's second seasonal cruise to Rockaway and on the boat's return, an even larger crowd awaited the GOP's annual moonlight sail. Reaching the height of her local popularity, the *Delaware* delivered her 3,000 day passengers to a Yonkers pier jammed with nearly 4,000 people, most of whom planned to take the moonlight cruise . . . However, the era of happy family trips was coming to an end.

By summer, 1941, America still maintained an uneasy peace while much of the world was again engulfed in conflict. New Yorkers were acutely aware of how close America was to entering the hostilities as the news media presented daily accounts of horrors, bloodshed and the spread of war. Those who made trips through New York Harbor noted the ominous signs as one great liner after another shed her peacetime garb for grim war grey, and people on *State of Delaware* frequently cautioned one another to "forget" what they had seen in the harbor.

While there had been occasional disturbances on several of the local steamboats during the mid-depression period, some of which were attributable to generally depressed conditions, the attitude of 1941 was that of tension and fear. That tension was to have its impact on the venerable excursion fleet and before the end of the summer a number of incidents rocked the usually tranquil steamboats.

Early in the season Day Line's *Robert Fulton* took a moonlight cruise with the British-American Ambulance Corps which planned a fund drive for Britain. The event was marred by anonymous telephone calls which warned that the *Fulton* would be blown up if she made the cruise. No one knew whether the calls were from Nazi fifth columnists or ordinary pranksters, but 50 plainclothes detectives went on the sail just to search and observe. Fortunately, nothing happened. A few days later *State of Delaware* was the subject of anonymous calls warning of a bomb on board while she steamed to Roton Point, Connecticut. A thorough search produced nothing.

Before the end of the summer, however, the *Delaware* became involved in two serious incidents. One mid-August trip to Poughkeepsie was marred when some of her passengers became involved in a melee at Woodall Park. The following week the local Wilson office received anonymous telephone calls warning that counterfeit tickets had been sold for the steamer's August 17 Hudson River cruise. Although the validity of the information was questionable, long experience with people led the line's management to take no chances. The incident was reported to the New York police and extra patrolmen were requested at the pier as a precautionary measure.

When the *Delaware* steamed into her pier at West 132nd Street, a throng of over 6,000 people, more than twice the steamer's capacity, stood awaiting her arrival. The telephone warnings had been serious. Thousands held bogus tickets picturing an oceangoing freighter on one face. To make matters worse, not nearly enough extra police had been assigned to the pier.

At first, the crowd pushed and shoved in a lighthearted way but the throng's mood changed as those farthest from the boat pressed toward the gangplank. Lunch boxes broke and people fell. One patrolman urged the charterer's committeemen, who controlled the ticket collection and the boat's use, to open the gates and allow part of the crowd to embark, in an effort to relieve some of the pressure. Some order was restored after a Wilson representative ordered the steamer away from the pier. Many line personnel favored cancelling the excursion at the risk of being sued for breach of contract but the decision was not that simple.

Meaningful communication between the committee, line representatives and police had become almost impossible owing to the density of the crowd and the general atmosphere. Officials were worried over both the prospects of cancellation, and the problem of attempting to let some of the passengers embark to the disappointment of thousands of others. The latter course was deemed safer than frustrating everyone. The steamer was waved back to the pier but as she came alongside the crowd again stampeded forward, resulting in the fatal trampling of three women. Thereafter, tears replaced laughter and thousands lost interest, turned and went home. People had hurt themselves when seized by the herd instinct, the end product

*State of Delaware* makes one of her last trips through the verdant Hudson Highlands on August 17, 1941, the day of the bogus ticket melee at the West 132nd St. pier in New York. Kenneth E. Smith

of the petty greed that had motivated the counterfeit ticket scheme. About 1,200 actually took the sail.

Wilson's staff was shocked by the traumatic incident. No one with the line, the charter's organization or local police knew who had made and sold the bogus tickets, or how many might have been sold prior to the trip.

Captain Stenken was saddened but very angry over the incident and warned those on the cruise that he would put into the nearest landing and debark all passengers if even the slightest problem arose. However, the crowd was very quiet and no irregularities occurred. "She was," as one crewman said, "like a ghost ship." Shortly afterward, New York District Attorney Thomas E. Dewey led an investigation and those characters who had printed the fraudulent tickets were found and prosecuted.

However, the turbulent summer of 1941 was not yet over and a few days later pandemonium erupted on Sutton Line's *Clermont* while she was returning to New York from Hook Mountain. A wild melee ensued among her 2,500 passengers after one of them drew a revolver during an argument. Captain Chris Johnson radioed for police to stand by at the West 132nd Street pier. This time a small army was dispatched and patrol boats were sent to escort the boat to New York. Several passengers were taken to hospitals but the culprits eluded detection. These and other disturbances of the season generated a feeling of insecurity among excursionists and steamboatmen alike. A dangerous trend seemed to be developing, especially unwelcome to Wilson Line which had made the largest investment in the future of the excursion business.

Wilson had yet to achieve a desired line operation at New York but its overall position was far better than any other eastern line. It was the only company still building new river and bay boats at a time when other lines were quitting the field. The Day Line continued in bankruptcy and McAllister Navigation Company had been liquidated following its president's death in 1939. Shortly afterwards it was rumored that Meseck Line sought to merge with Wilson Line before acquiring the Day Line. Nothing, however, came of that proposition which, it was said, did not appeal to the Wilmington firm.

The Mandalay Line had lost its popular *Mandalay* in a collision with Eastern Steamship Line's *Acadia* in 1938. The Night Line, the Hudson's once dominant steamboat power, had given up in 1940 after a long decline. Two of its boats, *Trojan* and *Benjamin B. Odell*, had reportedly burned "mysteriously," while the once luxurious liners

View of *State of Delaware*, heading south from Yonkers, on July 6, 1940, taken from *Alexander Hamilton*. Edward O. Clark

*Rensselaer* and *Berkshire* (the world's largest overnight river steamer) were requisitioned by the government in a quiet but steady preparation for war. New York Harbor itself became less colorful when the historic Jersey Central flyers *Monmouth* and *Sandy Hook* succumbed to "progress."

Other steamers were being laid up, or fell victim to fires and hurricanes, social change, or their owners' lack of determination. Still others were to be swept away by global warfare, never to return to their peacetime careers. On the Delaware, the bankrupt Ericsson Line collapsed entirely following Pearl Harbor, just two years before marking its centennial. Wilson Line survived as the only steamboat company on the Delaware.

Together again in the Christina for the last time in 1941 are (l. to r.): ferry *Washington;* streamliner *Mount Vernon* and *Dixie* (outboard); *Liberty Belle* and *City of Washington*, with *State of Pennsylvania* and *State of Delaware* (outboard). The same fleet never regrouped following Pearl Harbor. Walled Fort Christina Park and "The Rocks" are to the left of Wilson properties. Photo: Edwin K. Anderson, Wilson Line Collection

## Chapter VIII

# Streamliners and Showboats

By the mid-1930s the Wilson System had become an eastern institution that stretched from New York to Norfolk. Yet, while its big developments had taken place away from the Delaware, the home services remained the most important. Fourteen of the system's nineteen vessels still ran on the Delaware and its local fleet of Wilson liners and Delaware-New Jersey ferryboats carried over three million passengers yearly.

However, the depression had forced fares down to the "less than a penny a mile" rate of the nineteenth century. Daily sailings were less frequent than in the past but competing with the Pennsylvania Railroad was no longer a concern. As before, Wilson Line was an integral part of the region's way of life and in contrast to the line's new services at Baltimore, New York and Washington, the home fleet retained much of its traditional appeal of utter simplicity.

The new modern look began to show on the Delaware in 1938 when *City of Philadelphia* was earmarked for total reconstruction, like old *Brandywine*, into an ultramodern four-decked excursion "streamliner." The *Philadelphia's* reconstruction was carried out by Baltimore's Maryland Shipbuilding and Drydock Company and by saving her basic hull and engines, costs were kept below $200,000. A wholly new boat of her class would have cost over three times that amount. Changed beyond recognition, the "new" boat was rechristened *Liberty Belle*, a name which maintained her special association with the city of Philadelphia

*Liberty Belle's* maiden voyage announcement in the Wilmington press, June 3, 1938. Wilmington *Every Evening*

and marked the start of Wilson's series of boats named *Belle.*

Like the jazzy *Dixie, Liberty Belle* was streamlined, steel and sturdy. She too offered 2,500 passengers functional comforts and fireproof safety. Wilson Line's president George Junkin proudly told stockholders that her renovation would "give Wilson Line the best fleet of excursion steamers in the United States. Every modern device for safety has been employed and the line itself has developed many new features which can be found only on these steamers."

Totally transformed in 1938, *Liberty Belle,* ex-*City of Philadelphia,* was considered "The Delaware's First Streamliner." Courtesy: The Mariners Museum, Newport News, Va.

*Liberty Belle* was intended for summer use only on either the Philadelphia or Riverview Beach lines. (Her use in New York for the 1939-40 World's Fair was considered but never materialized.) With her debut, her tall-stacked former sister ships *City of Camden* and *City of Wilmington* now looked decidedly old-fashioned. *Liberty Belle* returned to the Philadelphia line on May 27, 1938, under Captain Edwin Savin and she was acclaimed anew on what may be called her second maiden voyage. This time she was hailed as "the Delaware's first streamliner." However, many missed her original profile. Those who knew her as *City of Philadelphia* in their youth rather resented the "mod" look, but children of the 1930s thought highly of her streamlined style.

The *Belle's* 7 P.M. sailings were billed as "The Dance Cruise" from Wilmington, and company ads asserted: "It's new! It's different! Now, for the first time from Wilmington, you can have fun on the river on a nightly dance cruise on the magnificent new *S.S. Liberty Belle.* Dance to your favorite Wilmington Orchestra on the biggest ballroom afloat. Sails every night! Coming?" She also made a similar cruise from Philadelphia at 4:30 P.M. It was billed as "The Sunset Cruise." At both cities thousands of couples turned out nightly for an evening of fun and romance on the river. These five-hour, 62-mile round-trip dance marathons cost but 50 cents.

Besides the scheduled trips, group excursions were as popular as ever out of Wilmington, Chester and Philadelphia. In Delaware, the biggest industrial outing of them all was the perennial du Pont excursion, a strictly Wilmington event with Wilmington boats, industry and people. Contrary to a popular notion, not everyone in Wilmington worked for the du Pont organization, but thousands did, and in this relatively small city it seemed that everyone knew someone associated with a du Pont facility. On du Pont's annual boat ride day, the whole town appeared to converge on Wilson's Fourth Street Wharf.

As in the past, the du Pont Company distributed red, white and blue pins in the shape of cans of explosives to identify its employees. However, the outings became more daring in the 1930s and instead of a routine day trip, the excursion combined a sunset sail, a shore picnic and a moonlight cruise. With an end to prohibition, there were well-patronized cocktail bars on the Wilson liners for the first time in the company's history.

In 1936, *State of Pennsylvania* could handle the du Pont outing alone but a few years later she needed help from *Liberty Belle.* Together they could accommodate up to 6,000 du Pont employees. In 1939 the du Pont program called for the two steamers to board passengers at 5 P.M. and sail at 5:30 P.M. Both landed at Riverview at 6 P.M., after a half-hour's cruise out the Christiana and down the Delaware.

At Riverview, thousands went ashore to enjoy a picnic supper under multicolored lanterns. The more energetic took a swim in the pool or danced at the pavilion.

As a bonus, those who wished could again board *State of Pennsylvania* at 8:30 P.M. for a moonlight cruise on the Delaware, including concert and dance music and supervised movies on the top deck. Contemporary pop tunes people enjoyed on

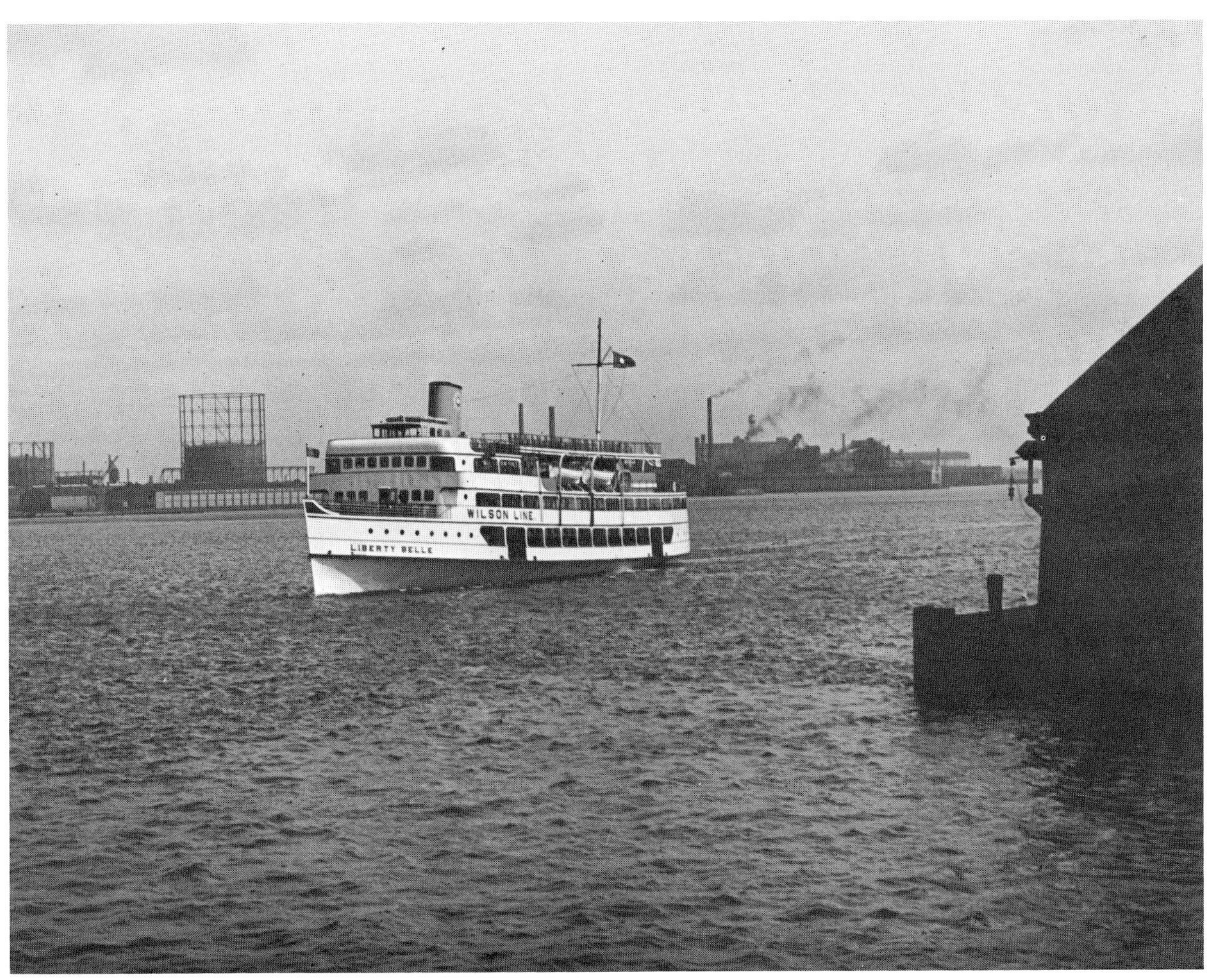


Glistening under morning sun *Liberty Belle* arrives at Philadelphia from Wilmington in 1938. Wilson Line, Inc.

board included *Indian Love Call, Oh, Johnny* and *The Beer Barrel Polka. Pennsy* returned to Riverview at 10:45 P.M., 15 minutes before both boats steamed back to Wilmington, their brightly lit decks crowded with fun-loving humanity. Technically, the annual party was over shortly after midnight but as always, the trips provided so much fun that they generated topics for conversation for months afterwards.

Of the Delaware fleet, *State of Pennsylvania* carried the biggest crowds and was perhaps the hardest working of all. Making two daytime and one nightly "Showboat" trip each twenty-four hours meant steaming about 160 miles. For her crew this meant being on their feet for nearly 18 hours. Understandably, her men were less than enthusiastic over the "Showboat" cruise from Philadelphia that capped an already long day. Like her sister in New York, the *Pennsy* offered a complete floor show and a swinging dance band. She also provided a dance team which demonstrated the latest steps, a barrel jumper and a lineup of dancing chorines. Music was continuous from the time the crowds embarked until the steamer returned at midnight.

Opening night of her 1938 "Showboat" season prompted one Philadelphia newspaperman to do an in-depth report. For the enthusiastic, gay crowd of passengers he found showgirls doing a precision "Rockette" step out on *Pennsy's* bow and the ship's band playing with gusto. However, the reporter emphasized *Pennsy's* skipper's reaction to all the "fun and frolic" on board.

Apparently *Pennsy's* master didn't really approve. In the *Bulletin* reporter's words: "There was only one sour face on the boat last night. It belonged to Captain Carl Phillips, who had piloted *State of Pennsylvania* for nearly 12 years and has been a riverman for nearly 30. 'To think,' Captain Phillips said as *Pennsy* backed from her dock, 'that I'd come to the point where I'd be skipper of a boat painted aquamarine and carrying a bunch of dancing cuties!' "

Captain Phillips' remarks typified the views of senior personnel and senior passengers alike. It wasn't the way the old Wilmington Steamboat Company would have done things, but the present generation enjoyed show business on the boats.

The highlight of the line's 1938 season was the dedication of Wilmington's new Fort Christina Park, timed to coincide with the three-hundredth anniversary of the arrival of the first Swedish colonists in America. The event generated considerable national interest, and local committees worked

New York *Daily News* ad for summer steamboat excursions, July 5, 1940.

tirelessly to assure its success. The land on which Fort Christina stood and "The Rocks" on which the Swedes first set foot had been Wilson Line property for many years and the line had made the area available to the state of Delaware for preservation as an historic landmark. (In Wilmington the landing of the Swedes at "The Rocks" was fully as significant to "New Sweden" as that of the Pilgrims at Plymouth Rock to New England. The Christiana River had been named for a young 17th century Queen of Sweden and the town on its banks was called Christinehamn until the English gained territorial control and it was renamed Wilmington.) The official spelling of the river's name was changed from "Christiana" to "Christina" coincidental with the anniversary.

To commemorate the 1638 Swedish landing, a monument of stone, immortalizing the arrival of the *Kalmar Nyckel* and the *Vogel Grip,* was presented to the people of the United States by the Kingdom of Sweden.

On the morning of June 27, 1938, Swedish American Line's luxury liner *Kungsholm* arrived off Wilmington after completing a special sailing to the Delaware for the event. On board were Sweden's Crown Prince Gustaf Adolf and Crown Princess Louise (later King and Queen of Sweden), Count Folke Bernadotte and many other Swedish and Finnish notables. President Roosevelt had arrived at Wilson Line's wharf the previous night.

Unfortunately, *Kungsholm* was late, Crown Prince Gustaf Adolf was ill and heavy rains fell on Wilmington. The Wilmingtonians, undaunted, turned out by the thousands. *Kungsholm* finally arrived escorted by two U. S. Navy destroyers and the light cruiser *USS Savannah* roared a 21-gun salute. Nationwide radio broadcasts were conducted over CBS and NBC, while Station WDEL informed Delaware and a special Swedish-language broadcast was relayed abroad.

Earlier that morning *State of Pennsylvania* left Philadelphia for Fort Christina with some 2,500

As President Franklin D. Roosevelt looks on, Crown Prince Bertil of Sweden speaks at the June 27, 1938 ceremonies marking the Swedish Tercentenary. Delaware State Archives

members of Swedish-American organizations and the Swedish American Line's staff. En route, she exchanged salutes with *Kungsholm* and for a brief moment there was some concern when most of her passengers rushed to one side for a better view. However, there was no serious cause for alarm with *Pennsy's* exceptional stability. *Liberty Belle* went alongside *Kungsholm* to transfer hundreds of

Despite torrential rain, thousands of smiling Swedish and Finnish-Americans on *State of Pennsylvania* exude enthusiasm at the Swedish Tercentenary ceremonies. Delaware State Archives

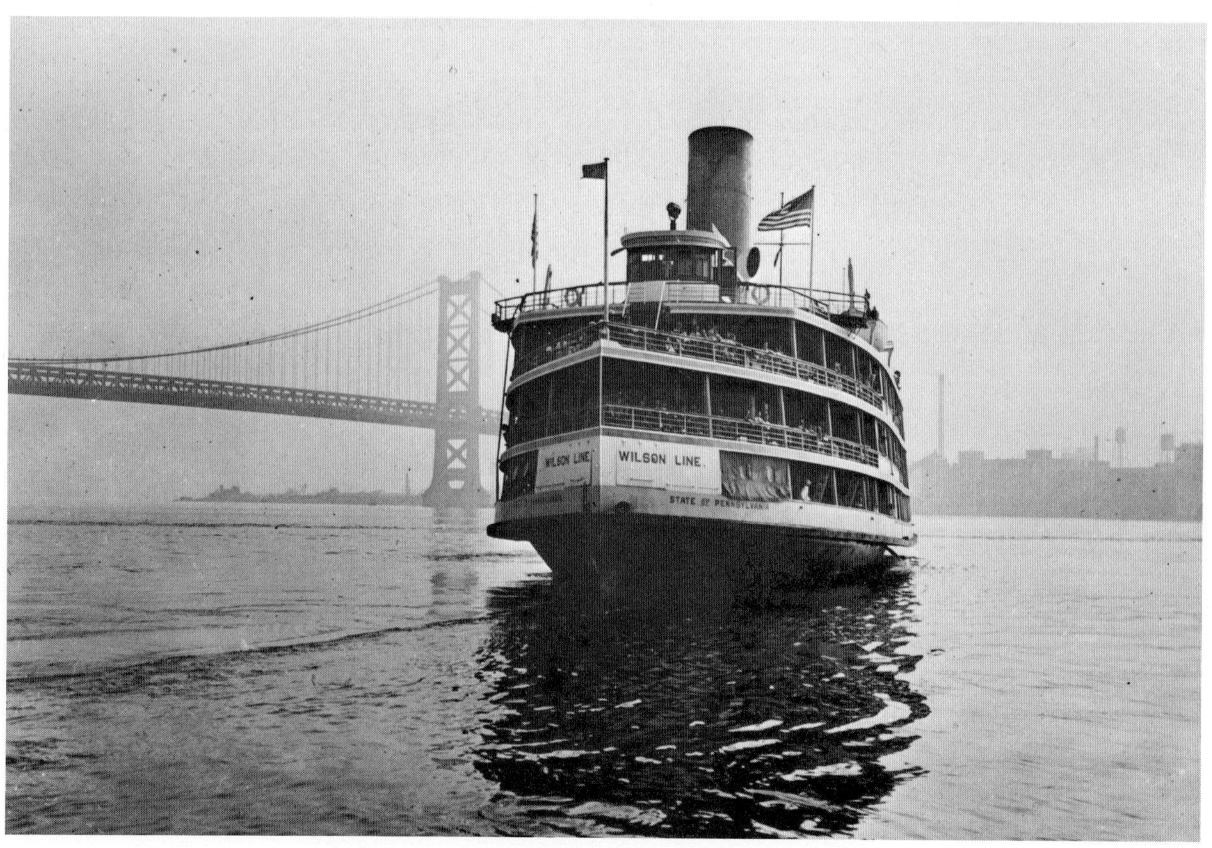


Framed by the Ben Franklin Bridge, "showboat" *State of Pennsylvania* sets out from Philadelphia on August 31, 1941. R. Loren Graham

Swedish dignitaries and tourists to the new park.

The arrival of *State of Pennsylvania* turned out to be the most exciting event of the morning, as the big day's schedule lagged and the weather became increasingly dismal. Thousands aboard and ashore waited hopefully for some activity. From the shore, news photographers beckoned *Pennsy's* passengers to cheer and wave handkerchiefs. *Life* magazine later ran a photo of the jam-packed steamboat captioned, "Swedish Sardines." Actually, more dramatic views of humanity on Wilson liners could easily be captured during any average excursion season.

When President Roosevelt and the Swedish royalty finally arrived, a military band was playing valiantly while rain dripped from their instruments and a crowd of 5,000 stood patiently under trees and umbrellas, ankle-deep in mud. Princess Louise's orchid hat drooped and notables in full military regalia were thoroughly soaked. Nevertheless, the event was markedly cheerful. Crown Prince Gustaf Adolf addressed the gathering via special radio broadcast from his shipboard suite, and all agreed that Wilmington had witnessed a great day.

Labor Day traditionally marked the close of the annual excursion season and in 1939 Wilson ads reminded parents that "Fall will soon be here and it will be back to school, so why not take the youngsters for a last trip on the river before the summer ends?" Actually, the trips were an education in themselves, developing in young minds a fuller appreciation for the river and its importance to Delaware Valley industry and world trade. The line distributed free guides to the "American Clyde," stimulating even more interest.

Many a young Philadelphian discovered these aspects of Delaware Valley life when he first boarded a Wilson liner for a trip to Pennsville. While this stretch from Philadelphia to Riverview Beach was no longer as scenic as it once had been, it offered much of historic and industrial interest. After backing out from her Chestnut Street Wharf with two long blasts, *State of Pennsylvania* passed near the Ben Franklin Bridge and offered a good view of the New York Shipbuilding Company's yards at Camden. The boat then turned south and headed past Philadelphia's waterfront lined with freighters from distant lands. She proceeded round the river's "Horseshoe Bend" to pass League Island Naval Shipyard, the world's largest, with its impressive assortment of naval craft.

Farther south, the boat would pass Hog Island, site of the mammoth World War I shipyard and what remained of its once-famed 50 shipways. (John Fitch had experimented with his steamboat near that site in 1786). Next came Little Tinicum Island and the Sun Shipbuilding yards, after which *Pennsy* made a landing at Chester to board a few hundred additional passengers. She then steamed past the oil refineries at Marcus Hook, and, after passing Wilmington in the distance to starboard

Captain Horace Wilson shortly before his death in 1938. He passed away at New York after completing an ocean cruise. Mrs. Frances W. Richardson

and the big du Pont plants at Deepwater and Carney's Point to port, arrived at the long Pennsville pier where a large sign greeted passengers with "Welcome to Riverview Beach." A short distance to the south Wilson's auto-passenger ferryboats arrived and departed every few minutes, to and from New Castle.

On the Delaware, children always comprised a high proportion of day trip passengers. They talked freely with officers and crew questioning them about navigation, engineering, boat handling, sights on shore, the "old days" on the river, where the other Wilson boats had gone, and other matters. Even though many of the youngsters never rode *City of Washington*, *State of Delaware* or *Brandywine*, their parents had, and what became of the boats was of great interest. Children who made frequent trips often developed friendships with their favorite conversationalists on the boats and many teenage girls suffered temporary broken hearts over the "sailors" they wouldn't see again after the summer season ended. Year after year sadness marked the close of the excursion season as Wilson Line shifted back to its winter commuter-freight operation.

Sadness also tinged the thoughts of Wilson Line's oldtimers on September 29, 1938, when news reached Wilmington that Captain Horace Wilson, the man who had led "The Great White Fleet of the Delaware" during most of the line's history, had died in New York. He was 76 and had just completed a cruise to Bermuda. His death came less than a decade after his retirement and although he had seen little of the line that still bore his family's name, he had continued to play an active role in Wilmington's business and social life.

Captain Wilson had maintained his captain's license and his memberships in many organizations, including the Delaware Society of Sons of the American Revolution, of which he had once been president. His membership was possible through his mother's family, named Engelman, which had settled in the territory from Holland in colonial times. He had been a leading Delawarean in many fields but he was remembered most as one of the great steamboatmen of the Delaware.

By 1939, Wilson Line began to think about a Boston operation and when Boston's Nantasket Beach Steamboat Company prepared to liquidate,

Hibernating at Wilmington in 1941 are (l. to r.): *State of Pennsylvania, City of Washington, Mount Vernon, Liberty Belle, Dixie* and *City of Wilmington* undergoing conversion. Wilson Line, Inc.

Captain John Emering discusses the day's events with members of the Mount Vernon Ladies' Association of the Union on board *Mount Vernon,* May 16, 1940. Wilson Line Inc.

After her reconstruction *Mount Vernon* bore no resemblance to the *City of Camden* she had been. She took over Potomac operations in 1940. Wilson Line, Inc.

Wilson expressed an interest in acquiring its steamers *Nantasket, Mayflower, Allerton* and *Town of Hull.* However, B. B. Wills, the one-man competitor of the Wilson System, beat the Wilmington firm to the draw and took control of the old Boston line. All Wilson hopes for a Boston line were eliminated by U.S. involvement in World War II. Apart from this, almost all of the new Wilson Line's plans of 1929 were being realized.

Wilson's reconstruction program moved on a two-year formula and in 1940 it was *City of Camden's* turn for conversion. Her hull was stripped bare and towed to the Sun Shipbuilding yards, at Chester, for sponsoning. The hull was then towed to Wilmington where Wilson's own shipyard installed a new streamlined superstructure. Like *Liberty Belle,* she featured a jaunty, short stack with the "diesel look" that then dominated contemporary naval architecture.

During the spring of 1940, Wilson's Washington division launched an intensive publicity campaign on the new streamliner's behalf. Washington's manager, Harry Baker, told newsmen that "the boat is unnamed as yet, but there will be a name-selecting contest later on. *Mount Vernon* is the best bet to date." *Mount Vernon* it was and Wilson proudly advertised the former *City of Camden* as "One of the mightiest all-steel cruisers afloat . . .

*City of Wilmington,* the last of Wilson's combination passenger-freight steamers, being transformed into an excursion liner, January 27, 1941. Wilson Line, Inc.

Wilson Line's pacesetting design is again reflected in the 1941-built *New York,* America's first streamlined double-ended ferry. Edward O. Clark

weather-conditioned, sleek, beautiful and SAFE! Equipped with every modern convenience for your pleasure and enjoyment. . . ."

The press called *Mount Vernon* the finest expression of the streamlined riverboat ever developed in the United States, and referring to her ultramodern touches such as adjustable plate glass windows (which could be raised or lowered as required), chrome-topped railings, and glimmering nickle-plated whistle, one reporter commented: "Why, Mr. Wilson Line, you actually make us suffer!" *Mount Vernon* had the streamlined refinement of a lady and Washingtonians loved her on sight. She entertained over half a million of them in her first season.

Meanwhile, the homey *City of Washington* had been returned to the Delaware and the 220-foot *Mount Vernon* assumed the Mount Vernon-Marshall Hall line. A gala rechristening ceremony was held off President Washington's plantation on May 16 and Mrs. Horace Towner, president of The Mount Vernon Ladies Association of the Union performed the honors. The steamer's Potomac career began later in the day with a moonlight sail sponsored by Washington's Junior Chamber of Commerce. Afterwards, *Mount Vernon* settled down to a routine of two day trips and one moonlight sail daily. At the end of each season she usually made special sailings from the Naval Academy and public trips from Washington to Baltimore and Wilmington via the Chesapeake and Delaware Canal. Photos of her appeared in a number of Annapolis yearbooks to revive memories of trips the midshipmen had made to Baltimore for the Army-Navy football classic in the fall.

Efforts were also underway in the late 1930s to upgrade the Delaware-New Jersey Ferry's fleet and in 1937, 57-year old *Brigantine* was converted into a derrick barge for use at Wilson's repair facilities. That same year, two big propeller ferries, *Washington* and *Pittsburg*, were acquired from the Pennsylvania Railroad. The following year the venerable sidewheeler *Arctic* of 1879, the oldest active steamboat on the Delaware, also became a barge. She was replaced by the former Pennsylvania Railroad ferry *Cincinnati* after the latter was converted to uniflow drive. *Pennsville* of 1891 and *Long Beach* of 1880 were retired in 1940 and replaced by *Wildwood*, formerly of the Pennsylvania's Camden–Philadelphia ferry line.

The veteran *New Castle* of 1890 and *Cape May* of 1901 were withdrawn in 1941, marking the end of the sidewheel era on the Delaware. They were replaced by two new vessels, *New York* and *Florida*, the nation's first uniflow-powered, streamlined double-enders. These identical sister ships were built by Wilmington's Pusey & Jones Company for nearly $1 million.

While the "gold mine" operation between New Castle and Pennsville continued to gain importance, the older Penn's Grove-Wilmington service fared less well and was finally abandoned in 1942. The first ferry on the Delaware had begun in 1669 on the "Christeen Kill" (Christina River) and that tradition ended, after 273 years, without ceremony.

*City of Wilmington's* reconstruction was originally planned for 1942 but as World War II grew more menacing the line began stockpiling steel and advanced the *Wilmington's* alterations to 1941, following the same overall design as *Mount Vernon.* The line's shipyard forces worked in freezing snow and rain to complete her transformation by the spring of 1941 and, except for minor differences, she emerged identical to *Mount Vernon.* The former *City of Wilmington* was now *Bay Belle* and the line's year-round passenger-freight service became a memory.

"Baltimore's Beautiful *Bay Belle*" received a warm reception and Captain "Bill" Hunton could not have been prouder. Rechristening ceremonies, staged off Fort McHenry in Baltimore Harbor on the morning of May 28, 1941, were a public relations man's dream! Mrs. Millard E. Tydings, wife of the U.S. Senator from Maryland, smashed the bottle of champagne to make *"Bay Belle"* the steamer's official name as fireboats sent sprays of water high into the air and harbor craft roared salutes of welcome to Baltimore's rakish new steamboat personality. Baltimore's Mayor Jackson, prominent Marylanders and Wilson's staff stood at attention as a band played *The Star Spangled Banner* within yards of the site where Francis Scott Key had penned the words to the national anthem. (This became the custom for *Bay Belle's* passengers as they passed Fort McHenry.)

After the ceremonies, *Bay Belle* returned to Baltimore for public inspection. Her second maiden voyage took place on Decoration Day, as she sailed to Cambridge, Maryland. Regular service to Seaside Park began on June 8, and although Wilson called *Bay Belle* "the fastest excursion liner out of Baltimore," the 110-mile round trip was still a bit too long for her reduced, post-modernization speed. About a quarter of a million Baltimoreans made pleasant trips on *Bay Belle* during her first season, but some of the passengers

The Penn's Grove ferry *New Castle* makes one of her final crossings from Wilmington, September 1, 1941. Wilson Line operated the last side-wheelers on the Delaware. R. Loren Graham

Veteran *Cincinnati* crosses the Delaware in 1937 on "that gold mine" operation between New Castle and Pennsville. Courtesy: The Mariners Museum, Newport News, Va.

who had formerly ridden *Dixie* missed the older boat. *Dixie* had returned to the Delaware River to serve as a spare boat.

While Wilson Line was rebuilding *City of Wilmington,* Pusey & Jones was completing the system's largest boat, a huge auto-passenger transport for Virginia Ferry Corporation's Little Creek route. This new steamer was 300 feet long and nearly 2,000 tons. Like *Del-Mar-Va* and *Princess Anne* she was powered by steam uniflow engines that would give her a service speed of 19 miles per hour. She was given the romantic name of *Pocahontas* on September 16, 1940. Built at a cost of $1,225,000, *Pocahontas* was the most expensive ferryboat ever built in the United States and she was one of the most impressive bay steamers ever seen on the East Coast. "*Pocahontas,*" commented *Marine Engineering and Shipping Age,* "must be ranked tops in attractive passenger facilities, carrying capacity and performance."

The new transport's capacity of 1,200 passengers and 100 vehicles was a valuable addition to Virginia Ferry Corporation's fleet as lines of waiting traffic grew longer at its terminals which displayed large signs announcing "Gateway to the North" at Little Creek and "Gateway to the South" at Cape Charles. The Wilson-Pennsylvania operation carried some 220,000 vehicles and over 600,000 passengers across the Chesapeake in 1941 and with the nation climbing out of the depression, far greater traffic was anticipated.

As a result of the promotion of the Ocean Hiway many motorists heading north or south used both the Chesapeake and Delaware services of the Wilson System. For those who could afford the ferry services, a short, relaxing cruise, dining while overlooking the blue waters of the Chesapeake, was just the right formula for pleasant touring.

The huge *Pocahontas,* built in 1941, departs from Little Creek, Virginia. Courtesy: The Mariners Museum, Newport News, Va.

Under post-1929 management, the Wilson System by 1941 had emerged from the brink of bankruptcy to operate a water transportation network of national significance. It now possessed the nation's largest and most modern fleet of river and bay steamers entertaining and transporting some 5 million passengers over 1 million miles yearly. The morale of the organization was high. Wilson had done the "impossible" and its feat became a unique success story in American maritime circles during one of the nation's worst depressions. Then came Pearl Harbor.

*Chicago* (left) and *Pittsburgh* pass on the Delaware, August 31, 1941. R. Loren Graham

## Chapter IX

# Wilson Goes to War

THE BEST plans of individuals and companies alike meant little after December 7, 1941, as the entire nation responded quickly with total commitment to the war effort. Wilson Line's immediate plans were postponed and its former history almost repeated itself. In World War I, its fleet had been expanded but none of its boats were laid up or taken over by the government. The World War II situation was far more complicated.

The war brought gas rationing and a halt to the manufacture of private cars. This meant a reduction in auto travel and lost business for both of the line's ferry systems. Auto limitation could have spurred Wilson's summer excursion services but the government placed high priority on fuel oil and this led to elimination of pleasure cruising until fuel supplies met the needs of naval and merchant ships. The government also needed seamen and all types of ships—including defenseless riverboats.

The war automatically postponed Wilson's plans for a Boston operation and new construction. It also ended *State of Delaware's* excursion service at New York and she returned to Wilmington for prolonged lay-up. As it developed, her peacetime career was over after 19 years. During that time she had carried over 18 million passengers under the Wilson banner. The system continued to operate in 1942 but uniformed Army and Navy personnel on weekend shore leave were increasingly in evidence throughout the fleet.

However, at Baltimore, the government saw more urgent use for the Wilson fleet than morale-building. The shipyards were working round-the-clock on a crash program to build a huge merchant fleet in a few years' time. Baltimore's yards, however, were quite distant from the city and, with gas rationing and auto scarcity, the government

Graceful *Mount Vernon* embarks civilians and servicemen on leave in Washington, August 30, 1942. Fuel restrictions curbed her services in 1943. R. Loren Graham

considered steamboats ideal for providing mass transportation for shipyard workers. As it had for the Hog Island yards in World War I, Wilson Line would again support this crucial war effort.

The U.S. Maritime Commission signed a contract with the line in 1942 for daily transportation services between Baltimore, Bethlehem Steel's Fairfield yard and Maryland Shipbuilding and Drydock Company's yards. Shortly afterwards *Liberty Belle* and *Dixie* were pressed into this service, carrying thousands of men daily from the city's recreation pier. To suit these commuter conditions, 16 turnstiles and a change booth were installed on the pier. *Liberty Belle* had barely begun this task when the Navy requisitioned her for use as an experimental ship for the Bureau of Ships.

Meanwhile, *Bay Belle* returned to her Baltimore-Seaside Park line two weeks earlier than usual. A. J. Dunn, Wilson's Baltimore manager said: "Our plans for this year have been laid out with the idea of supplying those who can't get away for vacations because of gasoline rationing or other reasons with some relaxation. We'll sail every night regardless of the weather and have planned a couple of all-day trips down to Cambridge to provide a variation."

Normal operations, however, were not possible. As the Baltimore *Sun* commented after one of its reporters made a trip:

*Dixie* transports shipyard men to Bethlehem's Fairfield yards in Baltimore, November 10, 1943. During World War I she carried du Pont powdermakers. Bethlehem Steel Corp.

"So, with blasts on her whistle, the steamer *Bay Belle* backed out of her slip, edged over to the docks along Key Highway and headed for the lower harbor.

"Those on board, if they weren't dancing below, saw a harbor that had undergone material changes in the year elapsed since *Bay Belle* sailed on her maiden voyage. Gone were the brightly painted freighters that used to line the Pratt Street and other wharves. In their stead were grim, grey craft waiting to be loaded or standing by for repairs. The docks below Fort McHenry were a sea of light under which night gangs sweated over repairs. The noise of the riveters echoed back and forth across the harbor and blue flares of welder's torches stood out like neon signs . . . only a few autos passed by the docks as the steamer slipped out into the Patapsco." *Bay Belle's* career was soon halted by fuel restrictions. By 1943 she too went on the shipyard run, teaming briefly with *State of Pennsylvania.*

*Bay Belle's* sister ship, now *USS Liberty Belle (IX-72)*, had been reassigned to the Commandant, Fifth Naval District, on June 5, 1942. She was painted navy grey and went into service out of the Naval Mine Warfare Test Station, Solomons, Maryland. The Navy altered her radically, removing her after superstructure and installing minesweeping gear on her stern for training purposes. She continued in this service until May, 1944.

The Navy also requisitioned *Christiana*, the line's last freight boat, and assigned her to the Seventh Naval District. This was *Christiana's* second call from Uncle Sam. As the lighthouse tender *Azalea* she had seen service on the Nantucket Patrol during World War I. Altered and dieselized by November, 1942, the Navy commissioned her as a miscellaneous auxiliary, *USS Christiana (IX-80)*. A year later she was redesignated *YAG-32* and served out of Tampa, Florida. Still later she was stationed off Nassau in the Bahamas as a seaplane tender and according to Navy records she saved the crew and their aircraft which crashed in her vicinity on July 19, 1944. Her naval service ended in July, 1945 after she had spent the early part of that year running ammunition and supplies from Florida to the Bahamas.

As the war continued, Virginia Ferry Corporation's transports and the Delaware-New Jersey ferryboats served what were now considered vital north-south transportation needs of military traffic and personnel. In 1943, however, Wilson's passenger fleet program underwent a complete reversal and when *Mount Vernon* arrived at Washington in the spring to resume operations, fuel restrictions were imposed and she was permitted only enough fuel to return to Wilmington. In effect, Wilson Line was restricted to the Delaware for the first time since 1930.

Stationed off the Bahamas in 1943, the radically altered *USS Christiana (YAG-32)* evokes memories of "Mr. Roberts." Navy Department

Even Delaware services were limited basically to the traditional Wilmington-Chester-Philadelphia line which the government recognized as a genuine transportation service. Direct service to Riverview was discontinued. However, with wartime restrictions on civilian use of the nation's railroads, the Philadelphia line enjoyed a temporary revival. Company ads in 1943 emphasized: "Passenger Transportation Service" and *State of Pennsylvania* and *City of Washington* each made five round trips daily between Wilmington and Philadelphia. Owing to war-related activities along the Delaware, the line had to warn: "No cameras, binoculars or flashlights allowed." One of the sad sights on the route was the wreck of the Ericsson Line's *John Cadwalader* which had burned and sunk while being prepared for service in England.

In early 1943, new decisions were being made in Washington that would place further demands on the Wilson fleet. Malaya, the world's main source of rubber, was in Japanese hands and Brazil, the original habitat of the rubber tree, was rediscovered as a source. Millions of rubber trees grew wild in the Amazon's jungles; rubber in Brazil was just waiting to be tapped—or so Washington was led to believe.

Unlike prewar crowds, this sun-bronzed *State of Delaware* group leaps ashore to report to rubber plantations on the Amazon during 1943. Reconstruction Finance Corporation

There were, however, many problems, including transportation of the crude rubber from Brazil's beautiful but treacherous "Green Hell" to the seacoast for transshipment to the United States. Good roads were nonexistent and the dense jungles were inhabited by anacondas and wild Indians. The U.S. Rubber Development Corporation (RDC) was formed in 1942 specifically to relieve the crucial rubber shortage, in cooperation with Brazil. Brazil allegedly lacked adequate vessels, so American boats were to be used.

By early 1943, the Rubber Development Corporation had collected an unorthodox fleet of its own for the Amazon assignment, including the Pennsylvania Railroad's *Virginia Lee,* the New York excursion steamers *Belle Island* and *Westchester,* Sound Steamship Line's *Cambridge,* and the Chesapeake steamer *Virginia.* The last two were being dismantled when RDC in desperation took title and repaired them. *Virginia Lee* and *Belle Island* (renamed *Col. James A. Moss*) had actually been reacquired from the British Ministry of Transport after they missed their convoy from Halifax. They were returned to New York and outfitted for Brazil despite the objections the Brazilians had to their suitability for the Amazon. On March 30, 1943, an additional $750,000 fund was authorized to acquire *State of Delaware.*

It was relatively easy. Small Craft Requisition 497 was prepared and on March 25, War Shipping Administration's Philadelphia manager wired RDC agents in Washington: "*State of Delaware* requisitioned, title to March 25, 9 A.M., Eastern War Time, simultaneous delivery Rubber Development Corporation"—(signed) Gormley Doyle, Yours United . . . For Victory." RDC's agents, Moore-McCormack Lines, promptly accepted the vessel.

Preparing the "Amazon boats" for the 4,000-mile ocean voyage was also relatively easy, but finding seamen willing to take boarded-up riverboats on an anticipated harrowing trip was far more difficult. If storms didn't sink them, they'd be sitting ducks for Nazi subs on the Atlantic, or so most seamen thought. One executive of Moore-McCormack told the writer half-jokingly that "I think the boats sailed undermanned: several of our office girls' names were added to round out the crew lists."

Unknown even to most Wilmingtonians, the boarded-up, grey-painted *State of Delaware* quietly slipped out of the Christina and down the Delaware on April 22, 1943, bound for a rendezvous with a convoy off the coast. Her secret destination: Belem, Brazil. She flew the Honduran flag to avoid U.S. and Brazilian red tape. Before long, people in New York and Wilmington were asking: "Whatever happened to *State of Delaware?*"

Part of the answer appeared in the July 9, 1943 edition of the Wilmington *News-Journal* which carried the front page headline: "Wilson Liner Makes Hazardous Trip to Brazil; Now on Amazon." The story revealed that veteran Wilson skipper Captain Edwin Savin, chief engineer Andrew

Anderson and a crew representing 40 nationalities had recently returned to the United States by Army air transportation.

It was also disclosed that the *Delaware* had arrived in Brazil on June 10. Later, Captain Savin indicated that he was "not at liberty to reveal much about the convoy" but he said it was attacked by submarines several times. He smiled when reporters asked if any of the ships were sunk and then replied: "The important thing is that we got the vessel safely delivered . . ."

Later, however, the captain admitted that the trip was the severest test of his career and he explained that: "Rounding Cape Hatteras was tricky . . . but the worst came when two of the convoy were sunk by torpedoes off the Bahamas. Then bad weather sent us scurrying for Cuban ports." *State of Delaware,* government records indicated, arrived at Belem on June 10, 1943 in "perfect mechanical condition." *Westchester* was less fortunate, nearly sinking after a storm tore off a 40-foot section of her guards. She limped into Miami for repairs and arrived at Belem on June 25.

When all the Amazon boats arrived at Belem they were turned over to Brazil's agents, Şervicio de Navegacao do Amazonas e Porto do Para (SNAPP), but it was some time before service between Belem and Manaus, the sweltering Amazon port some thousand miles inland, was begun. American journals with an inkling of the story highlighted the adventure. In 1943, *Life* reported that "The 'Battle of Rubber' being waged by Brazil is probably the biggest story in all South America." *Newsweek* soon carried a story titled "The Amazon Bubble," alleging that rubber from Latin America cost U.S. taxpayers as high as $500

Arriving at Manaus in 1943, *State of Delaware* prepares to transport rubber plantation workers and crude rubber 1,000 miles to Belem. Reconstruction Finance Corporation

A long way from home (4,000 miles away), grey-garbed *State of Delaware* rests at Belem, Brazil, after her extraordinary ocean voyage. Reconstruction Finance Corporation

a pound. Rubber Development's figures gave the cost as $.82 a pound.

During 1943 alone, the Amazon boats carried over 50,000 "soldados de barracha" (soldiers of rubber, as plantation workers were known in Brazil) between Amazon ports. Although Brazil wanted better boats than America sent, the steamers soon proved popular and *Belle Island* even set a few new speed records. Further, the American boats made much better time, averaging two and a half days from Belem to Manaus, compared with as many as 15 days for the wood-burning Brazilian boats which lost valuable time in refueling and siestas.

The whole program, however, suffered from insufficient planning, the lack of understanding of rubber, of the Amazon and of Brazil. Edward Laux, the man in charge of the American fleet working with SNAPP, told the writer in 1967 that: "Rubber Development's project was a mess from the start. Only after the vessels arrived in Brazilian waters was it found that they could have been fired upon for entering without clearance. The purpose of the project was to develop rubber by starting plantations along the Amazon but there were people with the project who didn't know that it took 11 years before a rubber tree yielded its first latex. Fortunately, the trees were of varying ages.

"Starting plantations posed problems too, including finding competent farmers. There were few. Finally, RDC accepted 'adventurers' (we called them 'bums') who received pay for manning a small plantation. Their equipment included rubber plants, a lantern, a kerosene stove, axes and a gun. We had heard about wild animals and wild Indians but I only saw quiet Indians myself. I

Remodeled *State of Pennsylvania* reflects her beauty in the serene Christina during the spring of 1944. Wilson Line, Inc.

Bound for the Army-Navy football classic at Baltimore, Naval Academy midshipmen embark *Mount Vernon* at Annapolis in 1945. Wilson Line, Inc.

When Wilson rebuilt its steamers, their original cast-iron stoves, like *Mount Vernon*'s above, were saved for "old-fashioned cooking." Wilson Line, Inc.

did, however, hear about other Indians who blew poison darts through shoots at the passing boats. We delivered supplies and picked up rubber, some of which had been deliberately filled with pebbles to give us a false weight. Our boats, however, did well under the circumstances. They were good in the Amazon's heavy currents." Although the Amazon boats did their bit for the war effort it was synthetic rubber which saved the day and kept the Allied war machinery equipped with tires and other urgently needed parts.

"Beautiful!" and "Like an ocean liner!" were among the public's reactions to the reconditioned *State of Pennsylvania* in 1944. Edward O. Clark

While *State of Delaware* was steaming the Amazon, her sister, *State of Pennsylvania,* was taken out of service for modernization in 1944. Both had been originally scheduled for up-dating but now only *Pennsy* was available. Using prewar stockpiled steel, Wilson Line personnel virtually rebuilt "old *Pennsy*" into one of the nation's most modern riverboats, and her streamlining was kept in harmony with her original lines. She was spared being renamed and sported a huge new stack which featured synchronized whistle-lights, a safety system for night steaming whereby two lights blinked simultaneously with the sounding of her whistle. In this, Wilson Line was at least 20 years ahead of the maritime industry in coordinating audio-visual signals.

A spectacular *State of Pennsylvania* was permitted to resume her Riverview Beach line in 1944, and with fuel restrictions lifted, *Mount Vernon* was prepared to return to the Potomac. By 1945, victory over the Axis powers was assured, *Dixie* and *Bay Belle* completed their wartime roles and the nation began to return to peacetime normalcy. Wilson's task was to pick up the pieces and rebuild the nation's largest river and bay operation. It did so with determination.

## Chapter X

# Postwar Boom and Gloom

WILSON LINE'S history was a continuous cycle of revivals following setbacks and periods of decline following spurts of notable success. The cycle was repeated very quickly in the immediate post-World War II period. The line's decline which began with Pearl Harbor ended with victory in 1945 and as America returned to peace, prospects for the Wilson System improved dramatically.

However, from the moment its revival seemed assured, a new prospect loomed as a threat to the line's continuation. That prospect was the eventual replacement of the line's Delaware-New Jersey ferry services by a bridge envisioned in the *Delaware River Crossing Act* passed by the State of Delaware in 1945. It would mean the end of the ferry service and without the year-round earnings from its gold mine, time was running out for the Wilson System.

Nevertheless, Wilson's management set out to surpass the fleet's prewar performance and each of the passenger steamers was thoroughly overhauled

*Princess Anne* as she appeared after her modifications in 1946. Her original design had been too artistic to be fully functional. The Pennsylvania Railroad Company

An architect's concept of a postwar Wilson liner that never materialized. George G. Sharp, Inc.

and returned to operation one by one. By 1945 the sleek *Mount Vernon* had reestablished herself as Washington's most popular steamer despite competition from B. B. Wills' Potomac River Line.

Wilson resumed prewar plans for a Boston service but other operators maintained a line to Provincetown and durable competitor B. B. Wills operated the popular Nantasket Beach run. Wilson then decided to start a Boston Harbor sightseeing operation and *Dixie* was readied for the assignment in the spring of 1946. "Dixie," however, was not an appropriate name for New England so the old boat was renamed a third time, becoming *Pilgrim Belle*.

Wilson Line hesitated to send a boat named *Dixie* to Yankee Boston. Hence, she was renamed *Pilgrim Belle* in 1946. Wilson Line, Inc.

Massive *Pocahontas,* flagship of the Virginia Ferry Corporation's Little Creek fleet, makes a routine crossing of the Chesapeake on May 5, 1946. John L. Lochhead Photo. Courtesy: The Mariners Museum, Newport News, Va.

Without a line, Wilson advertised *Pilgrim Belle* as "The Largest Sightseeing Steamer on the Atlantic Coast" and she made several trips daily from historic India Wharf. Whatever she lacked in appearance she made up in personality and she became a surprising success. Few boats at her age were ever expected to start a new service but "old *Brandywine*" always had an aura about her that won a following. In her sixty-first year she held the distinction of being America's first radar-equipped excursion steamer.

New *Delaware Belle,* America's first major diesel-powered passenger riverboat, prepares for her trials from Wilmington, September, 1946. Wilson Line, Inc.

Next on Wilson's agenda was resumption of operations at Baltimore where *Bay Belle* had served briefly before Pearl Harbor. The line arranged a new route to Betterton, Maryland, on the beautiful Eastern Shore of Chesapeake Bay. She was ready for her peacetime chores in 1946 and the line signed an agreement which allowed docking at the Betterton Yacht Club's pier. Wilson also purchased Gale Farms, a 235-acre tract located between Tolchester Beach and Rock Hall, Maryland, as a potential site for a new resort destination.

B. B. Wills revived the Tolchester route with *Bear Mountain* and in 1948 put a new *Tolchester* on that line as a replacement for the previous *Tolchester* which had been destroyed by fire in 1941. The new competitor turned out to be *Bay Belle's* erstwhile sister ship *Liberty Belle.* Wisely or not, Wilson Line had refused to reacquire her after the war, owing to her rundown condition. In 1947, another group had reconditioned her and renamed her *Asbury Park* for use on the racetrack run between New York and Atlantic Highlands, New Jersey. In 1948, B. B. Wills acquired her for his Baltimore service and Wilson's twin *Cities* of 1910 found themselves in the ironic position of being keen competitors for the next eight years, carrying hundreds of thousands of Baltimoreans each summer for different owners. In 1951, *Bay Belle* became the first American day boat with television shows when station WBAL-TV broadcast the popular dance show "Aboard the *Bay Belle*" every Sunday evening.

To replace *State of Delaware,* Wilson proceeded in 1946 with construction of a new 3,400-passenger vessel of about the same size. Her hull and superstructure were built by the Lancaster Iron Works of Perryville, Maryland, and Mrs. Lawrence C. Campbell, wife of Wilson Line's vice-president, christened her *Delaware Belle* on June 27, 1946. Wilson completed the vessel's outfitting at its own Wilmington yards.

*Pilgrim Belle's* passengers seem attentive to descriptions of Boston Harbor sites beaming over the steamer's loudspeaker system, June 16, 1946. R. Loren Graham

*Pilgrim Belle* departs from Boston's historic India Wharf with her youthful "Indians" celebrating a modern "Boston Tea Party," July 27, 1949. Wilson Line, Inc.

*Delaware Belle* added new laurels to Wilson's record of pioneering, being America's first large diesel-powered passenger riverboat. She was also the nation's first entirely glass-enclosed excursion vessel. Postwar costs were rising and the switch from steam to diesel was intended to keep operating costs down. However, after building a few more diesel *Belles,* the line concluded that the dependability of steam offset the apparent economy of diesel drive. Diesels also proved less attractive to passengers. Even so, *Delaware Belle* could have been exceptional had more attention been given to her spartan interiors.

Nonetheless, *Marine Engineering* commented: "To say that *Delaware Belle* is ideal for the purpose would probably be making an understatement . . ." A. V. S. Olcott, longtime president of the traditionalist Hudson River Day Line, wrote

Passengers on *State of Pennsylvania* view Summit Bridge on the C & D Canal, September 14, 1946. Donald C. Ringwald

*State of Pennsylvania's* passengers greet fellow travelers on another vessel during a Chesapeake and Delaware Canal cruise. The Steamship Historical Society of America, Inc.

*Bay Belle's* passengers customarily came to attention when the "Star-Spangled Banner" was played by the steamer's band off Fort McHenry. Courtesy: The Mariners Museum, Newport News, Va.

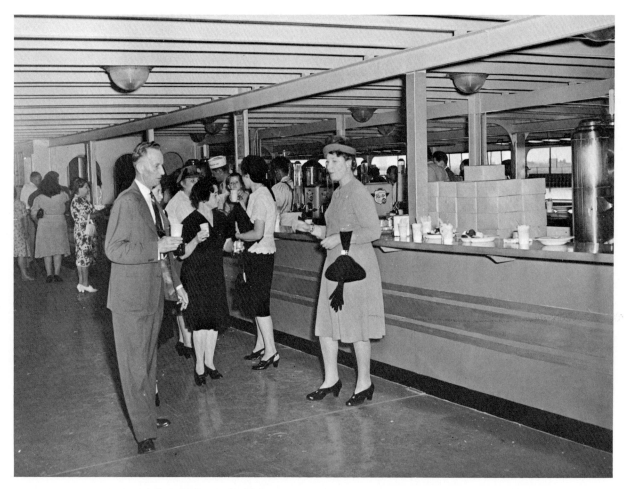

Fresh- or salt-air cruises spurred appetites and that extra-snack business which helped postwar steamboat lines to survive. Wilson Line, Inc.

to an associate: "She's quite a boat, with about the same capacity as *State of Pennsylvania.*" Olcott was one of many maritime executives invited to *Delaware Belle's* trials on September 10, 1946. Her maiden voyage was a special sailing from Annapolis to Philadelphia with thousands of midshipmen bound for the Army-Navy football game.

*Delaware Belle* entered the Philadelphia-Riverview run in the spring of 1947, teaming up with *State of Pennsylvania* while the veteran *City of Washington* continued on the Wilmington-Philadelphia line for which she was built in 1888. From Massachusetts to Virginia the Wilson boats enjoyed new prosperity but the certainty of the new Dela-

*State of Pennsylvania's* "big ship" impression is captured by this 1946 view near Chester, Pennsylvania. R. Scozzafava

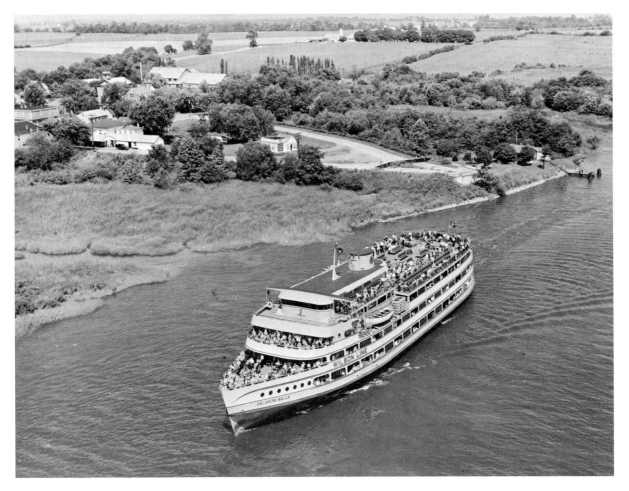

*Delaware Belle* brings city dwellers to clean air and a view of Maryland's green farmlands along the Chesapeake and Delaware Canal, September 3, 1947. Edward O. Clark

ware River bridge tempered all of the line's postwar investment plans and construction of new tonnage after *Delaware Belle* was considered unfeasible.

After 1947 the line made the best of this situation by purchasing surplus naval craft for conversion into excursion boats and bay transports. In 1947, one PCE(R) was being converted into a day boat for Wilson Line while an LST and an LSM were being rebuilt into an auto-passenger transport and a tanker for the Virginia Ferry Corporation. Other LST's and PC's were acquired for future conversions.

The fleet's revival was also reflected by increasing net earnings which rose from a low of $172,080 in 1945 to $322,803 in 1946. By early 1947, earned surplus had risen to over $1 million and all three Wilson operations grossed over $1 million yearly. However, as late as 1947, Wilson had yet to receive full payment for the requisitioned *State of Delaware* and final settlement was less than half the original agreement. Meanwhile, the government had auctioned the *Delaware* in Brazil to Guaracy Almeida Costa. She was subsequently taken another thousand miles south to Rio de Janeiro where she changed hands several times more among speculators who had many plans for her,

*Asbury Park,* ex-*City of Philadelphia,* sails from New York in July, 1947, with a crowd of horseracing fans bound for Atlantic Highlands, New Jersey. John C. Mills

Wilson's postwar "family" portrait at Wilmington, 1947, includes (l. to r.): *City of Washington, Pilgrim Belle, Mount Vernon, Bay Belle, State of Pennsylvania* and *Delaware Belle.* A. N. Sanborn

including operation on the sea between Angra dos Reis, Brazil and Buenos Aires, Argentina. About 1951, tentatively renamed *Guaruja,* the former Wilson liner sank at the Guanabara Shipyards in Niterói while laid up during alterations.

In 1948 the first of three former naval patrol craft, *PCE(R)-854,* was transformed by Wilson's own staff into a trim, 2,900-capacity diesel-powered excursion vessel. She was rechristened *Liberty Belle* and considered a replacement for the steamer whose name she assumed. The new *Belle* was originally built in 1943 by the Pullman Standard Car Company in Chicago, Illinois. During the war she had seen service in the Caribbean and off the Panama Canal Zone.

She could not have been built by a commercial yard for less than a million dollars but Wilson saved over half that by doing its own conversion work, most of which was accomplished while the boat was waterborne. The line was proud of her and somehow she proved a far more personable boat than the more expensive *Delaware Belle.* In the spring of 1948 *Liberty Belle* replaced *Pilgrim Belle* at Boston and opened a new line to Plymouth, site of the famed rock at which the Pilgrim Fathers landed.

*PCE-854,* in the Chicago River, November, 1943, bore no resemblance to the Wilson liner she was to become after World War II. The National Archives

Wilson boasted that *Liberty Belle* (II) was the "world's newest, most advanced excursion vessel . . ." but for all that, she rolled heavily when operated briefly to Provincetown. However, despite occasional diesel breakdowns on the Plymouth route, she managed to evoke considerable enthusiasm. At the end of her first season she made a few more calls at Provincetown where her reappearance prompted a second warm reception and one newspaperman reported that "she was a most impressive sight as she appeared over Long Point and moved across the harbor up to Town Wharf." This boat had personality and many grew to like her even if she was a diesel and "sounded like a bus."

The ingenuity of Wilson Line at work: (Top) *PCE-854,* minus superstructure, begins her metamorphosis into an ultramodern excursion vessel. (Bottom) With her hull heeled to starboard, Wilson shipyard staff adds sponsons to *PCE-854* in the spring of 1947. Wilson Line, Inc.

*State of Pennsylvania's* actual transfer to New

York came 12 years after the line's announcement of the change. Wilson had hoped to revive the Roton Point, Connecticut, service abandoned by *Belle Island* in 1941 but the park had been converted into a private country club, partly through efforts of community interests opposed to "any more Coney Islands here." With that prospect gone and the line again blocked from a Bear Mountain route, Wilson settled instead on a revival of the old line to Rockaway Beach. *State of Pennsylvania* began service between Jersey City, New York and Rockaway in May, 1948.

Although the revival was slow, Yonkers proved a bright spot on *Pennsy's* schedule when she sailed every Monday from that city. Within weeks her cruises were reminiscent of her sister ship's prewar successes and initially many thought she was *State of Delaware,* modernized and renamed. Many were astounded to learn that the prewar favorite was then in Brazil. Like her sister ship, *Pennsy* won a big following, especially among the youngsters, and on Mondays carried more people from Yonkers than she did from all of New York throughout the rest of the week.

As always, the "Pennsylvania Polka" was played at boarding time and on the way crowds sang "Cruising down the river . . . on the beautiful *State of Pennsylvania,*" to the music of Jack Constance's orchestra. After a short while Yonkers children gave her several new nicknames, including "Pencil" and "the black stack excursion."

*State of Pennsylvania's* triple-chambered, deep-toned whistle was a treat to hear and to see in action as feathers of white steam floated from both

Wilson shipyard men install superstructure framing on the future *Liberty Belle* (II) at Wilmington during the winter of 1947-8. Wilson Line, Inc.

Nearly completed, *Liberty Belle* (II) (far right) poses with her Wilson sisters at Wilmington in the spring of 1948. Edward O. Clark

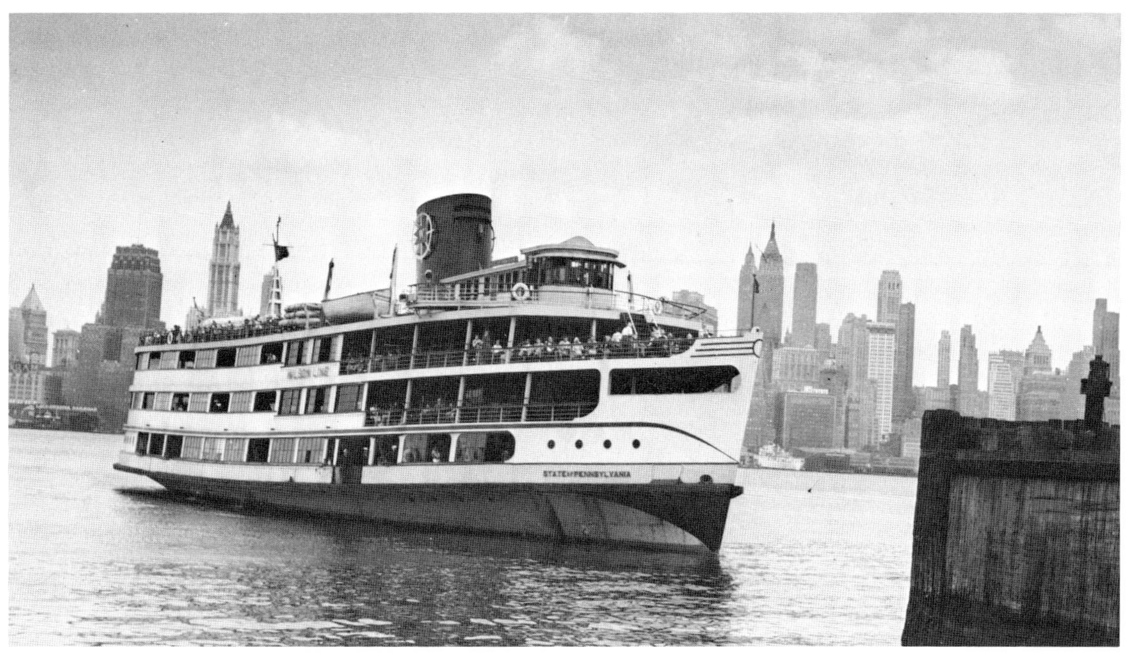

With New York's skyline as her background, *State of Pennsylvania* arrives at Jersey City on August 7, 1948. Harry Cotterell, Jr.

Queens Borough president James Burke (holding child) debarks from *State of Pennsylvania* after she completed the first postwar steamboat trip to Rockaway. Wilson Line, Inc.

*Liberty Belle* (II) embarks a capacity crowd of 2,900 at Plymouth, Massachusetts, in 1948. R. Loren Graham

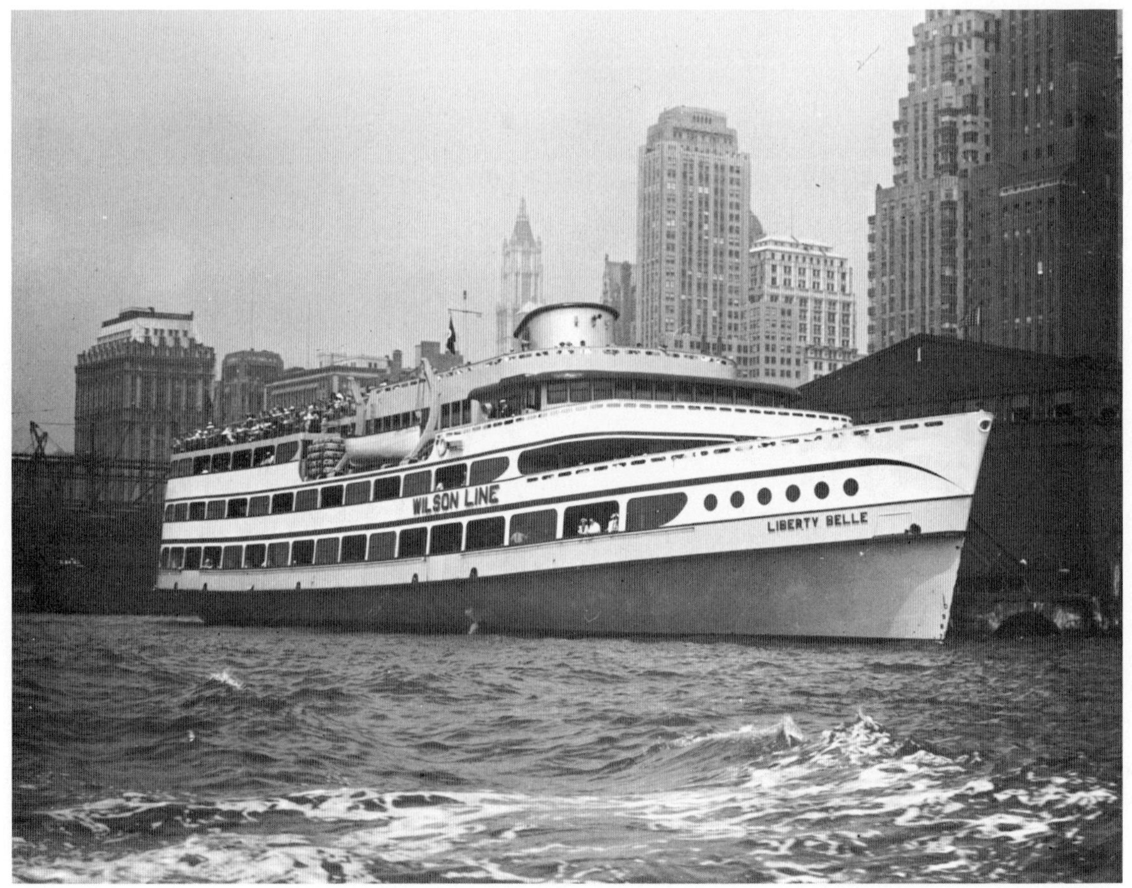


*Liberty Belle* (II) makes a landing at Pier 1, Manhattan. Stars of stage and screen frequented her Actor's Equity moonlight cruises. Edward Gibbs

sides of the ventilator slots on her massive stack. Children thrilled over the magnificent sound of her whistle and eagerly awaited her signal exchanges with other harbor craft, especially the sidewheeler *Clermont* which she often passed on the lower Hudson. While youngsters often exclaimed "Wow!" after hearing the powerful tone of *Pennsy's* blasts, they often laughed when the sidewheeler responded with her series of four chimes, each progressively lower in tone, which made a feeble, almost infirm impression. But, as in the past, Yonkers youths admired all of the "voices" of the riverboats.

It was still a time when steamboats entertained the young and a *State of Pennsylvania* cruise through New York Harbor meant interesting views and sounds, whether when passing ocean liners, or famous landmarks such as the Statue of Liberty, or any number of situations that made boat rides high adventures for children. Adults also enjoyed the sights, dancing in the ballroom or simply relaxing in an armchair on deck, especially at sunset when the lights of New York's skyline began to glow. The scenery varied on the rivers and bays served by the Wilson liners but all of the trips brought pleasure to millions of Americans.

These were good years for Wilson Line as passenger volume again rose toward the prewar level of two million passengers annually. It was still a pleasant business entertaining and transporting people happily content to enjoy the simple pleasures of the boat trips. This, however, was not to last as more and more people acquired cars and drove to local resorts during the summers.

The postwar period also brought boom times to Wilson's Delaware ferries and the Chesapeake transports. In 1948, over two million vehicles used the Delaware-New Jersey fleet and the Chesapeake boats transported 1,160,425 passengers and over

Representing two eras of Wilson Line: *Liberty Belle* (II) (left) and *State of Pennsylvania* are at Rockaway shortly before sailing time, 1949. Wilson Line, Inc.

396,000 vehicles between Cape Charles and Little Creek, Virginia.

Virginia Ferry Corporation also needed new vessels and in 1948 a World War II LST was reconstructed into a two-decked transport. This 327-foot vessel was renamed *Northampton* and entered the Little Creek run on November 4, 1948, with a capacity for 66 autos and 630 passengers. *Northampton* was no beauty but she was interesting and upheld the Wilson tradition for innovation by possessing the first "bow thruster" ever installed on an American merchant vessel. The "thruster," or cycloidal propeller, powered by its own engine and able to turn in any direction, was intended to facilitate dockside maneuvering. The scheme subsequently was copied by deep-sea operators with larger vessels. The third new boat of 1948 was a small LSM converted into a fleet tanker for the corporation. She was renamed *Kiptopeke.*

In the spring of 1949, Wilson Line completed

*Northampton,* a converted LST, joined the Little Creek fleet in 1948. She was America's first commercial vessel with a bow thruster. Courtesy: The Mariners Museum, Newport News, Va.

Sailing for B. B. Wills, the former Wilson liner *Liberty Belle* became "the" *Tolchester* in 1949, continuing an old Baltimore tradition. Courtesy: The Mariners Museum, Newport News, Va.

the conversion of *PC-1258* into the 258-foot, 3,000-passenger *Boston Belle*. She was a very simple boat but Wilson called her "A ship of glamour . . . rakish, yachty, long and low—she's a sleek, all steel beauty from stem to stern." Actually, her main assets were speed, roomy decks and exceptional safety provisions, including total fireproof construction and 64 watertight compartments. She also featured ship-to-shore phones and radar. Otherwise, she followed the trend towards utter simplicity in design. Like the rest of her fleet running mates, she received the Class A-1 rating of the American Bureau of Shipping, a rating few non-Wilson riverboats possessed.

Wilson placed the new *Boston Belle* on the Plymouth line in 1949 and on Sundays she made popular 13-mile Cape Canal cruises to Buzzard's Bay. *Liberty Belle* was placed on the Rockaway line at New York, replacing *State of Pennsylvania. Pennsy* remained at New York to handle charter traffic and ran once weekly from Bayonne and Elizabeth, New Jersey, to Rockaway. However, an intra-fleet rivalry affecting crews and passengers alike soon developed between those who favored the older steamboat and those who preferred the newer diesel boat, to the extent that the two boats might

**WYCIECZKI ŚRODOWE**

W Każdą Środę, Począwszy od 28-go Czerwca do 30 Sierpnia z Wyjątkiem 18-go Lipca

**z ELIZABETHPORT do ROCKAWAY BEACH**

Statek Przybija w Rockaway do Miljonowego Parku Przyjemności.

PLAYLAND

DARMO WSTĘP DO MIDWAY

DARMO DWA RAZY DZIENNIE

Wyczyny Samolotowe

WSZELKIE JAZDY

Zabawy - Przyjemności

DARMO KĄPIEL, czysta, piękna, zdrowotna plaża i deptak

Odjazd z Elizabethport . 10- arano 3:30 po poł.
Przyjazd do Rockaway Beach 12:30 w poł. 6-a w.
Odjazd z Rockaway Beach 12:45 w poł. 7-a w.
Przyjazd do Elizabethport 3:15 po poł. 9:30 w.

BILET OKRĘŻNY

DOROŚLI $1.00 DZIECI 50¢

Podatek włączony

Statek luksusowy S.S. State of Pennsylvania, o pojemności na 3,300 pasażerów. Cudowna wycieczka 2½-godzinna naokoło dolnych wybrzeży portu nowojorskiego. Spędzicie dzień na plaży.

Odjazd z Recreation Pier w Elizabethport
Telefon BErgen 4-7180

The ad is in Polish but the meaning of steamboat trips was international, June 30, 1950. *Nowy Swiat*

MOONLIGHT SAIL
SATURDAY, JUNE 10
BROADWAY REVUE & DANCING
Leave 8:45 P. M. Every Saturday
Battery Park, Pier 1
UP THE HUDSON VIA BEAR MT. SHOW BOAT $1.50
SUTTON LINE, Inc., 24 State St. WH. 3-6255

$1.00 Incl. Tax . . . Children 35c
Modern Steel Motor Vessel
NORMANDY
SIGHTSEEING
3 Hour Lecture Cruise
AROUND MANHATTAN ISLAND
Leaves Pier A, Battery Park 10:30 AM & 2:30 PM
DIgby 4-2397 GEdney 4-0101
BOATS FOR CHARTER

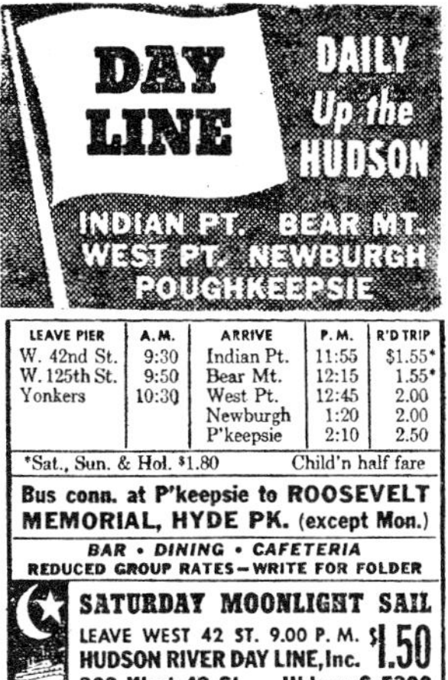

Weekday, Rd. Tr. fare: Ad. $1.50, Chil. 70c
Sun. & Hol., Rd. Tr. fare: Ad. $1.75, Chil. 70c
MOONLIGHT SAILS — SAT. — $1.50
Lv. Ex. Pl. Jersey City 8 p.m.
Bat. Pl. N.Y.C.—8:45 p.m.
MESECK LINE 17 BATTERY PL., N. Y. BOwling Green 9-1966

Only TAKE A LECTURE CRUISE Children
$1.00 SIGHTSEEING 35c
AROUND MANHATTAN ISLAND
M. V. MANHATTAN
LVS. PIER 1, BATTERY PARK
12-3-6 P. M. DAILY
PHONE BU. 2-6121

Although many steamboat lines succumbed during World War II, New York still enjoyed a variety of sailings in 1949. The New York *Daily News*

have been operated by different owners. In the meanwhile, the entire boating community was shocked by A. V. S. Olcott's announcement in the winter of 1948 that the venerable Hudson River Day Line had reached its end. During World War II Wilson Line had referred all of its requests for New York charters to the Day Line and, although the nation's two biggest boat lines were long-time rivals, there was much admiration among Wilson personnel for their old-fashioned competitor.

Rivalry of a serious nature developed at Boston

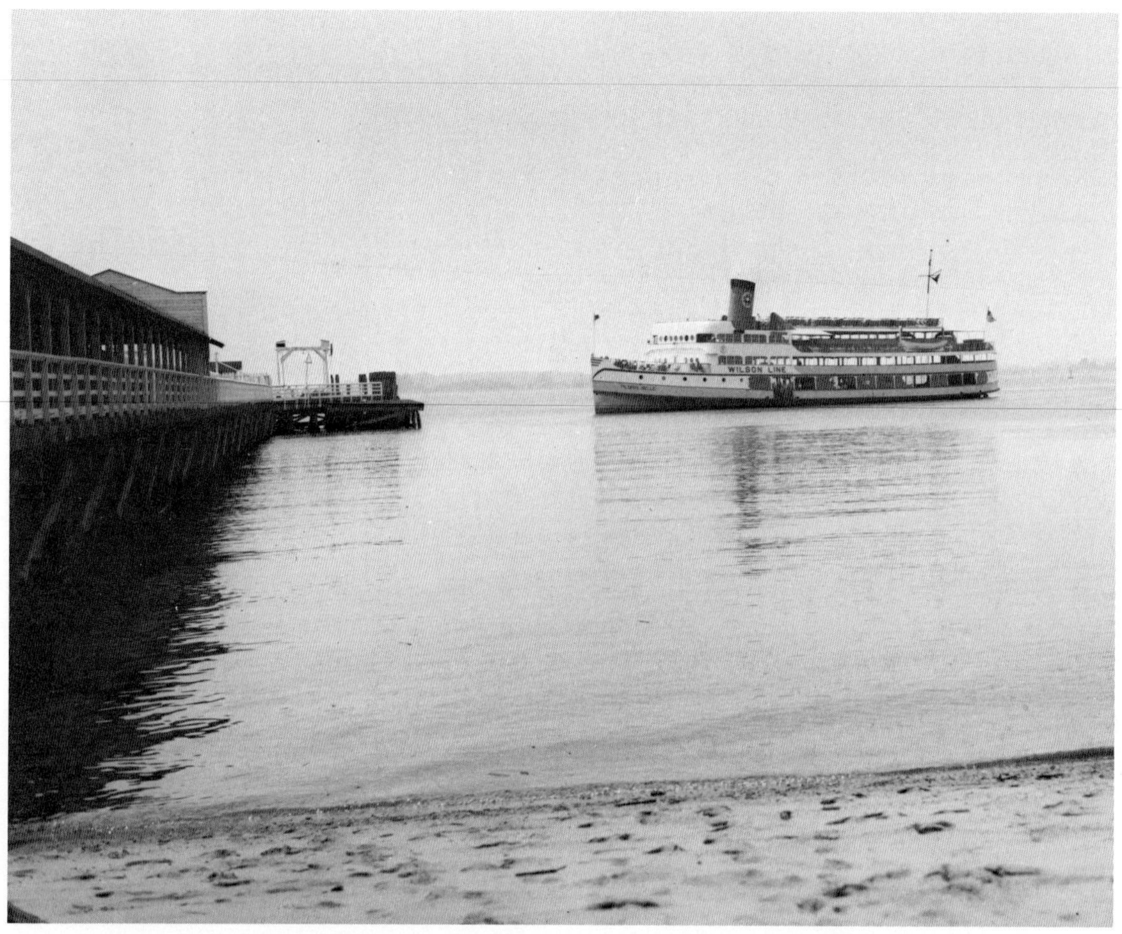


Returning to the Delaware in her 63rd year, the dowager *Pilgrim Belle* prepares to land at Riverview Beach on June 14, 1948. Harry Cotterell, Jr.

*Pinellas,* ex-*Wilmington,* was a Tampa Bay double-ended ferryboat when this view was taken in June, 1949. Joseph and Richard Braun

when *Boston Belle* began triangular trips between Boston, Plymouth and Provincetown. Running to "P-town" brought her into direct competition with B. B. Wills' *Holiday,* the dieselized former Chesapeake steamer *Virginia Lee* which had been operated by Virginia Ferry Corporation in 1933. She was the only "Amazon boat" to return to America after World War II. B. B. Wills purchased her in Brazil in 1948 and hired a crew to bring her home. Hatteras in the winter of 1950 while bound for a new operation at Houston, Texas. In the spring of 1951 she was sold to Wilson Line which had her rebuilt for service with the Virginia Ferry Corporation. Given a new "spoon" bow for head-on loading and renamed *Accomac,* she could carry 1,200 passengers and 70 vehicles. Her career had come full circle when she returned to the Chesapeake waters for which she had been built.

*State of Pennsylvania* (lower center, left) has her bow under a Jersey City ferry shed formerly used by Pennsylvania Railroad, May, 1948. The Port of New York Authority

This modern day steamboat war between two diesel boats climaxed a quarter-century of competition between the Wills and Wilson operations. The rivalry was now evidenced by court battles, gimmicky ads and friction between the crews. Bostonians were divided in their loyalties but many correctly predicted the outcome would be a Wilson victory.

The Wills-Wilson war ended in Wilson's favor after *Holiday* was battered by a storm off Cape

By 1950, the Virginia Ferry Corporation carried nearly 500,000 vehicles and 1,349, 924 passengers on its virtually flawless round-the-clock service. Its five radar-equipped transports made 44 crossings daily, exclusive of the Pennsylvania Railroad's Cape Charles-Norfolk service operated by the venerable *Elisha Lee.*

On May 1, 1950, the company transferred its northern terminal from Cape Charles to a new million-dollar terminal at Kiptopeke Beach, thus

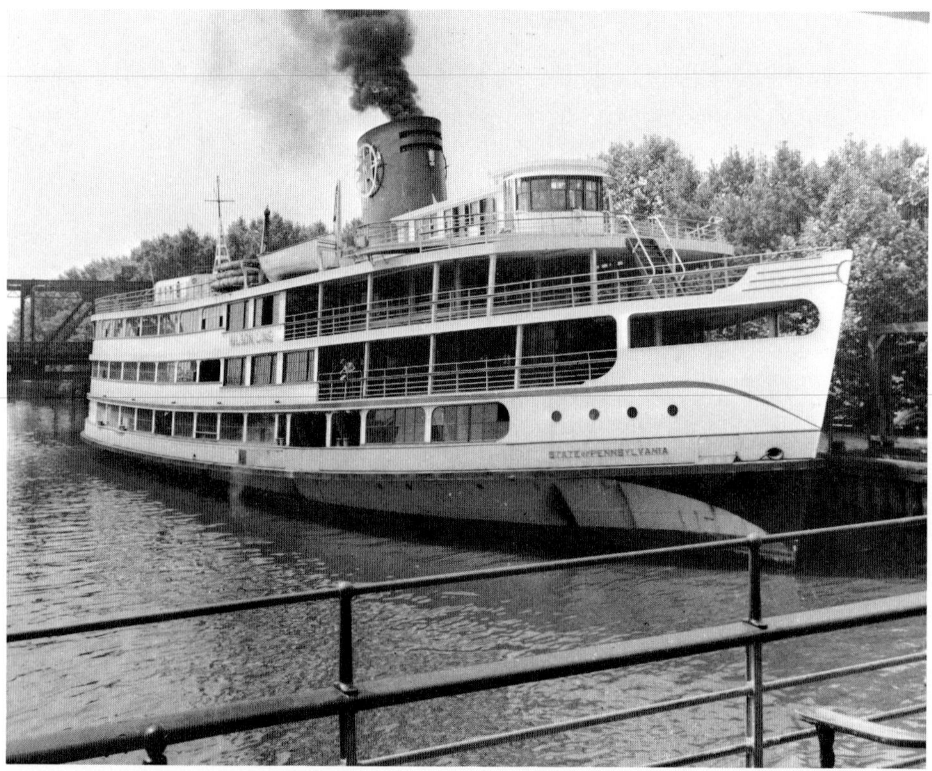

*State of Pennsylvania* at Wilmington, September 8, 1950, after completing her 200-mile trip down the Atlantic coast. Francis Palmer

Sporting a new stem to accommodate bow loading, *Accomac,* ex-*Virginia Lee,* returned to the Chesapeake in 1952, running on the Little Creek ferry. Wilson Line, Inc.

shortening the crossing by 8 miles and permitting a faster schedule, more trips daily and a greater capacity. Kiptopeke had not been selected as a terminal earlier owing to its exposed position near the Atlantic but the problem was finally solved by the purchase of nine World War II cement ships which were sunk to form a breakwater. With service and Wilson Line was content to acquire old boats. In 1948 the Pennsylvania Railroad's *Philadelphia* was purchased, followed by the ferryboats *Newark* and *Chicago*. New slips were also built at New Castle and Pennsville to accommodate eight boats now running about 288 crossings daily at headways of every five minutes and less.

Delaware-New Jersey Ferry Company's *Jersey Shore* (right) and *Wildwood* are at New Castle, Delaware, shortly before completion of the Delaware Memorial Bridge. The Steamship Historical Society of America, Inc.

*Washington,* shown at Pennsville, New Jersey, was the last steamer to make the Pennsville-New Castle crossing on August 15, 1951. The Steamship Historical Society of America, Inc.

*Accomac* joining the fleet, traffic rose to 561,840 vehicles and 1,626,323 passengers.

Superficially, the Wilson System seemed to be in an enviable position. However, no new boats were built for the Delaware-New Jersey Ferry Company after World War II. Time was running out on that The service, moreover, continued to out-earn the parent Wilson Line in which so much more had been invested in the postwar period.

Ironically, the Wilson System was on the verge of disintegration owing largely to its own longstanding efforts in promoting the Ocean Hiway.

Some 3,380 Southern New England Telephone Company employees embark *State of Pennsylvania* at New Haven for a cruise to Rye in 1952. Southern New England Telephone Company

*State of Pennsylvania's* passengers enjoy sunset on Long Island Sound after a long day of recreation at Rye Beach, New York, in 1952. Southern New England Telephone Company

North-south traffic continued to increase at an unprecedented pace, so much so that the public required new superhighways and higher speed. The boats were now too slow for people in an increasing hurry. In effect, Wilson had out-progressed itself and was about to founder in the midst of unparalleled success.

The new Delaware River bridge approached completion in 1950, the last full year of operation for the Delaware-New Jersey Ferry Company, and during that year the ferry fleet carried a record 3,143,000 vehicles and about 7 million passengers. The entire system's traffic had reached a new peak with its huge fleet carrying nearly 4 million vehicles and 10 million passengers. Yet, without its perennial gold mine, the Wilson System would never be the same, if it could in fact survive.

In May, 1951, Delaware-New Jersey's *Wildwood* was sold to Rhode Island's Jamestown-Newport ferry. That month, *Pittsburgh* was wrecked by fire, repaired and returned to service—an odd-looking craft minus her second deck. Meanwhile, negotiations continued with the State of Delaware over compensation for the New Castle-Pennsville route in condemnation proceedings.

An independent engineering firm rated Delaware-New Jersey's assets as worth $2.2 million while Wilson claimed $7.3 million. Having made a fortune over the years, Wilson Line finally settled for $2,500,000 or about 125 times the price paid by Captain Horace Wilson for control of the Pennsville operation in 1927!

The sentimental value of the system had also risen over a quarter-century and the passing of these boats was a personal loss to many residents of New Jersey and Delaware. The final crossings were slated for August 15, 1951, and many people went to the waterfront for a last trip. At 8:45 P.M., *Philadelphia*, better known locally as "Smokey Joe." was the first to end her career. When she tied up, all the operating boats wailed forlorn salutes and the mournful din of the incomparable steam whistles was repeated as each boat completed her last trip. At 11:30 P.M., the diesel *Jersey Shore* left Pennsville and the 60-year-old *Washington* departed from New Castle, marking the end of an era.

At one minute past midnight, the massive new Delaware Memorial Bridge was opened to traffic from the recently completed New Jersey Turnpike. (Although Frederick K. Reybold, Wilson Line's public relations chief, had lobbyed for years to forestall the construction of this bridge until the company's rights were protected, his brother, Lt. General Eugene Reybold, chief of the U.S. Army Corps of Engineers, had once been in charge of its building program.)

Actually, Wilson Line was proud that its efforts had led to the need for both the new turnpike and the bridge, but the sentiment of the moment was sadness for the displaced employees of the Delaware-New Jersey Ferry Company. The ever-busy, ever-running fleet was seen no more and the Delaware was less colorful for its passing.

The line had completed nearly 26 years of service and during that time its fleet had safely carried over 68 million passengers and more than 30 million vehicles. The State of Delaware subsequently sold its 10 boats for over $600,000. *New York* and *Florida* went to Norfolk and *Jersey Shore* went to the Delaware River Ferry Company's Chester, Pennsylvania-Bridgeport, New Jersey service. The older steamers were sold for scrap. Once again, setback had followed success.

## Chapter XI

# Years of Decline

THE WILSON LINERS were in excellent condition in the early 1950s and they still attracted bigger crowds each summer than the attendance at most major league baseball games. At every port of call along the eastern seaboard children were still excited at the prospect of a trip aboard one of Wilson's streamliners, and people of all ages still enjoyed the gay and happy atmosphere of the trips.

The line seemed generally in good shape but appearances were deceptive. Gross earnings stood at $1,313,667 for the summer of 1951 while expenses had risen to $1,268,858. Only three of the eight passenger boats in operation—*Delaware Belle, Boston Belle* and *Mount Vernon*—had shown a profit for the year. Being the nation's largest river and bay passenger steamboat service on the coast meant little to stockholders who saw profits falling rapidly.

Like other surviving operators, Wilson Line was caught in the squeeze between increasing costs on one hand and social and economic factors on the other. All lines were losing out to the auto, and all lines were experiencing a new type of passenger—disruptive and discontented—from a changing society.

Because of this new type of patronage, while it represented no more than a fraction of annual volume, most of the Wilson liners and boats of other lines experienced some occasional but serious disturbances and riots before the end of the decade. Adverse publicity following such incidents discouraged traditional patronage. The troublesome groups, reflecting problems in society and in themselves, were quite indifferent to any line's reputation or to the fact that they might damage not only a company's boat but also her good name.

The sleek *Boston Belle,* second of Wilson's three remarkable Navy PCE conversions, is bound for Plymouth, Massachusetts, July 7, 1949. R. Loren Graham

Unfortunately, the news media too often reported what had happened on what boat of what line, giving no clue as to why something happened and who was responsible. Boating personnel had to be prepared for almost anything. Operating a pleasure business with a wide variety of volatile crowds was becoming tedious, at best. Fortunately, however, the vast majority of passengers were well behaved and good-humored.

People of all ages enjoy a Cape Cod Canal cruise on *Boston Belle,* July 31, 1949. Sagamore Bridge is astern. R. Loren Graham

*Boston Belle's* passengers embark amidst Provincetown's salty surroundings, August 31, 1952. R. Loren Graham

The WILSON LINE of MASS.
LUXURY LINER BOSTON BELLE
Through the years of extensive experience in the operation of excursion vessels, the Wilson Line have become masters in the art of providing pleasure-bent excursionists with the finest features, the most up to date marine construction afloat! Features that assure luxury liner comfort and recreation you will long remember, for serving comfort and re-creation is the business of the Wilson Line. Whether you're taking the one hour cruise to Nantasket, or the one hundred mile ocean cruise to Provincetown or the delightful moonlight dance cruise each evening at 9 you'll notice that you are the prime consideration of the Wilson Line. To this end each Member of the staff and the highly trained, courteous, crew are dedicated.
W
BOSTON BELLE
Boston's harbor is dotted with islands that once felt the Pirates boot and knew the cannonade of early wars. Such interesting sights as famed Gallup's Island, Boston Light, Nantasket, Hingham Harbor, Charlestown Navy Yard, Logan Airport, Winthrop, Deer Island and Castle Island are only a few of the "musts" while you are sight-seeing in Boston!
Spend a romantic ONE DAY Vacation on Massachusetts Bay.


Wilson Line of Massachusetts ran services to both Provincetown and Nantasket Beach in 1952, with three vessels. Wilson Line of Massachusetts, Inc.

Wilson's 1952 season went well, particularly at Boston, where three boats, including the chartered steamer *Westport,* maintained the two-line services. However, one saddening note marred the season when *Pilgrim Belle* was battered by heavy seas off Montauk Point, Long Island, while returning to Wilmington. Thereafter, "old *Brandywine,*" the nation's oldest active passenger steamboat, was laid up permanently.

**100 MILE OCEAN CRUISE TO PROVINCETOWN**

(DAILY AND SUNDAYS)

- LEAVE BOSTON ............ 10:00 A.M.
  ARRIVE PROVINCETOWN ............ 1:30 P.M.
- LEAVE PROVINCETOWN ............ 4:30 P.M.
  ARRIVE BOSTON ............ 8:00 P.M.

TEL. PROVINCETOWN 1053

JUNE

| Su | Mo | Tu | We | Th | Fr | Sa |
|---|---|---|---|---|---|---|
| | | 1 | 2 | 3 | 4 | 5 |
| 6 | 7 | 8 | 9 | 10 | 11 | 12 |
| 13 | 14 | 15 | 16 | 17 | 18 | 19 |
| 20 | 21 | 22 | 23 | 24 | 25 | 26 |
| 27 | 28 | 29 | 30 | | | |

JULY

| Su | Mo | Tu | We | Th | Fr | Sa |
|---|---|---|---|---|---|---|
| | | | | 1 | 2 | 3 |
| 4 | 5 | 6 | 7 | 8 | 9 | 10 |
| 11 | 12 | 13 | 14 | 15 | 16 | 17 |
| 18 | 19 | 20 | 21 | 22 | 23 | 24 |
| 25 | 26 | 27 | 28 | 29 | 30 | 31 |

**MOONLIGHT DANCE CRUISE** NIGHTLY & SUN.

- LEAVES 9:00 P.M.
  RETURNS 12:00 MIDNIGHT

**WILSON LINE**

ROWES WHARF

344 ATLANTIC AVE., BOSTON HU 2-1000

*Special Group & Charter Rates*

— OVER —

**NANTASKET BEACH SCHEDULE**

| HU. 2-1000<br>LEAVE BOSTON | HULL 5-0100<br>LEAVE NANTASKET |
|---|---|
| ***MONDAYS THRU SATURDAYS*** | |
| 10:30 A.M. | 12:00 Noon |
| 1:30 P.M. | 4:00 P.M. |
| 5:15 P.M. | 6:30 P.M. |
| 8:45 P.M. | 11:00 P.M. |
| ***SUNDAYS ONLY*** | |
| 10:30 A.M. | 12:00 Noon |
| 1:30 P.M. | 3:00 P.M. |
| 4:30 P.M. | 6:00 P.M. |
| 7:30 P.M. | 9:00 P.M. |
| 9:00 P.M. | 11:00 P.M. |

**CRUISE TAKES ONE HOUR EACH WAY**

*Schedule Subject to Weather Conditions and to Changes Without Notice*

**NANTASKET DANCE FROLIC**

1¼ HOURS SHORE LEAVE
AIR COOLED DANCING

Leave Boston 8:45 P.M. Leave Nantasket 11:00 P.M.

*Special Group & Charter Rates*

91 — OVER —

Provincetown and Nantasket Beach schedules, 1952. Wilson Line of Mass., Inc.

At the same time, Wilson was converting *PCE-1207* into a 258-foot, three-decked passenger vessel quite similar to *Boston Belle.* She came out in the spring of 1953 and was named *Sea Belle.* This last of Wilson's naval craft conversions did not display the fine streamlining that had characterized earlier efforts, and perhaps the line might have been wiser not to have made the conversion. Nevertheless, *Sea Belle* was the largest of the big boats built by Wilson Line. She teamed up with *Boston Belle* at Boston in 1953, as *Pilgrim Belle's* replacement on the Nantasket Beach line. Boston operations, incidentally, had grown from a minor service in 1946 to surpass Philadelphia as the most important one. Over half a million Bostonians now boarded the Wilson liners each summer.

One of the happiest events in *Boston Belle's* career took place on September 19, 1953, when she literally "sailed down memory lane," making a special Fall River Revival Trip from Massachusetts to New York via Long Island Sound. The Fall River Line, one of the East Coast's old-time favorites, still evoked nostalgia and many who embarked on the flag-bedecked *Boston Belle* wore the romantic costumes of the turn of the century. The trip was but one of many events staged in celebration of the 150th anniversary of the founding of Fall River, Massachusetts, and a thousand good-natured people turned out for the memorable sail. *Boston Belle's* interiors naturally couldn't compete with those of the Fall River Line's "floating palaces," and were not intended to, but there was unanimous praise for Wilson Line's handling of the entire affair. Banners reading "On the Old Fall River Line" were draped over the Wilson liner's sides and serving on her were captains Norman Strickland, Frank Bunce and Albert Johnson —all of whom, significantly, were former Fall River Line veterans who now found employment on the old but seemingly ageless Wilson Line.

The Wilson system itself was in its twilight years and now faced the certainty that a huge vehicular crossing would be built across the Chesapeake, a project considered to be virtually impossible a decade earlier. Wilson's stockholders were increasingly dubious about the future and liquidation was considered inevitable. In fact, it had been a fairly well-known "secret" that the Wilson Line was for sale ever since the completion of the Delaware Memorial Bridge.

Ironically, one of those interested in acquiring the line was its perennial competitor, B. B. Wills. As did others, he felt that Wilson Line would be a bargain at $1 million but nothing materialized in 1952. At that time not one of the Wilson liners could have been reproduced for less than $1,250,000 by a commercial shipyard.

Virginia Ferry Corporation continued to set new records but it had a curious problem—while its fleet had expanded, its carrying capacity actually declined due to the increased lengths of postwar vehicles. It was also racing against time and progress and the cost of even one new transport, estimated at $3.3 million, was beyond reason. Its solution was to "jumboize" or lengthen its vessels and *Princess Anne* was the first to undergo the operation. She was taken to the Maryland Shipbuilding

*Mount Vernon* sports the yellow and white "layer cake" colors devised after City Investing Company purchased the Wilson Line in 1955. Wilson Line of Washington, Inc.

Many knew the Wilson Line as an Eastern steamboat institution but few knew what kept it going while others failed. No one, viewing the line's enormous turnouts, the interesting debutante parties on *Bay Belle,* Pearl Mesta's parties for foreign dignitaries on *Mount Vernon,* the motion picture stars entertaining themselves on *Liberty Belle,* and the hundreds of thousands of youngsters having fun on the fleet, could believe that the biggest of all surviving lines was about to give up. Yet, it was preparing to do just that.

& Drydock Company's yard at Baltimore, cut in two and given a new 90-foot mid-body. Alterations cost $775,000—more than her original construction cost. She emerged as a 350-foot "oceangoing dachshund" and was faster than ever.

In 1954, the Little Creek fleet transported 652,923 vehicles and over 2 million travelers to match at last the annual summer passenger traffic of the Wilson Line. Shortly thereafter, arrangements were made to jumboize *Del-Mar-Va* and Wilson Line sold out its interest in Virginia Ferry Corporation to its longtime partner, the Pennsylvania Railroad. It was rumored that the railroad sought to abandon the line, and a group of Virginia legislators introduced a bill in the state senate to acquire the Little Creek service. The Pennsylvania had just previously abandoned its Cape Charles-Norfolk service and had sent old *Elisha Lee* to the scrapyard. That move had triggered a storm of public protest in the greater Hampton Roads area and Virginians were in no mood for further abandonments.

RELAX, DINE, MAKE BETTER TIME!
NORTH-SOUTH
fun ROUTE
CHESAPEAKE BAY FERRIES
SAVE TIME!
CHESAPEAKE BAY FERRY COMMISSION

A slightly modified Virginia Ferry Corporation brochure issued by the Chesapeake Bay Ferry Commission. Chesapeake Bay Ferry Commission

Wilson Line had by now lost both of its vehicular gold mines and the only remaining segment of its once extensive system, Wilson Line itself, prepared to sell out. Practicality had carried the day and that meant total liquidation. Few people, however, were prepared for the January 1, 1955 announcement that Wilson Line, its fleet, terminals and other properties, had been sold for $1 million, just as B. B. Wills had anticipated.

*State of Pennsylvania* and *Bay Belle* (right) make preseason excursions from Philadelphia's Municipal Pier, May 21, 1955. Edward O. Clark

In the embittered words of one Wilson employee: "It was an absolute steal!" Frank Weber, the line's former general manager, told the writer: "We could never survive relying solely on our passenger boats. Our work wasn't easy but we liked our business of operating river and bay boats and entertaining people. However, times had changed and boat trips no longer meant what they once had . . . Of course, we would have wanted to continue."

Wilson Line, Inc. had seen many good times and some bad and, while the system was growing, it had earned more than any other operator in its field. All in all, Wilson Line, Inc. realized about $9 million in liquidation.

The line's new owner was City Investing Company of New York, a giant among the country's investment firms, and its chairman, Robert W. Dowling, appointed Lawrence C. Campbell (the former Wilson vice-president) president of the reorganized Wilson Excursion Lines. Once again general expansion plans were discussed but many felt that the old line's spirit of survival had gone. Being an investment rather than an independent company also affected employees' morale. That morale had been high and proud, for besides building the nation's largest and most modern river and bay fleet, Wilson Line, Inc. and its two longest-lasting ferry subsidiaries had transported about 145 million passengers and 38 million vehicles without losing a single passenger, according to a company spokesman, excluding accidents which occurred on piers, or suicides.

The passing of Wilson Line, Inc., a phenomenon of American water carriers from 1929 to 1955, was as much of a shock to its rivals as to its many friends who now asked incredulously, "How *could* Wilson have given up?" George B. Junkin, the line's able and only president, retired from steamboating, later becoming a director of the Pennsylvania & Atlantic Railroad, the Wellington Fund and other firms. Also retiring was Wilson's amicable public relations chief, Frederick K. Reybold, 80-year-old great-grandson of Major Philip Reybold, the "Peach King of Delaware." "Old Fred" was well liked, and known as a raconteur who enjoyed

*PCE-1207* is being cut in two and lengthened at Wilson shipyard in 1952. She emerged as the long, low *Sea Belle* in 1953. Sanborn Studio, Wilmington, Del.

The completed 253-foot *Sea Belle* is at Wilmington, shortly before her departure for Boston in the spring of 1953. Edward O. Clark

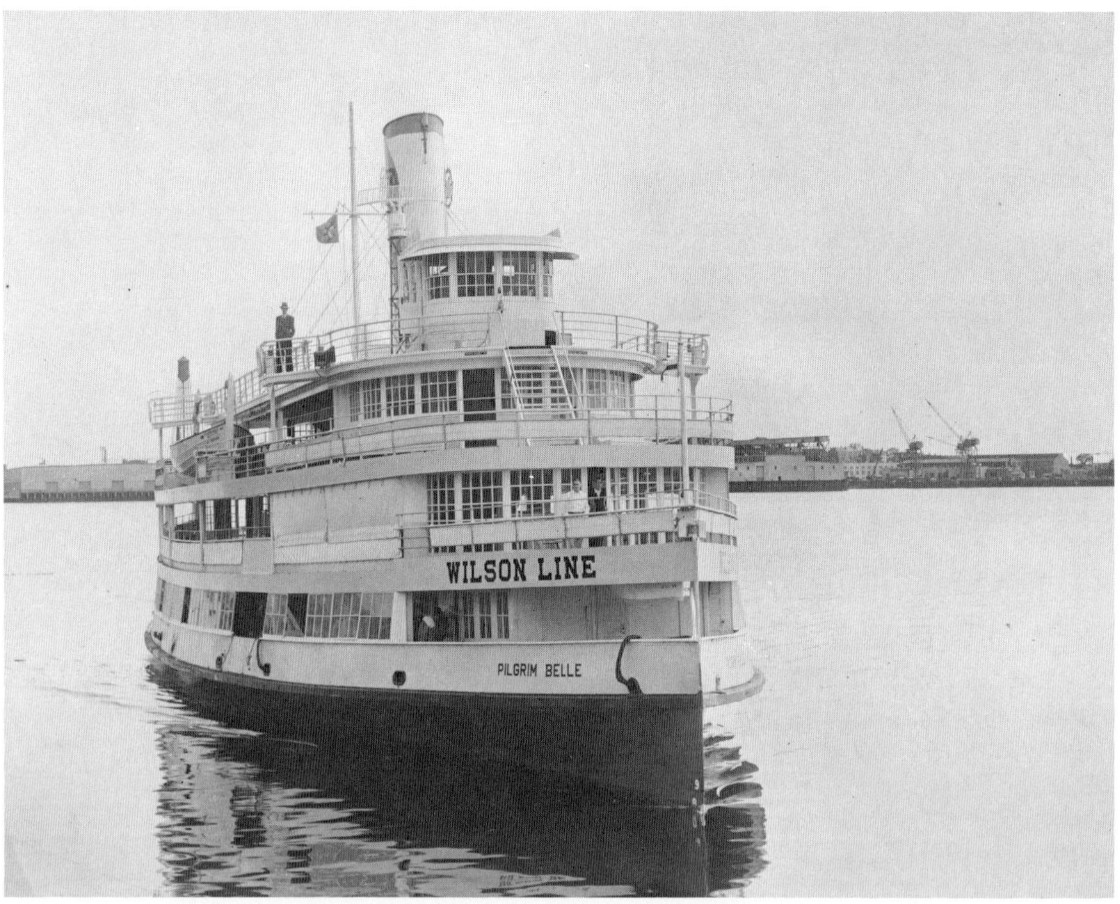


The second *Pilgrim Belle,* ex-*City of Washington,* ex-*City of Chester,* sails from Boston in 1955, her 67th year of service. Wilson Line, Inc.

*Boston Belle* arrives at Rye Beach, New York, June, 1956. She often made New York sailings before reporting to Boston. Franklin B. Roberts, Jr.

recounting tales of the "good old days" on the Delaware to the pleasure of all listeners. Wilson Line was poorer without both men.

One of City Investing Company's first steps was to give the Wilson liners a "bright new look" consisting of alternate bands of yellow and white on their superstructures with an irregular band of red on white stacks. The change was well intended but crews and passengers alike objected to the scheme as being too dazzling, almost "psychedelic." One crewman thought that "it made the boats look like clowns," and one woman who had patronized the fleet for years considered sending a tube of a well-known brand of toothpaste to the line's president, for as she put it: "I don't care where the yellow goes, just so long as it goes!" Unfortunately, the yellow remained.

There were fleet changes, too, in 1955 as *State of Pennsylvania* exchanged places with *Hudson Belle,* the former *Delaware Belle,* and the venerable *City of Washington* became the second *Pilgrim Belle,* taking over the Nantasket line while *Sea Belle* underwent alterations for a new service at Houston. Of all the line's name-changing, none seems to have amused people more than the two *Pilgrim Belles* at Boston. There, one witty Bostonian differentiated between the former *Dixie* and the former *City of Washington* by referring to the first as "the Pil" and the second as "the Grim." "The second Pilgrim," he added, "should have been named *Puritan Belle!*"

*Hudson Belle,* ex-*Delaware Belle,* passes New York's magnificent skyline on the East River during the summer of 1955. Wilson Line, Inc.

In another effort to reinvigorate the business, stars of stage, screen, radio and television were booked for appearances on evening "Showboat Cruises" for the 1955 season, including big-name entertainers such as Bob Carroll, whose "Belle, Belle, My Liberty Belle" was always a favorite on

*Liberty Belle,* Eydie Gorme and Steve Lawrence, Teresa Brewer, Alan Dale, Felicia Sanders, Polly Bergen, Rusty Draper, Bob Eberle, Betty Madigan, The Fontaine Sisters, and several leading rock and roll groups. The ballrooms on the older boats had by now seen every dance fad from the Charleston

National stars of stage, screen and television were featured on Wilson Excursion Lines' "showboat" series during the 1955 season.

to Rock and Roll. Times changed but some of the same boats kept right on going as a common link between generations. No line had ever spent so much on entertainment, but the result was only a modest success.

For all its efforts, the new Wilson Line met repeated reversals. The most serious came on June 22, when *Pilgrim Belle (II)* grounded in fog off Spectacle Island in Boston Harbor with 272 passengers on board. Fortunately, the steamer's crew kept order and helped everyone to safety with aid from the Coast Guard. The old boat flooded to her main deck but was subsequently raised, repaired and finished out the season. After that, however, she never returned to service. Boston operations were also plagued by interruptions and lost patronage due, among other things, to the collapse of part of the Provincetown pier, a polio outbreak and bad weather.

Another costly setback came when *Sea Belle* went to Houston in October of the same year. She did not have a line and not surprisingly, the venture proved an utter fiasco. She had been air-conditioned, against the better judgment of senior staff and at very great expense. She was America's first air-conditioned riverboat but that meant little to people who preferred fresh air, open decks and sunshine. It might have been an asset in Houston's climate but there was no demand for a boat service at the Texas port.

In 1956 Wilson personnel went aboard the iron-hulled *Pilgrim Belle (I),* removed company insignia and painted over her name. Their sad task was to ready the dowager of the line for the scrapyard. "Old *Brandywine*" had lived through almost everything since her heyday in 1885, when she was one of the world's fastest propeller steamers, to her present state as an abandoned derelict of a once jaunty streamliner of the 1930s. In her long life she had participated in great, spirited races, steamboat wars, historic events, good times and bad, thousands of trips with the du Pont powdermakers

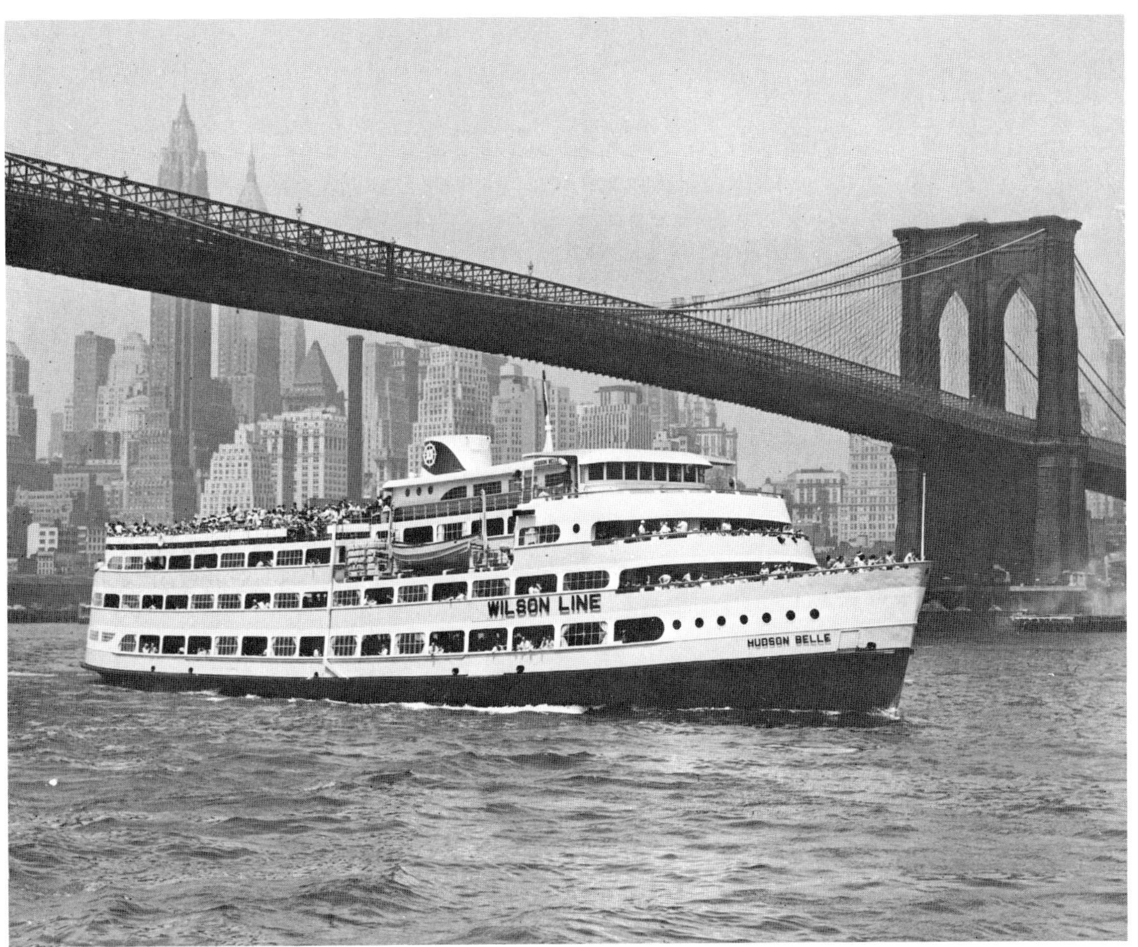


*Hudson Belle* passes under the venerable Brooklyn Bridge on a morning trip to Rye Beach, New York, during the summer of 1955. Wilson Line, Inc.

and thousands more trips providing pleasure to millions of families.

In an "obituary" appearing in *Steamboat Bill,* the journal of The Steamship Historical Society of America, historian Edward O. Clark noted poignantly that ". . . she rewarded her builders and owners alike with 71 years of solid, unspectacular service." "Old *Brandywine*" had carried four gener-

Riverview Lines' *State of Pennsylvania,* in her "Little Red Floating Schoolhouse" color scheme, makes one of her last sailings on the Delaware, in 1960. Edward O. Clark

B. B. Wills' *Tolchester,* ex-*City of Philadelphia,* became a familiar personality in Baltimore Harbor during the 1950's. Edward Gibbs

ations of Delaware Valley people and had probably steamed more miles than any boat in Delaware River history. She was one of that old breed of steamers of which old-timers used to say "they built them better than they knew."

The liquidation of Wilson Line proceeded in 1957 when Riverview Beach and *State of Pennsylvania* were sold for a $280,000 promissory note to Riverview Lines, Inc., which continued her operation to the old beach. That sale left the home waters without a Wilson Line service for the first time since 1882. Later, *Pennsy* took some 20,000

*Delaware Belle's* special cruises to Trenton, New Jersey, 1953.

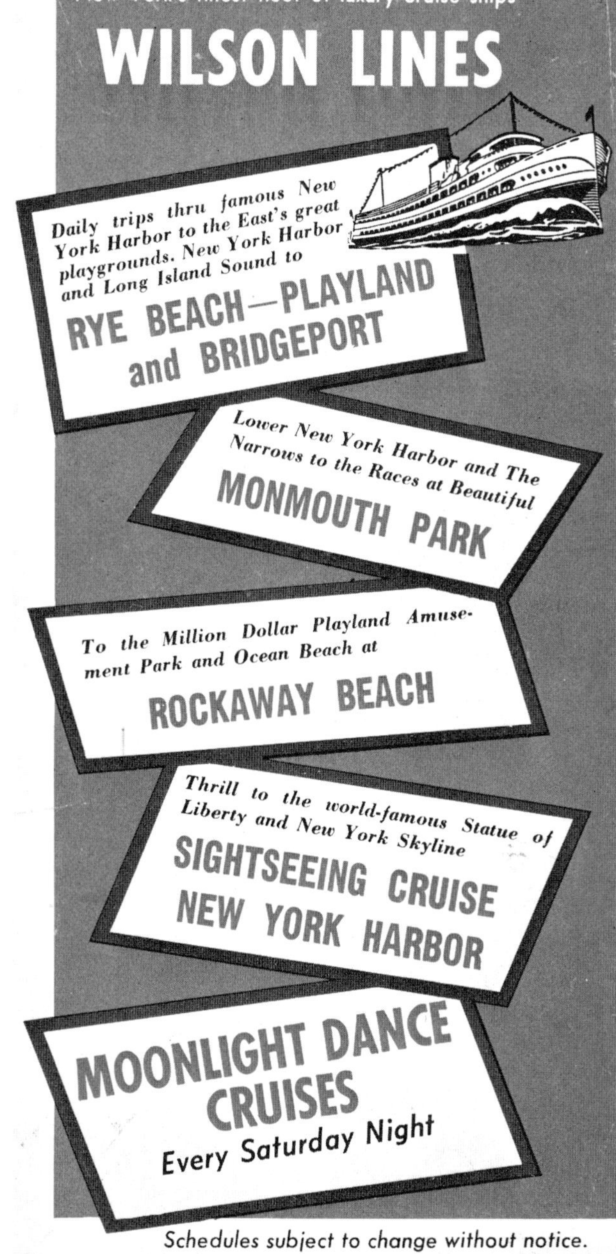


Wilson Line's New York operations in 1957, with sailings to Rockaway Beach, Rye Beach and Atlantic Highlands, three once-prized routes.

Meseck Line's *John A. Meseck,* veteran of the Normandy invasion, was acquired by City Investing Company for Wilson Line in 1957. Franklin B. Roberts, Jr.

*Isla del Tesoro* (Treasure Island), *ex-Liberty Belle* (II), bears the name of Nueva Gerona as her new home port shortly before setting sail for Cuba, 1958. Wilson Line, Inc.

Philadelphia children on educational harbor tours and she was nicknamed "The Little Red Floating Schoolhouse."

About the same time that *Pennsy* was farmed out, *Bay Belle* was chartered to the Baltimore and Annapolis Railroad, painted silver and operated to Tolchester and Betterton under the Wilson-Tolchester Steamship Company, which had no connection with the Wilson Line. The year before she had been operated to Tolchester and Betterton in a Wilson-Wills cooperation effort. In the meanwhile, her erstwhile sister ship, now *Tolchester*, was sold for the rather ignominious role of gambling ship on the Potomac. She was again renamed, becoming *Freestone*. Such was the fate of old boats.

At New York, where Wilson once had difficulty obtaining a single line, Wilson Excursion Lines had purchased in 1957 Meseck Line's staunch *John A. Meseck* for about $250,000. She was continued on her route to Rye Beach on the Westchester shore of Long Island Sound. (Captain Meseck had long recognized the decline of his

Interior view of *Liberty Belle* (II) resembles an aircraft carrier's hangar during conversion at Wilmington, Delaware, in 1958. Wilson Line, Inc.

Side port is one of the new features incorporated during Wilson Line's conversion of *Liberty Belle* (II) to an auto-passenger transport. Wilson Line, Inc.

Crown Princess Michiko of Japan is feted aboard *Mount Vernon* in September, 1960. *Mount Vernon* frequently entertained visiting royalty and other celebrities. Wilson Line of Washington, Inc.

route and, as it developed, the *Meseck* never paid for her cost to Wilson Line.) The line also operated *Liberty Belle* to Rockaway and *Hudson Belle* to Atlantic Highlands.

In 1958, Wilson sold the popular *Liberty Belle* to the Isle of Pines Steamship Company for about half a million dollars and Wilson's staff converted her into an auto-passenger transport for the Caribbean. *Liberty Belle* had won a legion of fans at New York and even *The New York Times*, reporting her sale, called her "Old *Liberty Belle.*" Her new owners renamed her *Isla del Tesoro* (Treasure Island) and she set forth for Cuba, flying the Cuban flag, on December 11, 1958. After a very rough trip, of which Wilson skipper Captain Johansen said "It was a miracle she made it," she began running the 60-mile ocean route between Batabano, Cuba and the Isle of Pines. (And people used to get seasick off Coney Island while dancers wobbled on her ballroom deck!)

Shortly after, she was commandeered by Fidel Castro's communist regime and allegedly had been used to carry political prisoners to detention camps on the Isle of Pines. "Luckily," Wilson men said, "we received last payments just before Castro took everything." From smiling, excited youngsters bound for amusement parks to glum prisoners bound for incarceration had been quite a change.

Another liquidation step followed in 1959 with the sale of the always successful *Mount Vernon* and the Washington Division to Marylander Joseph I. Goldstein, a man who held an optimistic view of the potential of water transportation. The division was restyled the Wilson Steamship Corporation but continued to use the "Wilson Line" trade name. Goldstein had enthusiasm, many ideas and was soon called "The Aristotle Onassis of the Potomac." One branch of the Wilson Line seemed destined to survive.

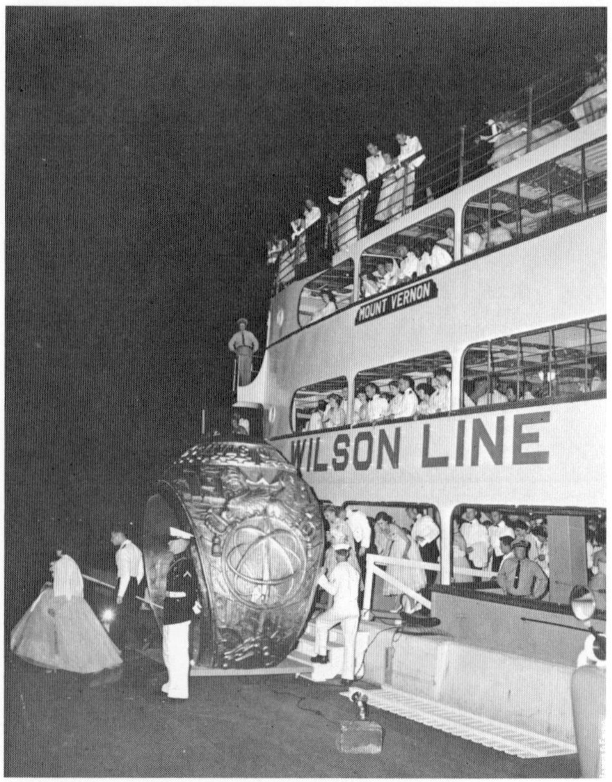


Graduating midshipmen and their belles disembark at Annapolis after their unique "Ring Dance" aboard *Mount Vernon,* April, 1960. Wilson Line of Washington, Inc.

## Chapter XII

# Last of the Steamboats

IN September, 1960 *State of Pennsylvania* made her last excursion from Philadelphia to Riverview Beach. The cheerful sound of the "Pennsylvania Polka" would never again be heard from her crowded decks. *Pennsy* was subsequently retired at Wilmington and returned to Wilson ownership. Her owners began to receive many requests from her fans for her whistle, her bell and other parts.

"It is amazing," Wilson Shipyard president John Gravdahl told the writer, "how many people hold an affection for that vessel and have requested mementos from her."

*The Diplomat,* a former New York sightseeing yacht, joined the Wilson Line of Washington in the late 1950's. Wilson Line of Washington, Inc.

The writer subsequently purchased her brass whistle for preservation and while loading it into his car at Wilmington was met by an employee of the Pennsylvania Railroad, Wilson's ancient competitor. The gentleman was taking his son on a tour of historic sights in Wilmington and when he realized that this was *State of Pennsylvania's* whistle he called to his son and said, "I want you to see the whistle that came from a boat I rode when I was your age. What wonderful times we all had on *State of Pennsylvania* and other Wilson liners. Nobody took the train then. The boats were the thing! I'm so sorry you'll never have a chance to ride them. There'll never be days like those again."

The venerable *City of Chester,* the East Coast's last iron-hulled passenger steamboat, now known as *Pilgrim Belle (II),* was towed to a scrapyard at Fieldsboro, New Jersey, shortly after *State of Pennsylvania's* retirement. During her 72-year career as the line's "old reliable" she had steamed over 2 million miles and had carried over 30 million passengers. Moreover, despite her age, she had remained the fastest of the fleet. Like *Pennsy,* she was always considered "warm and homey," more like the old Wilmington Steamboat Company than the successor Wilson Lines.

And now, even the new breed of Wilson Liners were disappearing. In the spring of 1961 *Boston Belle* was sold to Rosario, Argentina and renamed *Ciudad de Rosario (City of Rosario).* She completed the 5,000 mile voyage to South America with ease and there began a new career. In April, 1961, Wilson Steamship Corporation, which then

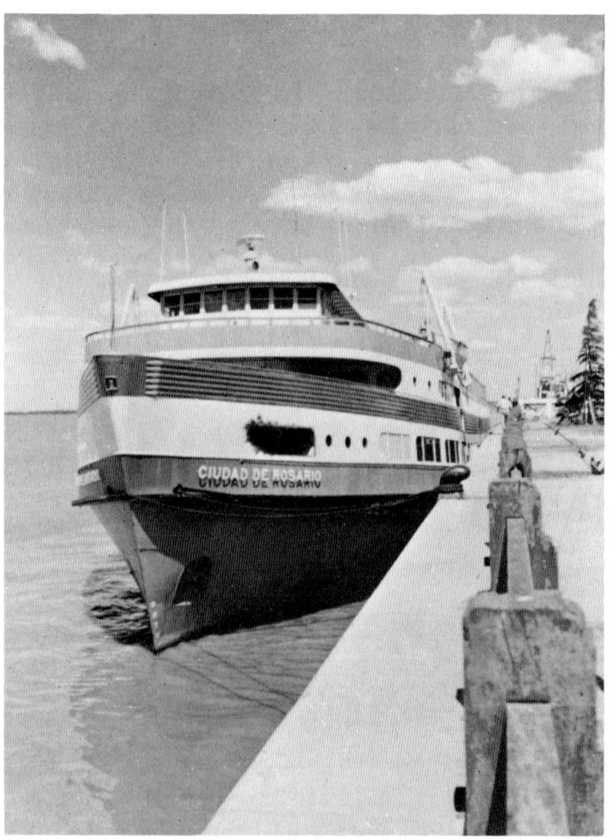


*Ciudad de Rosario,* ex-*Boston Belle,* shown at Rosario, Argentina, in 1963, is one of the Wilson fleet scattered throughout the western hemisphere. Donald Nevin

*Chippewa Chief,* built in 1959, was acquired by Wilson Line of Washington to carry small groups. Wilson Line of Washington, Inc.

operated *Mount Vernon* and two sightseeing yachts, *Chippewa Chief* and *The Diplomat,* purchased the Wilson Excursion Lines from City Investing Company, including steamers *John A. Meseck* and *Bay Belle* and the diesels *Hudson Belle* and *Sea Belle,* for over $1.5 million. It was a courageous bid to revive the remnants of the Wilson System. City Investing Company retained ownership of its modernized shipyard at Fourth Street Wharf, Wilmington.

However, Wilson abandoned Boston operations in 1961 and in their place B. B. Wills employed *S.S. Potomac,* the former Wilson liner *City of Philadelphia,* on the Nantasket line. In Boston people quipped: "If Wilson won't, Wills will." Wilson's *Sea Belle* took over the Philadelphia service while *Bay Belle* remained at Baltimore. *Hudson Belle* and *John A. Meseck* operated at New York.

Unfortunately, the 1961 season was marred by an inter-union jurisdictional dispute, difficulties with passengers and financial problems. Hopes for a fleet-wide revival were dim and all of the boats, except *Mount Vernon,* were subsequently laid up and returned to City Investing.

*Mount Vernon* brings another fun-seeking crowd to Wilson Line's own 370-acre Marshall Hall Amusement Park in the summer of 1962. Wilson Line of Washington, Inc.

By the summer of 1961 Joseph Goldstein had nine boats, including two new sightseeing craft, *Martha Washington* and *Dolly Madison.* His boundless enthusiasm for the future of water transportation was further reflected in plans for new commuter operations, an overnight service between Norfolk and Baltimore and the operation of large hydrofoils along the coast from Boston to Miami, competing with airlines.

The last of the excursion days was at hand and the boats idled away each summer at Wilmington, their decks barren of life except for the sparrows. Many who passed by Fourth Street Wharf often stopped to look at the stoic fleet lying silent with-

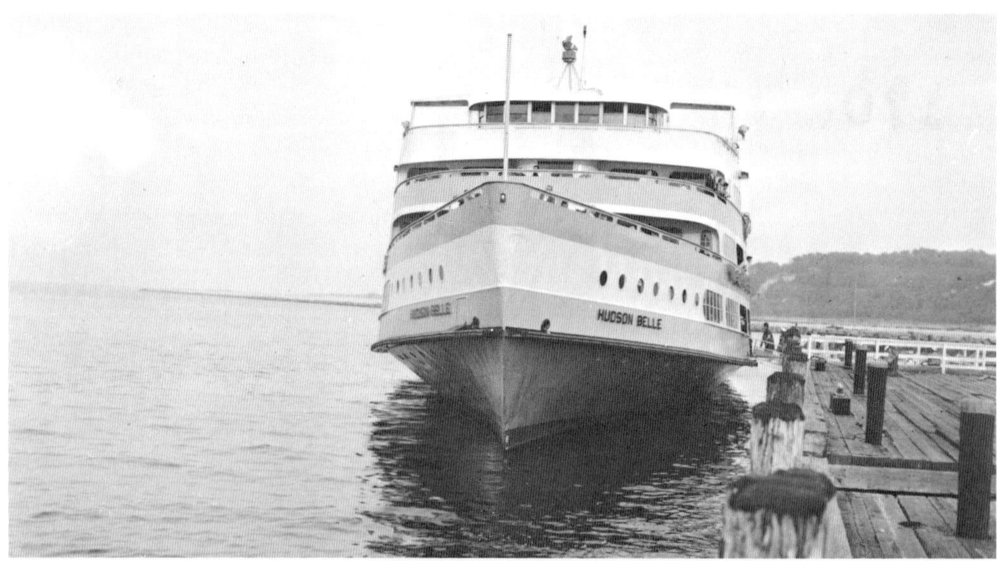


*Hudson Belle* at Atlantic Highlands, New Jersey, in the summer of 1961, her last season at New York Harbor. John C. Mills

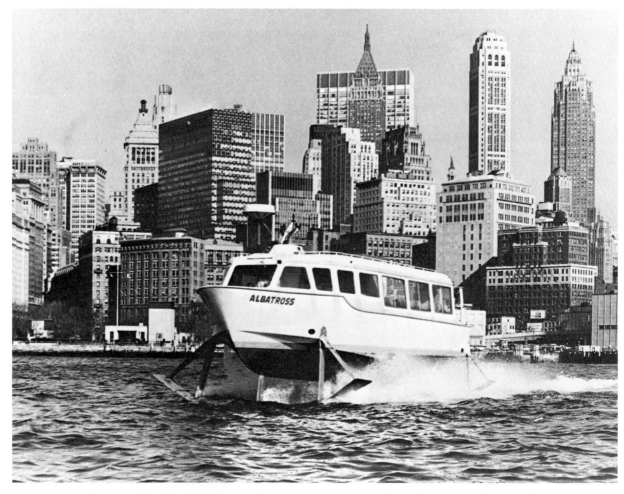

Continuing Wilson's pioneering tradition, the hydrofoil *Albatross,* America's first hydrofoil licensed to carry passengers, skims across New York Harbor in 1962. American Hydrofoil Lines

out its happy crowds, roaring whistles and music wafting from the ballrooms. "What fun we used to have on the old Wilson Line," people would say.

It hadn't mattered that these forlorn vessels were just riverboats. Each of them had been a personality in her day and had provided countless happy times for millions of people. That mattered.

Wilson tradition, pioneering was again evidenced in 1962. That year Wilson Shipyard completed a 34-foot, 40-knot hydrofoil which was christened *Albatross*. She was America's first hydrofoil licensed by the Coast Guard to carry passengers.

Wilson Line's operations in Washington continued successfully into the 1960s. *Mount Vernon*

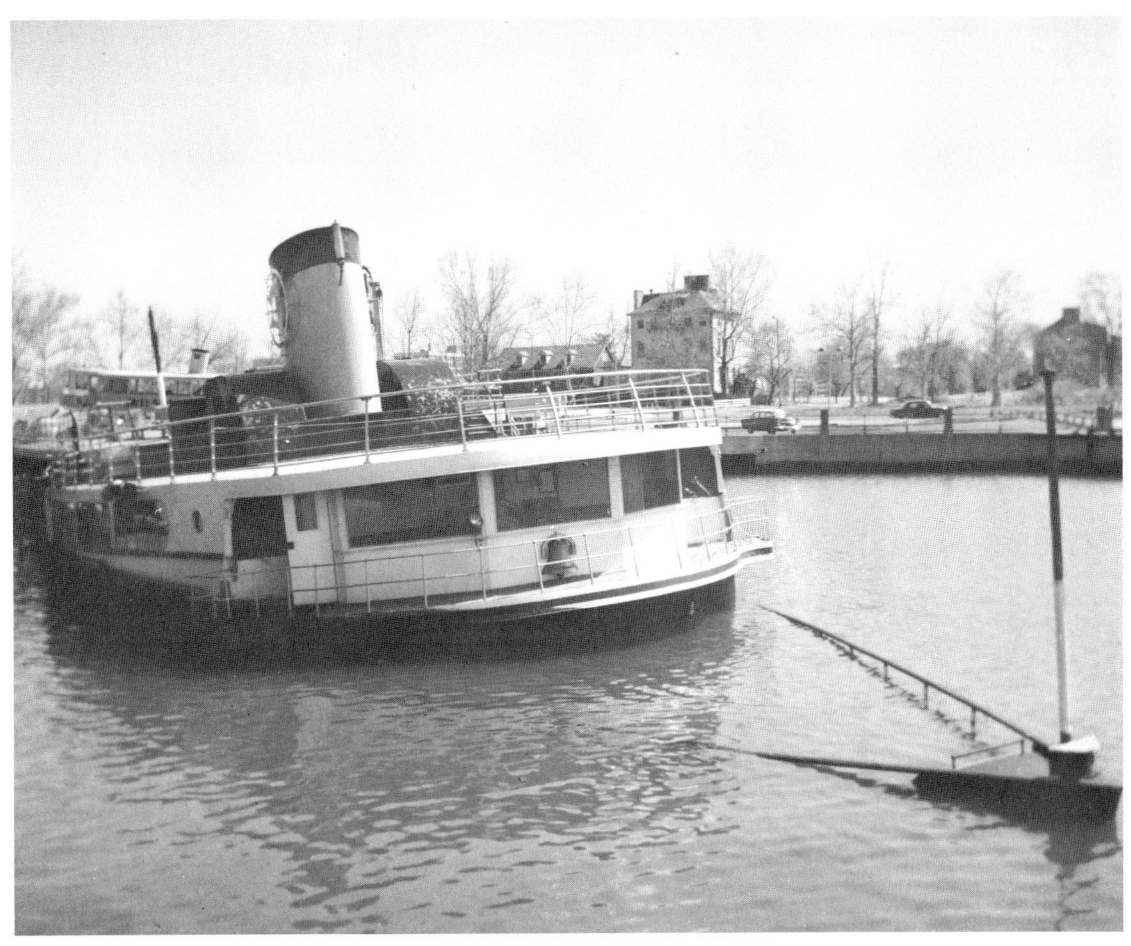

A sight that saddened many Washingtonians: *Mount Vernon* after she foundered at her Washington pier during the winter of 1963. Peter T. Eisele

Yet, the pressures of America's supercivilization had completely overtaken the riverboats from coast to coast. Progress had won, but people had lost, especially the youngsters, who would never enjoy river and bay trips on a big steamer. A river trip was one less activity available for people's enjoyment in the "new leisure time."

As City Investing Company phased out of actual boat operations it gradually built up Wilson Shipyard and placed it under the able direction of U. S. Merchant Marine Academy graduate John Gravdahl, previously mentioned. While City Investing Company was not very familiar with the

was still Washington's leading hostess to children and foreign dignitaries and the fleet continued to carry well over half a million passengers yearly. However, tragedy struck *Mount Vernon* when she foundered at Pier 4 on January 5, 1963 during winter lay-up. No one was on board in the 14 hours during which water seeped into her hull via a cracked valve. The steamer sat upright on the bottom of the Potomac.

News of *Mount Vernon's* misfortune spread quickly and local newspapers headlined the story on page one, displacing what might have been considered more important events. After 22 years of virtually flawless performance, *Mount Vernon* was a local institution unto herself. As one Washingtonian phrased it: "Some of us even wept over her loss. She was, after all, one of Washington's 'personalities' and she symbolized our youth . . . Washington loved that boat." She was subsequently raised and laid up on the Potomac but plans for her reconstruction failed to materialize.

As her replacement, Wilson Line of Washington reacquired *Hudson Belle* in time to open the 1963 season. In a gala ceremony at Mount Vernon, she was renamed *George Washington* on April 5, the 231st anniversary of President George Washington's own christening in 1732. The honors went to Mrs. Frances F. Beirne, regent of the Mount Vernon Ladies Association of the Union, the organization which has maintained the First President's plantation home since 1853.

Wilson Line of Washington continued to provide river trips but, without *Mount Vernon*, this last of the Wilson Lines ceased to be a *steamboat* operator. In 1965, it acquired two hydrofoils, *Wilson I* and *Victory I*. A third, *Wilson II*, was added in 1966. However, while the hydrofoils operated well, they proved too fast for comfortable sightseeing, and were subsequently placed on sale.

Throughout its history Wilson Line was known for its "firsts" but its scattered fleet also left its mark for memorable "lasts" of American steamboating. In 1960, *State of Pennsylvania* was the last

Mrs. Frances F. Beirne, regent of the Mount Vernon Ladies' Association of the Union, christened *George Washington*, ex-*Hudson Belle*, on April 5, 1963. Looking on (l. to r.) are: Douglas Smith, president, National Savings and Trust Company, Senator Glenn Beall of Maryland, Joseph I. Goldstein, president, Wilson Steamship Corporation and George Thomas Washington, Circuit Judge, U. S. Court of Appeals, D. C. District, a direct descendant of Colonel Samuel Washington, younger brother of the nation's first president. Wilson Line of Washington, Inc.

steamboat to regularly ply the Delaware, ending an era begun by John Fitch over 173 years earlier. *Mount Vernon's* last trip in 1962 ended steamboating on the Potomac, started by Captain O'Neale and the steamer *Washington* over 150 years before, and in 1961, *Bay Belle* made the last regular day steamboat trip on the Chesapeake, a practice begun in 1813 by the steamer *Chesapeake*.

that day the "poor man's ocean liners" were through and, although the new bridge offered great savings in travel time, the last sailings of the boats drew far more public attention.

Like Wilson's Delaware River ferries, the Little Creek fleet had out-progressed itself and ended while enjoying a booming business. Between 1933 and 1956, the Virginia Ferry Corporation's fleet

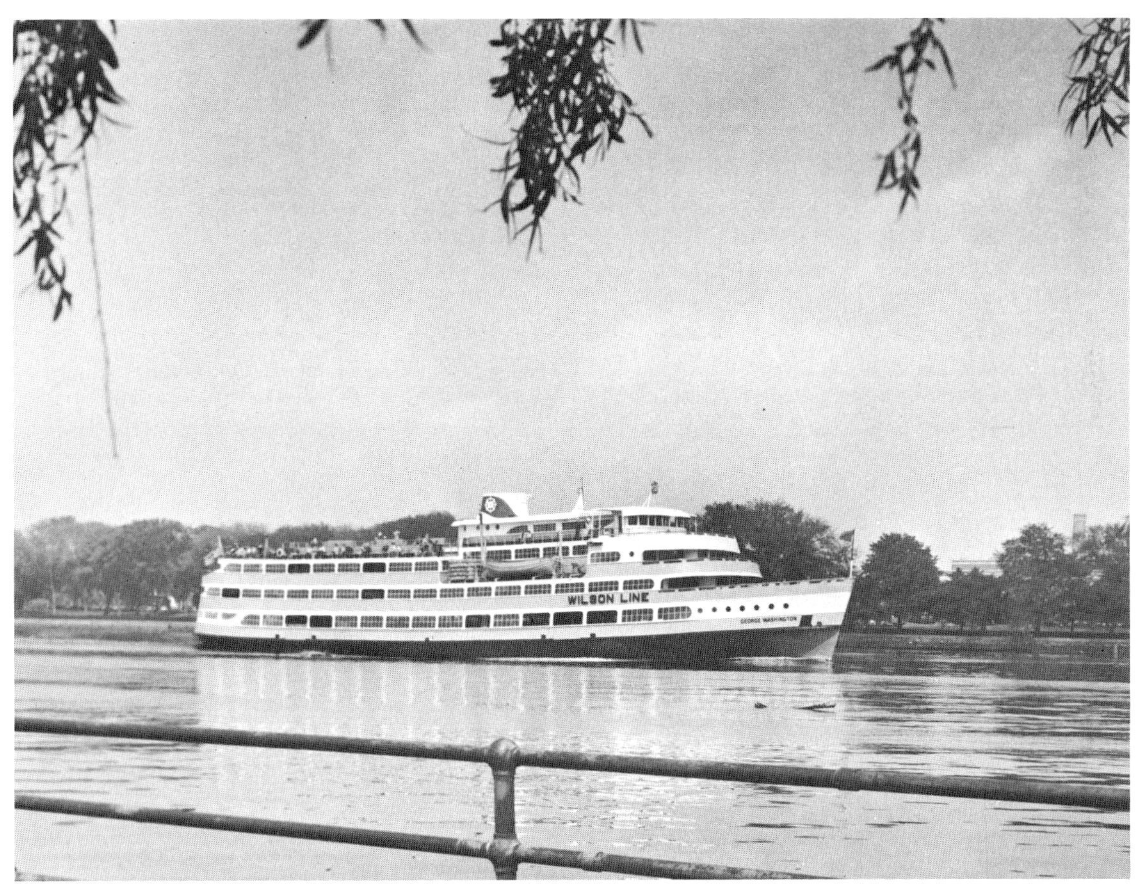


*George Washington* on the Potomac during the summer of 1963. She is the last of the once huge Wilson fleet still operating under the trade name of Wilson Line. Wilson Line of Washington, Inc.

The Old Bay Line, last of the night lines on the bay, gave up in 1962. It could trace its tradition back to little *Eagle* in 1815. The same vessel, running on the Delaware in 1814 under Captain Moses Rogers, represented the forerunner of the old Wilmington Steamboat Company which evolved into the "Wilson Line."

The former Virginia Ferry Corporation transports which had been acquired by the State of Virginia in 1956 were the last steamers to cross the Chesapeake. Their time ran out on April 15, 1964, when the mammoth 17.5-mile, $200 million Chesapeake Bay Bridge-Tunnel opened to traffic. On

had carried over 25 million passengers and over 8 million vehicles, earning $42 million. Between 1956 and 1964, the fleet had carried another 16 million passengers and 6 million vehicles, earning $37 million. The Wilson-Pennsylvania Railroad "adventure" of 1933 had well proven its worth. Since operations began, the fleet had steamed nearly 9 million miles. It had been one of the world's greatest bay services and now it too belonged to the past.

Millions, north and south, watched television newscasts as cameramen recorded the last sailing, made by *Pocahontas* from Little Creek at 6:15 P.M.

The 340-foot *Cape May,* ex-*Del-Mar-Va,* steams across Delaware Bay in 1964. Delaware River and Bay Authority

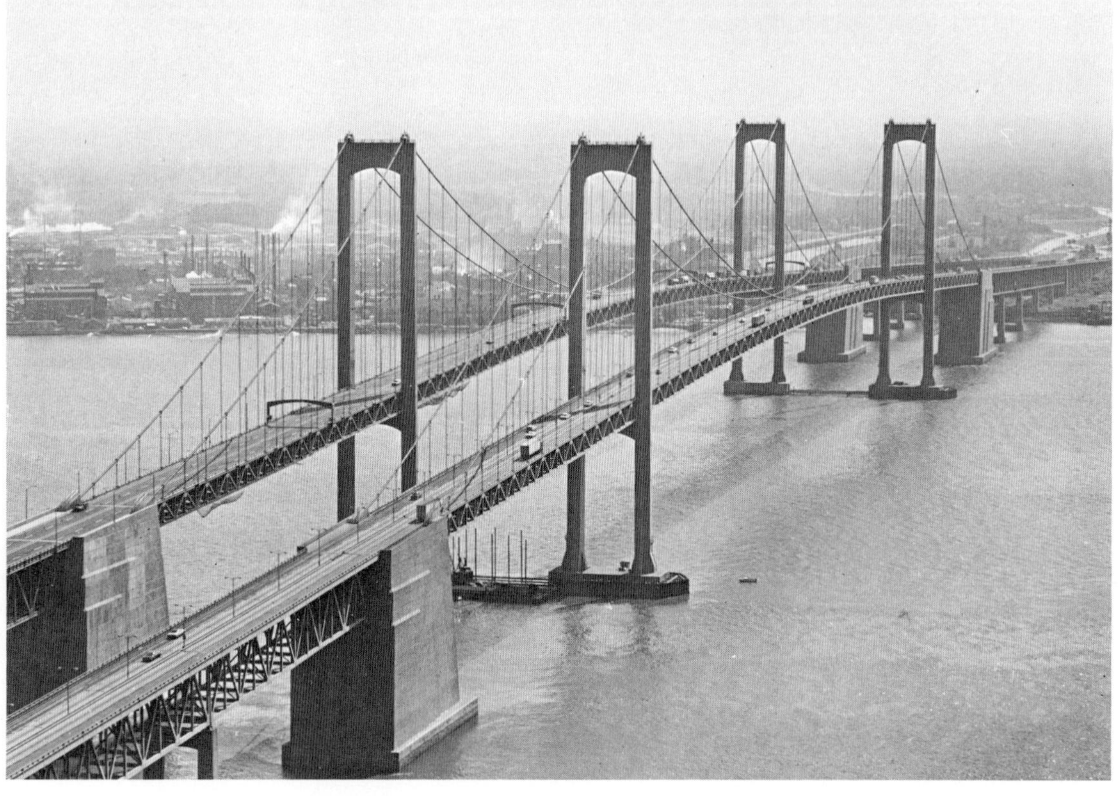

A "twin" span of the Delaware Memorial Bridge was completed in 1967. Since replacing Wilson's ferries in 1951, the bridge has been used by more than 375,000,000 travelers in more than 187,000,000 vehicles. Delaware River and Bay Authority

Her long mournful blasts symbolized an end to the era of short sea voyages across the Chesapeake. Progress had eliminated another pleasant and irretrievable phase of American life. Thereafter most of the fleet found employment on the new Cape May, New Jersey-Lewes, Delaware, crossing begun by the Delaware River and Bay Authority.

In the late 1960s former Wilson liners were to be found throughout the Western Hemisphere. Besides the former Virginia Ferry Corporation's vessels on Delaware Bay, two former Delaware-New Jersey Ferry Company ferryboats, *Florida* and *New York*, renamed *Jamestown* and *Newport*, had found employment maintaining ferry service between Newport and Jamestown, Rhode Island. They were the last of steam on Narragansett Bay, just as the Virginia Ferry steamers will be the last on Delaware Bay.

The former Wilson liner *State of Delaware* lay abandoned at a "ship's graveyard" on the south side of Rio de Janeiro's Guanabara Bay. During a trip to Rio in 1967 the writer investigated her whereabouts and found that she had sunk in a deep channel. Local residents, however, smilingly recalled her name. Ironically, a political poster nearby promoted votes for a Brazilian with the unlikely name of Wilson.

*Boston Belle* could be found at Rosario, Argentina and the former Virginia Ferry Corporation tanker *Kiptopeke*, now *Sandra*, operates on the coast of Ecuador. *Northampton* operates from Mexican ports. In the Caribbean, *Liberty Belle (II)* is working out of Cuba with a smaller vessel named *Pinero*, none other than Wilmington Steamboat Company's *City of Trenton* of 1901. *Deepwater*, last renamed *Provincetown*, operated out of the Virgin Islands.

Most remarkable, however, is the fate of "Little *Wilmington*" which revived the Wilmington Steamboat Company in 1882. Displaced from ferry service by a bridge across Tampa Bay, she had been advertised in 1961 as "the largest fishing boat in Florida." In 1966, as *Pinellas*, she was reportedly sold for use on Brazil's Amazon River. In 1970, 88 years after her emergence from Cramp's shipyard at Philadelphia, she remains in service.

Wilmington Steamboat Company's twin *Cities* of 1910, *City of Wilmington* and *City of Philadelphia*, launched in a gala ceremony in 1909, were still active in the late 1960s. Rebuilt and renamed *Bay Belle* and *S.S. Potomac*, and operated by Sound Steamship Lines and B. B. Wills, respectively, they were found competing in the New York Harbor excursion trade in 1966, often moored bow to bow at local resorts. As one of *Bay Belle's* men commented: "If the two old sisters could talk, what notes they could exchange about their lives since 1909!"

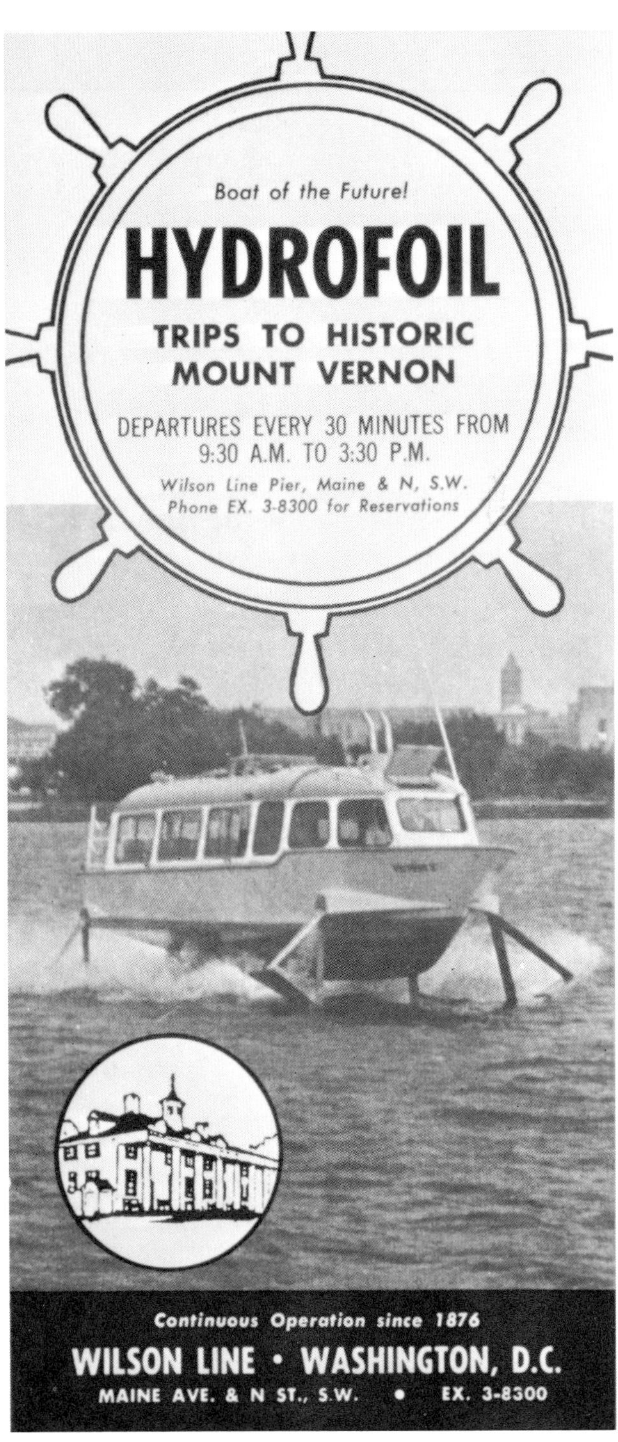


Wilson Line of Washington's first hydrofoil, *Victory I*, made over 40 knots and became, technically, America's fastest riverboat. Wilson Line of Washington, Inc.

An entertainers' party for the benefit of underprivileged children meant a "Mississippi Soirée" on *Bay Belle,* September 18, 1966. *Night Beat*

Moonlight Cruises

on Beautiful Tampa Bay

WHAT COULD BE MORE DELIGHTFUL THAN AN EVENING SAILING IN THE MOONLIGHT TO MUSIC AND DANCING ON TAMPA BAY

★ ★ ★ ★ ★

May be Chartered by Group or Organizations
Minimum charge - $165 up to 150 people

★ ★ ★ ★ ★

For further information contact us and we will be glad to arrange your outing to your satisfaction.

★ ★ ★ ★ ★

Tampa Bay Excursions, Inc.

500 PINELLAS POINT DRIVE SOUTH
ST. PETERSBURG, FLORIDA
5-3047 — PHONES — HE 6-5619
★ FREE PARKING ★

Salt Water

FISHING

MOTOR VESSEL

PINELLAS

Largest Fishing
Boat in the State of Florida
135 feet long — 28 foot beam
Wrought iron hull & Diesel Power
Radio-Telephone and Fish Finder
All crew members licensed under
UNITED STATES COAST GUARD

★ ★ ★ ★ ★

2 TRIPS DAILY — 7 DAYS A WEEK
8 A.M. - 12 Noon — 1 P.M. - 5 P.M.
Adults $2.00 — Children under 12 $1.00
— CAPACITY —
150 for fishing — 220 for Night Charter

★ ★ ★ ★ ★

Tampa Bay Excursions, Inc.

H. C. SPLANS and J. W. WINTERS, Owners
500 PINELLAS POINT DRIVE SOUTH
ST. PETERSBURG, FLORIDA
5-3047 — PHONES — HE 6-5619
★ FREE PARKING ★

Motor vessel *Pinellas,* running excursions from Tampa, Florida, in the early 1960's, was the barely recognizable "Little *Wilmington.*" Tampa Bay Excursions, Inc.

They were still carrying big crowds but their roles had changed. In 1910 they carried freight, and travelers who sat on their saloon decks looking at the Delaware's scenery or quietly reading a newspaper, much as rail commuters still do. In recent times, however, their second decks were often scenes of exuberant rock-and-roll marathons. The times changed and the boats have changed, but below decks the same durable steam engines that Harlan & Hollingsworth built in 1909 still propelled them along in the 1960s.

*S.S. Potomac* has been laid up at Baltimore since 1967 but she had become the last steamboat operated out of that port. *Bay Belle* continues at New

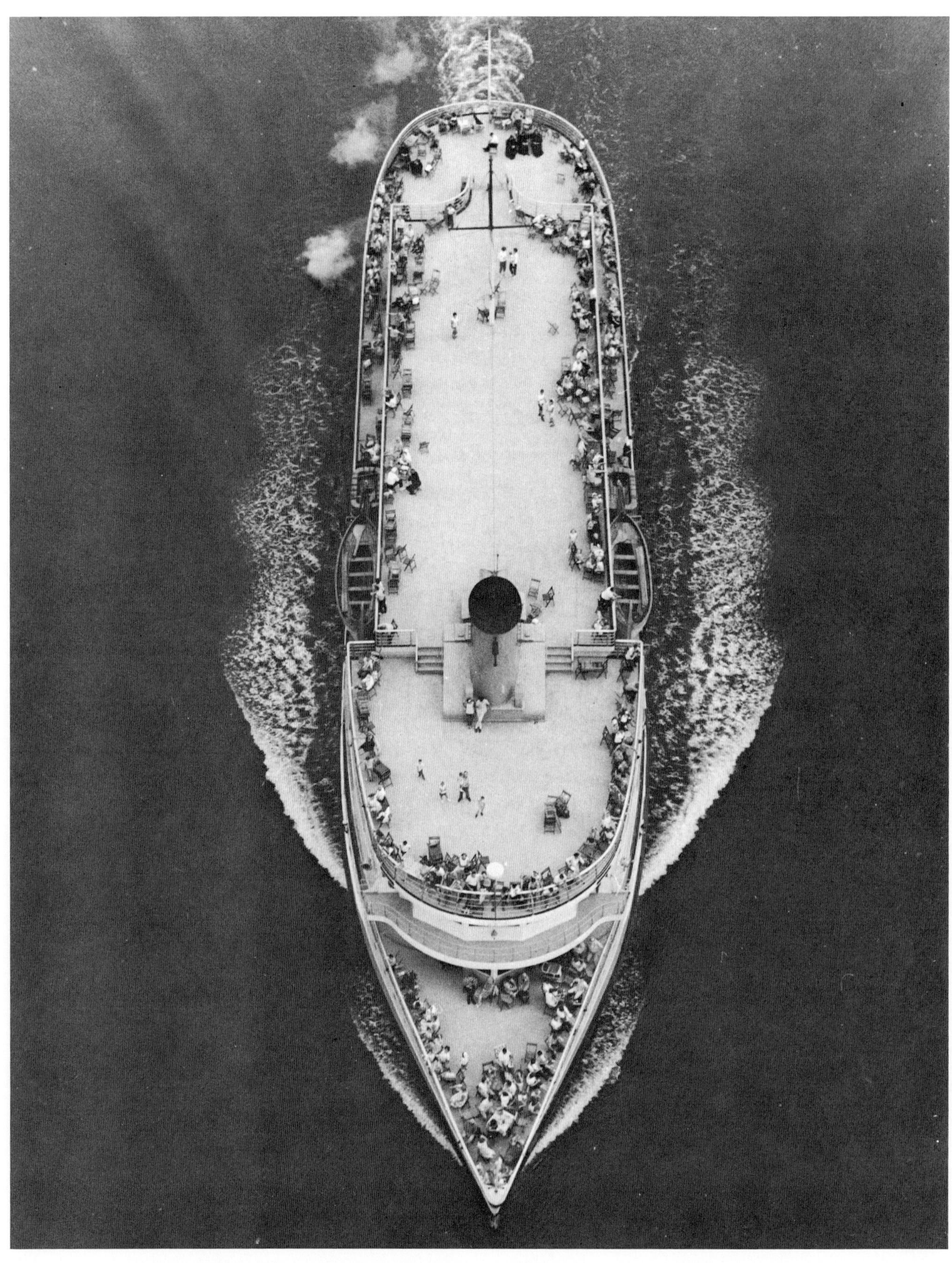

*Bay Belle* displays her streamlined form as she steams under the George Washington Bridge while bound from Yonkers, New York, to Rockaway Beach in 1966. Franklin B. Roberts, Jr.

York, running summer excursions and vying with the Day Line's *Alexander Hamilton* to be the last steamboat on the Hudson. Although the newest looking steamer on the coast, *Bay Belle* is the oldest active steamboat on the Atlantic seaboard. She is already considered the last steamboat operated from Long Island and Connecticut, from northern New Jersey ports and from Yonkers, New York, where she still keeps alive the old tradition of "going down the bay to Rockaway."

MONDAY & WEDNESDAY
CRUISE SPECIAL
from
YONKERS Recreation Pier to
ROCKAWAY'S PLAYLAND
• FREE admission to the Midway!
• FREE ocean bathing
• FREE Beach
OPEN EVERY DAY
ROCKAWAYS PLAYLAND
S.S. BAY BELLE
2400 PASSENGER LUXURY VESSEL
Don't fight traffic! A 3½ hour sail each way... through N.Y. Harbor. See the Manhattan Skyline from the Hudson River, pass the Statue of Liberty... sail under the famed Verrazano Bridge.
DANCING TO A LIVE ORCHESTRA
RESTAURANT • BAR • REFRESHMENTS
ADULTS ROUND TRIP $3.00
CHILDREN ROUND TRIP $1.50
no charge for children under 5
$50 Discount to Groups of 100 Adults or More
LEAVES 10 A.M. FROM
YONKERS RECREATION PIER
FOOT OF MAIN STREET
Leave Rockaway Beach 4:30 p.m. Arrive Yonkers 8 p.m.
Regular Monday & Wednesday Excursions starts June 12
SOUND STEAMSHIP LINES
YOnkers 5-5136

Sound Steamship Lines' *Bay Belle,* sailing from Yonkers to Rockaway twice weekly in 1966. *The Herald Statesman,* Yonkers, N.Y.

By 1969, *Mount Vernon,* ex-*City of Camden,* the third of Wilson's durable trio, had been converted into a school ship for the Seafarers International Union's training center at Piney Point, Maryland. *John A. Meseck,* veteran of the Normandy invasion, has also been sold to the union. "Old *Pennsy,*" laid up since 1960, had been sold to a real estate firm for possible conversion into a restaurant. In mid-January, 1970, *State of Pennsylvania* foundered in the icy Christina River not far from where she had been built. By 1970, only *Sea Belle* awaited buyers at Wilmington.

Joseph S. Wilson, last of the Wilson men, died in 1967. He had been mayor of Wilmington, Delaware, as had his father, Horace Wilson. Mrs. Frances W. Richardson

The line of Wilson men ended on February 5, 1967, when Joseph S. Wilson, grandson of the line's founder, died at his Wilmington home in his 79th year. After Wilson Line's sale in 1929, he became a founder of the Wilmington Marine Terminal and the Wilmington Board of Harbor Commissioners. In 1931, at 44, he entered the

University of Pennsylvania Law School and became a lawyer in 1935. Between 1941 and 1943 he served as president of Bellanca Aircraft Corporation and during World War II he was assistant West Coast director of the U.S. Maritime Commission. In 1946 he became mayor of Wilmington, following in the footsteps of his father, Captain Horace Wilson.

Eulogizing the passing of its former mayor, the Wilmington *Every Evening* in its editorial titled "Man of the Port of Wilmington" noted: "Many a Wilmingtonian remembers the Wilson Line steamboat days when the river was still a favored way of travel and transport between here and Philadelphia. . . .

"Those were the days when a father or mother

*S. S. Potomac,* ex-*City of Philadelphia,* on an excursion to Bear Mountain, New York, in 1964. Franklin B. Roberts, Jr.

*Sea Belle* (left) and *Bay Belle,* retired after the 1961 season, are shown at the erstwhile Pusey & Jones shipyard, Wilmington, Delaware, on March 19, 1964. They were for sale but the market for river and bay boats was very limited in the 1960's. R. Loren Graham or both would take the children by steamboat to Philadelphia for some shopping—a visit to Independence Hall and the Liberty Bell. What if the expedition took all day—much of the time at very leisurely speed on the river? That time wasn't wasted in the memory of those who had the privilege.

"Those were the closing years of Wilmington's long history as a river port and a shipbuilding town on the great estuary that has been called the 'American Clyde.' The Wilsons were part and parcel of this character that has put Wilmington on the map as much as (or more than) gunpowder-making did in the same century. . . .

"True, the lawyer and mayor and educational leader named Joseph Wilson may not have looked or acted like a steamboatman according to any popular notion of that calling. Yet, history has

After being laid up for five years, *Bay Belle* was reconditioned by Sound Steamship Lines, Inc., and returned to excursion work at New York in 1966. Franklin B. Roberts, Jr.

A Chinese-American group's flyer describes a *Bay Belle* outing in 1967.

already made sure of his niche as a man of what ship pilots call the Bay and River Delaware."

In 1969, Frederick K. Reybold died in Wilmington in his 94th year. Discussing the preparation of a Wilson Line history with Mr. Reybold in 1967, the author found him alert, highly enthusiastic and informative. He still spoke in the same friendly, matter-of-fact way as he had while the line's public relations director for 33 years. He urged the writer to "complete that book soon. I'd like to read it, but I'm 93, and haven't much time left." He died shortly before we could give this book to him.

By 1970 most of the men who had made the tradition of the Delaware had passed away. However, the tradition of John Fitch, Captain Moses Rogers, the Union Line, the Bush, Clyde, Warner, Reybold and Ericsson Lines, the Wilmington Steamboat Companies of 1820 and 1882, and the successor Wilson Lines—a spirited tradition of innovation—still survives. Interestingly, Wilson Line had come

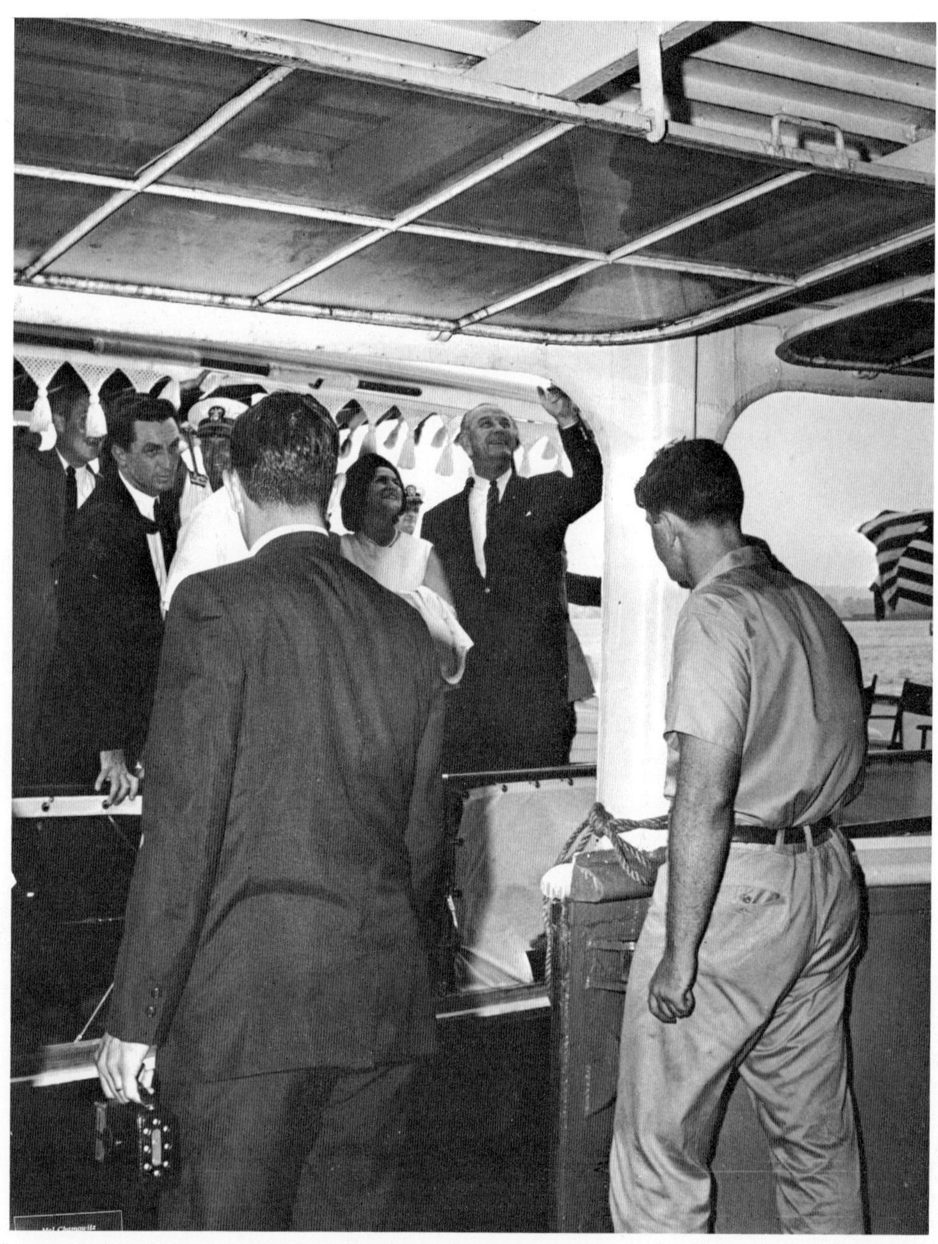

President and Mrs. Lyndon B. Johnson prepare to board *George Washington* on July 18, 1966. Wilson Line of Washington, Inc.

After being raised and repaired, *Mount Vernon* undergoes conversion into a schoolship at a Norfolk shipyard in 1968. Franklin B. Roberts, Jr.

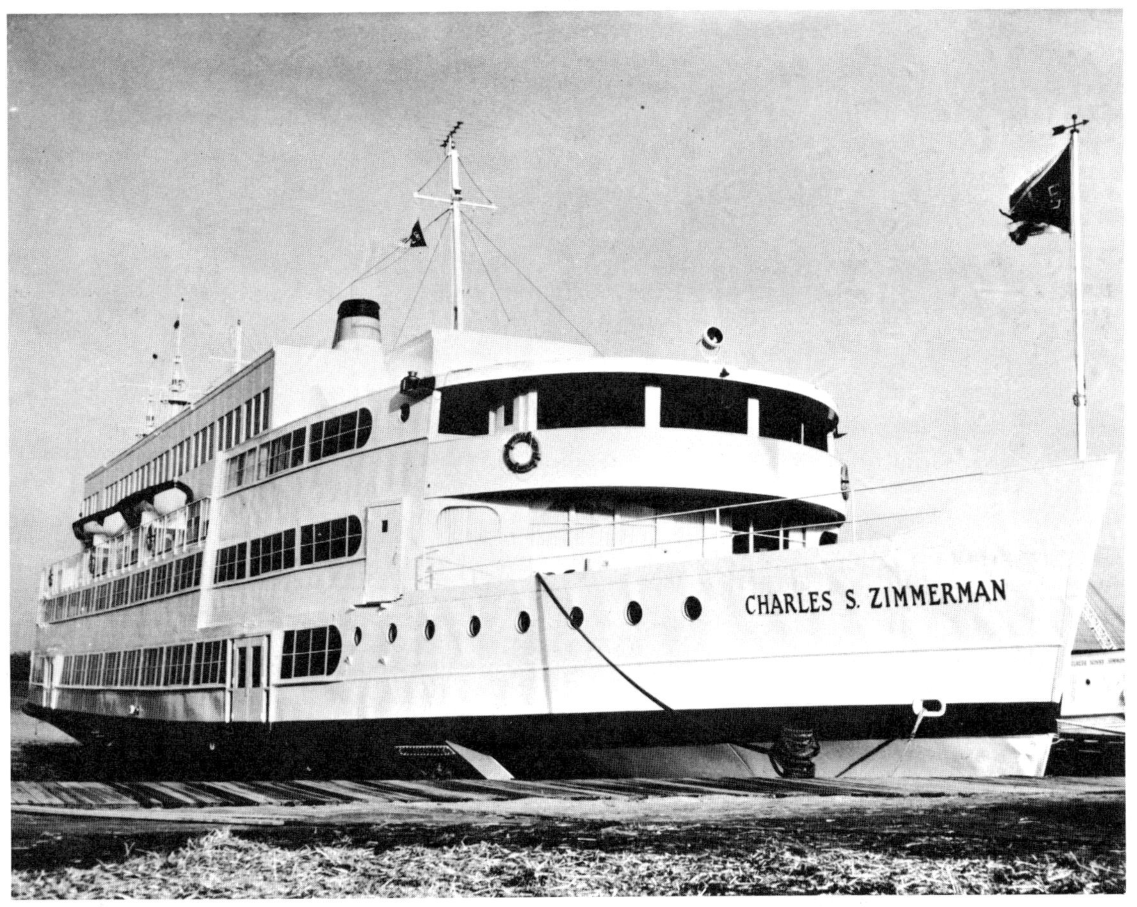


The former *Mount Vernon,* renamed *Charles S. Zimmerman,* begins her new career as a schoolship at The Harry Lundeberg School, Piney Point, Maryland in 1969. Seafarers' International Union

full circle, returning to the origins of its founder, J. Shields Wilson.

J. Shields Wilson had left shipbuilding to reorganize Wilmington Steamboat Company in 1882. Cramp's yard, Harlan & Hollingsworth and all the great yards of the 19th century were gone, but one of the few surviving shipyards on the Delaware—Wilson Shipyard at Fourth Street Wharf, Wilmington—continues to build and repair ships. Wilson had returned to shipbuilding.

Vanquished by "progress" and changing social conditions, the once-proud *State of Pennsylvania* foundered in the Christina on January 16, 1970. One newsman who had known her in his youth felt that she had "died of a broken heart." The News Journal Company

Wilson Line of Washington also continues the tradition of riverboat operations. It is ironic that while Wilson Line is regarded as a "notable Delaware River institution" with historic links to Delaware, New Jersey and Pennsylvania, the only surviving Wilson Line operates from Washington, D.C., where J. Shields Wilson was born in 1834.

In 1969 over half a million people enjoyed river trips on Wilson boats and on any typical summer morning one could still see excitement in the faces of thousands of young people awaiting a trip on *George Washington* to enjoy the adventure of sailing, of seeing the sights and of crossing the Potomac for a day of traditional amusements at Marshall Hall Park, as millions have before them.

People of all ages still see the beautiful Potomac the only complete way, by boat. Returning to Washington, thousands view the same sights and in late summer enjoy twilight on the river. After a day or evening aboard, the visitors go ashore hoping to make another boat trip in the future, just for the pleasure of it.

For nearly a century the more than 100 steamboats and other craft operated by the various Wilson Lines have given safe transportation and pleasure to over 250 million passengers. From the time J. Shields Wilson began tugboat operations in 1876 on the Delaware to the 1970s with hydrofoil operations on the Potomac, Wilson Line had always been a pioneer, doing things its own way and building vessels technologically ahead of their times.

Wilson Line may not have looked or acted quite like other steamboat lines, nor did it fit the popular notion of what a steamboat line should be. It was itself—and in many ways the greatest of all American steamboat lines. It was steamboating determined to survive, and it lived to operate the last of the steamboats. Perhaps the most important facet of its ingratiating personality was the fact that its personnel have always been kind to children. There should be many of them enjoying trips on the Wilson boats during the line's centennial year of 1976 and in the distant days ahead.

*Delaware,* ex-*Pocahontas,* continues to cross the Delaware in 1970, nearly a century after the first Wilson boats began steaming on the Delaware. Delaware River and Bay Authority

# Fleet List

# *Fleet List*

Fleet List of steamboats and other vessels owned or operated by J. Shields Wilson and Associates, 1876; Wilmington Steamboat Company of 1882—the "Wilson Line"; subsidiary and successor Wilson Lines, 1876-1970 (vessels of the earlier Wilmington Steamboat Companies are omitted).

Notes

Vessel measurements are those recorded in the Federal Government's List of Merchant Vessels of the United States; Lloyd's Register of Shipping and The Record of the American Bureau of Shipping.

No complete listing of all vessels owned or chartered and operated by the various Wilson Lines is available to include the years encompassed by the following list. A few vessels are included on the basis of newspaper records and human recollections. Allowance should be made for the likelihood that a number of vessels not appearing in this list may have been owned or operated by Wilmington Steamboat Company prior to 1920. Unless otherwise indicated, vessel dimensions are minimal lengths and widths. Vessels are listed in approximate chronology of acquisition or use.

Abbreviations for Fleet List Vessel Classification

STP - Steam, paddle wheel
SSC - Steam, screw
D - Diesel, screw
H - Hydrofoil
T - Tugboat
B - Barge
L.O.A. - Length, overall
O.G. - Max. beam over guards
P - Passenger
P-F - Passenger & freight
F - Freight
TK - Tanker
P-V-T - Passenger and vehicle bay transport
FY - Ferryboat (passenger and vehicle)
R - Rebuilt
* - Vessel chartered on occasion
** - World War II ship purchased for breakwater at Kiptopeke, Va.

Abbreviations Indicating Name of Operator

W.S.C. - Wilmington Steamboat Company, "Wilson Line", 1882-1929
W. & P. - Wilmington & Penns Grove Transportation Company
T. & St. P. - Tampa & St. Petersburg Transportation Company
C. - Christiana Ferry Company
N.J.-W. - New Jersey & Wilmington Ferry Company
D. -N.J. - Delaware-New Jersey Ferry Company
W.L. - Wilson Line, Inc., 1929-1955
V.F.C. - Virginia Ferry Corporation
W.E.L. - Wilson Excursion Lines, 1955-1960
W.L.W. - Wilson Steamship Corporation, 1958
(Wilson Line of Washington and subsidiaries)
W.L.F. - Wilson Line of Florida

(Continued next page)

| Name | Official Number | Tonnage Gross | Tonnage Net | Length | Beam | Depth | Horse-power | Built Year | Built Location | Owner/ Operator | Type |
|---|---|---|---|---|---|---|---|---|---|---|---|
| Blanche | 3079 | 94 | 47 | 83 | 17.9 | 10 | | 1878 | Phila., Pa. | J.S. Wilson | SSC, T |
| Wilmington | 80884 | 106 | 72 | 122 | 22.0 | 6.0 | 300 | 1882 | Phila., Pa. | W.S.C. | SSC |
| b-Pinellas | | | | | | | | | | | P-F |
| Twilight | 24788 | 466 | 371 | 176 | 27.4 | 6.9 | 900 | 1868 | Wilm., Del. | W.S.C.* | STP, P-F |
| Brandywine | 3318 | 407 | 215 | 177.5 | 25.1 | 8.5 | 1,000 | 1885 | Wilm., Del. | W.S.C. | SSC |
| b-Dixie | | 435 | 296 | 203.9 | 45.1 | 9.7 | | 1936 (R) | | W.L., W.E.L. | P-F |
| c-Pilgrim Belle | | | | 210.2(L.O.A.) | 47.6(O.G.) | | | | | | P |
| City of Chester | 126493 | 611 | 327 | 185.5 | 28 | 9.0 | 950 | 1888 | Wilm., Del. | W.S.C. | SSC |
| b-City of Washington | | 418 | 164 | 191.8 | 44.4 (O.G.) | 9.2 | 950 | 1926 (R) | | W.L., W.E.L. | P-F |
| c-Pilgrim Belle | | 420 | 166 | 197.0 | 45.0(O.G.) | 10.5 | 1,250 | 1931 (R) | | | P |
| | | | | 203.9(L.O.A.) | | | | | | | |
| John A. Warner | 13429 | 578 | 506 | 211.8 | 27.8 | 9.0 | 1,100 | 1857 | Wilm., Del. | W.S.C.* | STP |
| b-Burlington | | | | | | | | | | | P-F |
| Sylvan Dell | 115040 | 440 | 287 | 178 | 27 | 8.7 | 700 | 1872 | Bklyn., N.Y. | W.S.C.* | STP, P-F |
| Sylvan Glen | 23768 | 330 | 165 | 153.5 | 27 | 8.3 | 457 | 1869 | Bklyn., N.Y. | W.S.C.* | STP, P-F |
| Pleasant Valley | 20336 | 400 | 302 | 159.5 | 26.8 | 8.6 | 600 | 1870 | Keyport, N.J. | W.S.C.* | STP, P-F |
| John Sylvester | 13185 | 495 | 338 | 193 | 30 | 9.6 | 484 | 1866 | Jersey City, N.J. | W.S.C.* | STP, P-F |
| b-Starlight | | | | | | | | | | | |
| c-Favorite | | | | | | | | | | | |
| Thomas Clyde | 145173 | 625 | 570 | 212 | 31 | 7 | 1,000 | 1878 | Wilm., Del. | W.S.C.* | STP, P-F |
| Major Reybold | 17524 | 530 | 426 | 204.3 | 30.3 | 7.2 | 800 | 1853 | Wilm., Del. | W.S.C.* | STP, P-F |
| Fannie | 120140 | 220 | 133 | 132 | 22.9 | 7.6 | 250 | 1886 | Wilm., Del. | W.S.C. | SSC, F |
| City of Trenton | 127534 | 458 | 311 | 155.5 | 32.0 | 7.4 | 1,000 | 1901 | Phila., Pa. | W.S.C. | SSC, P-F |
| | | | | 162 (L.O.A.) | | | | | | | |
| b-Sagamore | | | | | | | | 1902 (R) | | | |
| c-Princeton | | | | | | | | | | | |
| d-Pinero | | | | | | | | | | | D |
| Quaker City | 20633 | 469 | 318 | 155.5 | 32.0 | 7.4 | 1,000 | 1901 | Phila., Pa. | W.S.C. | SSC, |
| | | | | 162 (L.O.A.) | | | | | | | P-F |
| b-Sieur de Monts | | | | | | | | | | | |
| c-Major L'enfant | | | | | | | | | | | |
| d-Gen'l. Mathews | | | | | | | | | | | |
| Queen Anne | 20624 | 651 | 410 | 203.3 | 52 | 8.6 | 1,000 | 1899 | Balto., Md. | W.S.C.* | STP, P-F |
| City of Wilmington | 207202 | 749 | 435 | 192.9 | 32 | 11.8 | 1,250 | 1910 | Wilm., Del. | W.S.C. | SSC, P-F |
| b-Bay Belle | | 622 | 423 | 200.6 | 48 (O.G.) | 12.1 | | 1941(R) | | W.L., W.E.L. | P |
| | | | | 220.5(L.O.A.) | | | | | | | |
| City of Philadelphia | 207201 | 749 | 435 | 192.9 | 32 | 11.8 | 1,250 | 1910 | Wilm., Del. | W.S.C. | SSC, P-F |
| b-Liberty Belle | | 622 | 423 | 200.6 | 48 (O.G.) | 12.1 | | 1938 (R) | | W.L. | P |
| c-U.S.S. Liberty Belle (IX-72) | | | | | | | | | | | |
| d-Asbury Park | | | | | | | | | | | |
| e-Tolchester | | | | | | | | | | | |
| f-Freestone | | | | | | | | | | | |
| g-S.S. Potomac | | | | | | | | | | | |
| Merchant | 201335 | 350 | 238 | 131 | 27 | 6.5 | 500 | 1904 | Phila., Pa. | W.S.C. | SSC, F |
| a-John P. Wilson | | | | | | | | | | | |
| Ulrica | 25293 | 205 | 171 | 105 | 22.6 | 7.8 | 110 | 1893 | Wilm., Del. | W.S.C.(W.&P.)N.J.-W.P. | FY, SSC |
| Fearless | 120945 | 656 | 471 | 160 | 35 | 15.6 | 450 | 1893 | Wilm., Del. | W.S.C. (W.&P.) | FY |
| Peerless | 20412 | 298 | 186 | 149 | 32.6 | 8.6 | 400 | 1872 | Wilm., Del. | W.S.C. (W.&P.) | FY, STP |
| City of Reading | 126560 | 576 | 445 | 145 | 30.1 | 11 | 450 | 1889 | Wilm., Del. | W.S.C. (W.&P.)W.L. | STP, FY |
| Arctic | 105876 | 394 | 284 | 145 | 30 | 7.8 | 453 | 1879 | Wilm., Del. | W.S.C.(W.&P.) W.L. | STP, FY |
| Cape May | 127566 | 714 | 532 | 156 | 30 | 13 | 620 | 1901 | Wilm., Del. | W.S.C.(W.&P.) W.L. | STP, FY |
| Long Beach | 140399 | 411 | 259 | 150.5 | 32 | 10.5 | 300 | 1880 | Wilm., Del. | W.S.C.(W.&P.) W.L. | STP, FY |
| Springfield | 117092 | 287 | 163 | 127 | 24 | 9.0 | 325 | 1901 | Wilm., Del. | W.S.C.* | SSC, P |
| F.W. Brune | 9493 | 296 | 201 | 129 | 23 | 7.6 | 350 | 1860 | Wilm., Del. | W.S.C. | SSC, F |

| | | | | | | | | | | |
|---|---|---|---|---|---|---|---|---|---|---|
| Baltic | 3181 | 398 | 289 | 145 | 30 | 7.8 | 500 | 1881 | Wilm., Del. | W.S.C., D-N.J., W.L. | STP, FY |
| b-Brigantine | | | | | | | | | | | |
| City of Camden | 214055 | 730 | 414 | 192.9 | 32 | 10.6 | 1,450 | 1916 | Wilm., Del. | W.S.C. | SSC, P-F |
| b-Mount Vernon | | 661 | 449 | 201.7 | 46.5 | 12.5 | | 1940 (R) | | W.L. | P |
| c-Charles S. | | | | | | | | | | W.E.L. | |
| Zimmerman | | | | 220.5 (L.O.A.) | 48 (O.G.) | | | | | W.L.W. | |
| Montauk | 20637 | 641 | 436 | 193 | 30.1 | 11.2 | 1,000 | 1902 | Balto., Md. | W.S.C.* | SSC, P |
| a-Queen Caroline | | | | | | | | | | | |
| Pokanoket | 150653 | 319 | 254 | 151.2 | 29 | 8.0 | 300 | 1894 | Bklyn., N.Y. | W.S.C. (T.&St.P.) | SSC, P-F |
| Favorite | 120967 | 399 | 271 | 127.6 | 30.6 | 8.2 | 1,000 | 1894 | Tompkins Cove, N.Y. | W.S.C. (T. & St. P.) C | SSC, P-F |
| Mandeville | 212235 | 467 | 200 | 179.6 | 32 | 8.6 | 650 | 1914 | Wilm., Del. | W.S.C. (T. & St. P.) | STP, P |
| a-Hanover | | | | | | | | | | | |
| c- William Penn | | | | | | | | | | | |
| City of Jacksonville | 126081 | 459 | 395 | 160.5 | 32.5 | 6.6 | 700 | 1882 | Wilm., Del. | W.S.C.* (T.& St.P.) | STP, P |
| Dolphin | 86299 | 491 | 341 | 209.0 | 28.3 | 9.1 | 507 | 1893 | Port Richmond N.Y. | W.S.C.* | STP, P |
| a-Glen | | | | | | | | | | | |
| b-Amphion | | | | | | | | | | | |
| Trenton | 110086 | 1,269 | 863 | 206.0 | 33.0 | 21.6 | 640 | 1873 | Wilm., Del. | W.S.C. | STP, P |
| a-Richmond | | | | | | | | | | | |
| b-Albion | | | | | | | | | | | |
| Deepwater | 204233 | 343 | 233 | 126.6 | 33 | 10 | 600 | 1907 | Phila., Pa. | W.S.C. | SSC, P |
| a-Boothbay | | | | | | | | | | | |
| b-Grampus | | | | | | | | | | | |
| d-Liberty | | | | | | | | | | | |
| e-Provincetown | | | | | | | | | | | |
| President | 125592 | 1,468 | 1,098 | 260.6 | 29 | 12 | 1,200 | 1877 | Greenpoint, Bklyn., N.Y. | W.S.C.* | STP, P |
| a-Columbia | | | | | | | | | | | |
| State of Delaware | 222971 | 814 | 336 | 219.1<br>226 (L.O.A.) | 48.9<br>59.5 (O.G.) | 10.6 | 2,900 | 1923 | Wilm., Del. | W.S.C., W.L. | SSC, P |
| b-Guaruja | | | | | | | | | | | |
| State of Pennsylvania | 223103 | 814 | 336 | 219.1<br>226 (L.O.A.)<br>235.5 | 48.9<br>59.5 (O.G.) | 10.6 | 2,900 | 1923<br>1944 (R) | Wilm., Del. | W.S.C.<br>W.L., W.E.L. | SSC<br>P |
| New Castle | 81299 | 721 | 454 | 196 | 37.4 | 14.1 | 540 | 1890 | Newburgh, N.Y. | W.S.C. (D.-N.J.)<br>W.L. | STP<br>FY |
| a-Whitehall | | | | | | | | | | | |
| Pennsville | 92259 | 725 | 457 | 196 | 37.4 | 14.1 | 540 | 1890 | Newburgh, N.Y. | W.S.C. (D.-N.J.)<br>W.L. | STP<br>FY |
| a-Montauk | | | | | | | | | | | |
| R. Hasburgh | (no information found) | | | | | | | | | W.S.C. | |
| Harding Highway | 91704 | 652 | 458 | 152 | 32.5 | 12.2 | 300 | 1884 | Newburgh, N.Y. | W.S.C. (D.-N.J.) | STP<br>FY |
| a-Manhattan Beach | | | | | | | | | | | |
| Penn-Jersey | 127157 | 757 | 515 | 148.8 | 38.0 | 13.2 | 600 | 1896 | Elizabeth, N.J. | W.S.C.* (D.-N.J.)<br>W.L.* | SSC<br>FY |
| a-Camden | | | | | | | | | | | |
| Christiana | 232860 | 423 | | 145 | 25.0 | 12.3 | 400 | 1891 | New York, N.Y. | W.L. | F, SSC |
| a-Azalea | | | | | | | | | | | |
| c-U.S.S. Christiana (IX-80) | | | | | | | | | | | |
| Foote | 168373 | 240 | 240 | 101.4 | 21.5 | 10.7 | | 1922 | Kingston, N.Y. | W.L. | B |
| J.C. Reichert | 126349 | 77 | 38 | 79.2 | 19.0 | 9 | 235 | 1884 | Tottenville, N.Y. | W.L. | SSC, T |
| a-Chauncey M. Depew | | | | | | | | | | | |
| b-N.Y. Central Lighterage Co. No. 10 | | | | | | | | | | | |
| c-New York Central No. No. 10 | | | | | | | | | | | |
| C. & O. Tug #8 | (no information found) | | | | | | | | | W.L. | SSC, T |
| West River | 204550 | 190 | 124 | 108.8 | 22.4 | 6.9 | 250 | 1907 | Milford, Del. | W.L. | SSC, F |
| Green Island | 210847 | 1,152 | 783 | 184.7 | 36.1 | 11.9 | 900 | 1912 | Wilm., Del. | W.L. | SSC, F |
| a-York | | | | | | | | | | | |
| c-Louise | | | | | | | | | | | |

| Name | Official Number | Tonnage Gross | Tonnage Net | Length | Beam | Depth | Horse-power | Built Year | Built Location | Owner/ Operator | Type |
|---|---|---|---|---|---|---|---|---|---|---|---|
| Betterton | 212471 | 355 | 236 | 121.3 | 24 | 7.4 | 300 | 1912 | Milford, Del. | W.L. | SSC, F |
| a-George F. Pierce | | | | | | | | | | | |
| Atlantic City | 212140 | 807 | 549 | 139.8 | 35 | 14.8 | 700 | 1914 | Wilm., Del. | W.L.* (D.-N.J.) | SSC, FY |
| a-Delaware | | | | | | | | | | | |
| Pennsylvania | 150848 | 1,352 | 857 | 244.3 | 40 | 14.8 | 3,300 | 1900 | Chester, Pa. | W.L.* (V.F.C.) | SSC, P-F |
| New York | 130450 | 770 | 523 | 207.5 | 31.1 | 12.4 | 689 | 1889 | Wilm., Del. | W.L.* (V.F.C.) | SSC, P-F |
| Maryland | 204242 | 1,369 | 827 | 249.5 | 40.1 | 14.1 | 1,900 | 1907 | Sparrows Pt. Md. | W.L.* (V.F.C.) | SSC P-F |
| Virginia Lee | 228015 | 2,158 | 1,189 | 291 | 50.1 | 16.5 | 2,400 | 1928 | Quincy, Mass. | W.L.* (V.F.C.) | SSC, P-V-T |
| b-Holiday | | | | | | | | | | | |
| c-Accomac | | | | | | | | | | | |
| Jersey Shore | 231169 | 636 | 432 | 194.9 | 43.1 | 14.6 | 925 | 1931 | Wilm., Del. | W.L. (D.-N.J.) | FY, D |
| Del-Mar-Va | 232813 | 1,496 | 821 | 249.8 | 59 | 19.5 | 2,800 | 1933 | Wilm., Del. | W.L. | SSC |
| b-Cape May | | 2,294 | 1,560 | 339.8 | 59 | 19.5 | 2,800 | 1955(R) | | (V.F.C.) | P-V-T |
| Iris | 150754 | 428 | 292 | 142 | 30 | 10.3 | 850 | 1897 | Phila., Pa. | W.L. | SSC-Lighthouse tender purchased for parts. |
| a-Plymouth | | | | | | | | | | | |
| Cincinnati | 126803 | 745 | 507 | 193.2 | 46.5 | 15.4 | 1,200 | 1891 | Elizabeth, N.J. | W.L. (D.-N.J.) | SSC, FY |
| Washington | 81386 | 739 | 503 | 193.2 | 46.5 | 15.4 | 650 | 1891 | Chester, Pa. | W.L. (D.-N.J.) | SSC, FY |
| Princess Anne | 235140 | 1,616 | 758 | 260 (L.O.A.) | 59 | 19 | 3,100 | 1936 | Chester, Pa. | W.L. (V.F.C.) | SSC, P-V-T |
| b-New Jersey | | 2,366 | 1,259 | 335.7 | | | | 1954(R) | | | |
| Pocahontas | 240352 | 1,862 | 1,266 | 282.7 | 65 | 16.2 | 3,825 | 1941 | Wilm., Del. | W.L. (V.F.C.) | SSC, P-V-T |
| | | | | 300 (L.O.A.) | | | | | | | |
| b-Delaware | | 2,542 | 1,728 | 358.7 | 65 | 19.6 | | 1957(R) | | | |
| New York | 240610 | 701 | 477 | 194.9 | 49.1 | 14.8 | 1,500 | 1941 | Wilm., Del. | W.L. (D.-N.J.) | SSC, FY |
| b-Norfolk | | | | | | | | | | | |
| c-Newport | | | | | | | | | | | |
| Florida | 240725 | 701 | 477 | 194.9 | 49.1 | 14.8 | 1,500 | 1941 | Wilm., Del. | W.L. (D.-N.J.) | SSC, FY |
| b-Richmond | | | | | | | | | | | |
| c-Jamestown | | | | | | | | | | | |
| Pittsburgh | 150741 | 794 | 540 | 200 | 46 | 15.2 | 540 | 1896 | Phila., Pa. | W.L. (D.-N.J.) | SSC, FY |
| a-Pittsburg | | | | | | | | | | | |
| Chicago | 127509 | 766 | 521 | 206 (L.O.A.) | 65 (O.G.) | 15.2 | 750 | 1901 | Port Richmond, N. Y. | W.L. (D.-N.J.) | SSC FY |
| Margate | 92499 | 642 | 406 | 145 | 32 | 14.4 | 650 | 1893 | Wilm., Del. | W.L. (D.-N.J.) | SCC, FY |
| a-Mauch Chunk | | | | | | | | | | | |
| Wildwood | 208345 | 809 | 550 | 152.9 | 36.7 | 13.0 | 650 | 1911 | Port Richmond, N.Y. | W.L. (D.-N.J.) | SCC, FY |
| Newark | 13994 | 749 | 509 | 192.5 | 46 | 15.0 | 750 | 1902 | Newburgh, N.Y. | W.L. (D.-N.J.) | SCC, FY |
| Philadelphia | 150806 | 826 | 561 | 191.0 | 46.1 | 15.2 | 1,800 | 1899 | Chester, Pa. | W.L. (D.-N.J.) | SCC, FY |
| Unnamed auxiliary pile barge | | | | 80 | 23 | 5 | | | | W.L. | B |
| Delaware Belle | 250603 | 908 | 617 | 221.1 | 52.5 | 13.7 | 2,000 | 1946 | Wilm., Del. | W.L. | D |
| b-Hudson Belle | | | | 236 (L.O.A.) | 54 (O.G.) | | | | | W.E.L. | P |
| c-George Washington | | | | | | | | | | W.L.W. | |
| Northampton | 256686 | 1,042 | 456 | 306.7 | 50.0 | 10.6 | 3,200 | 1943 | Jeffersonville, Ind. | W.L. (V.F.C.) | D, P-V-T |
| a-LST-63 | | | | 328 (L.O.A.) | | | | 1948(R) | | | |
| Kiptopeke | 256435 | 1,029 | 646 | 195.2 | 34.1 | 17.8 | 3,600 | 1944 | Houston, Texas | W.L. (V.F.C.) | D, TK |
| a-LSM-73 | | | | | | | | 1948(R) | | | |
| c-Sandra | | | | | | | | | | | |
| Hecla | 223176 | 53 | 36 | 59.3 | 23.3 | 6.9 | 150 | 1923 | Brookhaven, N. Y. | W.L. (V.F.C.) | D F |
| Liberty Belle | 255508 | 892 | 470 | 209.5 | 50 | 18.5 | 2,200 | 1943 | Chicago, Ill. | W.L. | D |
| | | | | 228 (L.O.A.) | 54 (O.G.) | | | 1948(R) | Wilm., Del. | W.E.L. | P |
| a-PCE(R)-854 | | | | | | | | | | | |
| c-Isla del Tesoro | | | | | | | | | | | |

| | | | | | | | | | | | |
|---|---|---|---|---|---|---|---|---|---|---|---|
| Boston Belle | 258021 | 1,049 | 888 | 237.5 | 50.7 | 14.6 | 2,880 | 1945 | Stamford, Conn. | W.L. | D |
| a-PCE-1258 | | | | 257.5 (L.O.A.) | 54 (O.G.) | | | 1949 (R) | Wilm., Del. | W.E.L. | P |
| c-Ciudad de Rosario | | | | | | | | | | | |
| Arthur Newell Talbot | 244542 | 4,826 | 3,405 | 350 | 54 | 35 | 1,300 | 1944 | Tampa, Fla. | W.L. (V.F.C.) | SSC, F, Cement** |
| Richard Kidder Meade | 245069 | 4,826 | 3,405 | 350 | 54 | 35 | 1,300 | 1944 | Tampa, Fla. | W.L. (V.F.C.) | SSC, F, Cement** |
| Willis A. Slater | 245071 | 4,826 | 3,397 | 350 | 54 | 35 | 1,300 | 1944 | Tampa, Fla. | W.L. (V.F.C.) | SSC, F, Cement** |
| Leonard Chase Wason | 245336 | 4,690 | 3,248 | 350 | 54 | 35 | 1,300 | 1944 | Tampa, Fla. | W.L. (V.F.C.) | SSC. F, Cement** |
| Robert Whitman Lesley | 246029 | 4,690 | 3,248 | 350 | 54 | 35 | 1,300 | 1944 | Tampa, Fla. | W.L. (V.F.C.) | SSC, F, Cement** |
| Edwin Thacher | 246120 | 4,690 | 3,248 | 350 | 54 | 35 | 1,300 | 1944 | Tampa, Fla. | W.L. (V.F.C.) | SSC, F, Cement** |
| Willard A. Pollard | 246758 | 4,680 | 2,738 | 350 | 54 | 35 | 1,300 | 1944 | Tampa, Fla. | W.L. (V.F.C.) | SSC, F, Cement** |
| William Foster Cowham | 246759 | 4,680 | 2,738 | 350 | 54 | 35 | 1,300 | 1944 | Tampa, Fla. | W.L. (V.F.C.) | SSC, F, Cement** |
| John Grant | 245773 | 4,690 | 3,248 | 350 | 54 | 35 | 1,300 | 1944 | Tampa, Fla. | W.L. (V.F.C.) | SSC, F, Cement** |
| City of Keansburg | 225904 | 1,037 | 551 | 231 | 43 | 12 | 1,500 | 1926 | Newburgh, N.Y. | W.L.* | SSC, P |
| Westport | 209877 | 246 | 167 | 125.6 | 21.2 | 8.8 | 450 | 1911 | Boston, Mass. | W.L.* | SSC, P |
| Accomac (see Virginia Lee) | 228015 | | | | | | | | | W.L. (V.F.C.) | D, P-V-T |
| Sea Belle | 265365 | 1,828 | 1,638 | 237.5 | 50.7 | 14.6 | 1,800 | 1943 | Morris Hghts., N. Y. | W.L.<br>W.E.L. | D, P |
| a-PCE-1207 | | | | 257.5 (L.O.A.) | 54 (O.G.) | | | 1953 (R) | Wilm., Del. | W.L.W.<br>W.E.L. | P<br>SSC, P |
| Tolchester (see City of Phila.) | 207201 | | | | | | | | | | |
| John A. Meseck | 225904 | 1,978 | 936 | 240.1 | 45.2 | 14.0 | 2,400 | 1929 | Quincy, Mass. | W.E.L., W.L.W. | SSC, P |
| a-Naushon | | | | | | | | | | | |
| The Diplomat | 229917 | 99 | 67 | 124.3 | 21.2 | 11.6 | 500 | 1930 | New York, N.Y. | W.L.W. | D, P |
| a-Stevana | | | | | | | | | | | |
| b-Ace | | | | | | | | | | | |
| c-Circle Line II | | | | | | | | | | | |
| d-Circle Line Sightseer IX | | | | | | | | | | | |
| e-Circle Line IX | | | | | | | | | | | |
| Mount Vernon | 279228 | 93 | 38 | 63.0 | 21.0 | 6.8 | 912 | 1959 | Nashville, Tenn. | W.L.W. | D, P |
| a-Chippewa Chief | | | | | | | | | | | |
| Dolly Madison | 286092 | 34 | 23 | 59.9 | 26.9 | 7.6 | 228 | 1961 | Warren, R.I. | W.L.W. | D, P |
| Martha Washington | 285596 | 34 | 23 | 59.9 | 26.9 | 7.6 | 228 | 1961 | Warren, R.I. | W.L.W. | D, P |
| Albatross | 289197 | 6 | | 33'10" | 11'4" | | 181 | 1962 | Wilm., Del. | Wilson Shpyd. Inc. | H, P |
| Commodore I | 268899 | 12 | 8 | 48.4 | 15.4 | 4.2 | 165 | 1954 | St. Augustine, Fla. | W.L.F. | D, P |
| Commodore II | 268900 | 12 | 8 | 48.4 | 15.4 | 4.2 | 165 | 1954 | St. Augustine, Fla. | W.L.F. | D, P |
| Pancoast I | 221709 | 13 | 9 | 62.3 | 12.9 | 3.3 | 260 | 1921 | Trenton, Mich. | W.L.F. | D, P |
| a-Altona II | | | | | | | | | | | |
| b-Centaur | | | | | | | | | | | |
| c-Byronic | | | | | | | | | | | |
| Pancoast II | 255161 | 14 | 9 | 62.0 | 13.3 | 5.8 | 270 | 1924 | E. Boothbay, Me. | W.L.F. | D, P |
| a-USCG-74318 | | | | | | | | | | | |
| Gray Line Sightseeing I | 249310 | 60 | 55 | 61.6 | 15.0 | 5.6 | 165 | 1946 | Elizabeth, N.C. | W.L.F. | D, P |
| Gray Line Sightseeing II | 249324 | 60 | 55 | 61.6 | 15.0 | 5.6 | 165 | 1946 | Elizabeth, N.C. | W.L.F. | D, P |
| Victory I | 2944878 | 14 | 11 | 31.9 | 11.2 | 4.0 | 181 | 1964 | Eddystone, Pa. | W.L.W. | H, P |
| Wilson I | 295586 | 14 | 11 | 34 | 11 | | | 1965 | | W.L.W. | H, P |
| Wilson II | 295585 | 14 | 11 | 34 | 11 | | | 1965 | | W.L.W. | H, P |
| Mt. Vernon Belle | 288098 | 17 | 9 | 49.8 | 11.9 | 3.0 | 200 | 1962 | Dubuque, Iowa | W.L.W. | D, P |
| a-Grove Belle Showboat | | | | | | | | | | | |

# Bibliography

# Bibliography

"An Incomplete Summary of How the Ocean Hiway Came About, and What Has Been Accomplished in the Past 25 Years." Wilmington, Del.: Prepared by the Ocean Hiway Association, 1958.

Braynard, Frank O.: *Famous American Ships,* New York: Hastings House, 1956.

———: *Lives of the Liners,* New York: Cornell Maritime Press, 1947.

———: *S.S. Savannah, the Elegant Steam Ship,* Athens, Ga.: University of Georgia Press, 1963.

Brown, Alexander Crosby: *Steam Packets on the Chesapeake,* Cambridge, Md.: Cornell Maritime Press, 1961.

Buell, Augustus C.: *The Memoirs of Charles H. Cramp,* Philadelphia: J. B. Lippincott, 1906.

Burgess, Robert H.: *Chesapeake Circle,* Cambridge, Md.: Cornell Maritime Press, 1965.

———; Wood, H. Graham: *Steamboats Out of Baltimore,* Cambridge, Md.: Tidewater Publishers, 1968.

Clark, Edward O.: "They Crossed the Delaware," in *Steamboat Bill,* Barrington, R.I.: The Steamship Historical Society of America, September, 1951.

Conrad, Henry C.: *History of the State of Delaware,* Wilmington, Del.: Published by the author, 1908.

*Cramp's Shipyard,* Philadelphia: Published by The Wm. Cramp Ship & Engine Building Co., 1910.

*Cramp's Shipyard, Founded by William Cramp, 1830,* Philadelphia: Published by The Wm. Cramp Ship & Engine Building Co., 1902.

Dayton, Fred Erving: *Steamboat Days,* New York: Frederick A. Stokes Co., 1925.

Elliott, Richard V.: *"Bay Belle* Steams Again," a history of the Wilson Line steamboat *City of Wilmington,* a-*Bay Belle,* 1909-1966, in *Steamboat Bill,* the journal of The Steamship Historical Society of America, Spring, 1967, pp. 14-23.

———: "New York's Vanished Steamers," in *The Lookout,* Seamen's Church Institute, New York, July-August, 1963, pp. 10-13.

Foster, George, and Zeil, Ron: *Steel Rails to the Sunrise,* a history of the Long Island Rail Road, New York: Van Rees Press, 1965.

Groh, Lynn: "Pleasure Is Their Business," a concise history of Wilson Line, in *Ships and the Sea,* Summer, 1956.

Hardy, A. C.: *American Ship Types,* New York: D. Van Nostrand, 1927.

*Hudson-Fulton Celebration, 1909, The,* 2 vols. prepared by Edward Hagaman Hall. Albany, N.Y., 1910.

*Janes Fighting Ships.* Sampson Low, Marston & Co., Ltd., London. Annual, various years.

Lincoln, Anna T.: *Wilmington, Delaware—Three Centuries Under Four Flags, 1609-1937,* Rutland, Vt.: Tuttle Publishing Co., 1937.

*List of Merchant Vessels of the United States,* 1868-1924. *Merchant Vessels of the United States,* 1925-present. Annual list. Washington: U.S. Government Printing Office. Various years for vessel data.

Lytle, W. M.; Holdcamper, F. R., editor: *Merchant Vessels of the U.S., 1807-1868,* publication No. 6 of The Steamship Historical Society of America, Mystic, Conn., 1952.

McAdam, Roger William: *The Old Fall River Line,* New York: Stephen Daye Press, 1955 Ed.

McKay, Henry Bacon: *Wilmington, N.C.—Do You Remember When?* Published by the author, Greenville, S.C., 1957.

Morrison, John Harrison: *History of American Steam Navigation,* New York: Stephen Daye Press, 1958 Ed.

Murdock, George W.: Collection of biographies of Hudson River and East Coast steamboats, in the New York Historical Society, New York, N.Y.

Osbourne, Alan: *Modern Marine Engineer's Manual,* 2 vols. Cambridge, Md.: Cornell Maritime Press, 1943.

Periodicals (General references). Files of *Harper's Weekly,* New York; *The Nautical Gazette,* New York; *Ships and the Sea,* Milwaukee; *Steamboat Bill,* Journal of The Steamship Historical Society of America, Staten Island, N.Y.; *International Marine Engineering* and *Marine Engineering/Log,* New York, and *The Maritime Reporter,* New York.

Richardson, John M.: *Steamboat Lore of the Penobscot,* Augusta, Me.: Kennebec Journal Print Shop, 1941.

Ringwald, Donald C.: *Hudson River Day Line,* Berkeley, Calif.: Howell-North Books, 1965.

Scharf, Thomas J.: *The History of Delaware, 1609-1888,* Philadelphia: L. J. Richards & Co., 1888.

Smith, Harry J.: *The Romance of the Hoboken Ferry,* New York: Prentice-Hall, 1931.

Stanton, Samuel Ward: *American Steam Vessels,* New York: Smith & Stanton, 1895.

"Swedes Celebrate 300 Years in America," in *Life,* July 11, 1938.

Tyler, David B.: *The American Clyde,* Newark, Del.: The University of Delaware Press, 1958.

______: *The Bay and River Delaware,* Cambridge, Md.: Cornell Maritime Press, 1955.

*Wilson Line Annual Reports,* general files, miscellaneous record and publications of Wilson Line, Wilmington Steamboat Company, New Jersey & Wilmington Ferry Co., Christiana Ferry Co., Penns Grove Transportation Co. and Virginia Ferry Corporation, covering period between 1882 and the present, at the headquarters of Wilson Shipyard, Inc., Wilmington, Delaware.

*Wilson Papers* and miscellaneous notes on the history of Wilmington Steamboat Company by Captain Horace Wilson and Joseph S. Wilson, in the possession of Mrs. R. Frances Wilson Richardson, Wilmington, Delaware.

# Index

# Index

Abbreviations used in this index to indicate types of vessels:

frt. freight boat
stbt. steamboat
tkr. tanker
M/V. motor vessel

# Index

CITY OF CHESTER
CITY OF TRENTON
CITY OF WILMINGTON
CITY OF PHILADELPHIA
NEW CASTLE
CITY OF CAMDEN
CAPE MAY
PEERLESS
FAVORITE
DELAWARE-NEW JERSEY FERRY CO.
WILSON LINE